Understanding Judaism

Melanie J. Wright

First published in 2003 by Orchard Academic,
16 Orchard Street, Cambridge, England, CB1 1JT

Typeset and design: H. Oppity and L. Beak

ISBN 1-90328303-5 (paper)
ISBN 1-90328304-3 (cloth)

All photographs in this work were taken by Melanie J. Wright.
Cover illustration: the synagogue of Cos.

Understanding Judaism

Melanie J. Wright

Orchard Academic

Contents

Preface and *Apologia*

Why is this book different from all other books?

For many Jews, be they intensely committed to or largely distanced from religious concerns, the celebration of *Pesach* (or Passover) is one of the earliest and most vivid of childhood memories. It is also one of the Jewish religious practices most familiar to non-Jews. The Passover meal or *seder*, during which consumption of symbolic foods is punctuated by the rehearsal of the ancient story of the deliverance of Hebrew slaves from bondage in Egypt, is shared by the carefully observant and by many secular Jews. One of the reasons for its ongoing popularity is that it encapsulates so many of the features that make Judaism and Jewish tradition so vibrant and interesting to engage with. Since medieval times, in the Western world the *seder* ritual has been opened by the youngest child present, who asks four questions (in earlier periods and still today in, for example, Yemeni tradition, the adult leading the *seder* poses the questions and the children respond):

Mah nishtanah....?

Why is this night different from all other nights? On all other nights we eat either leavened or unleavened bread. Why on this night, do we eat only unleavened bread?
On all other nights we eat all kinds of herbs. Why, on this night, do we eat especially bitter herbs?
On all other nights, we do not dip our herbs in any condiment. Why, on this night do we dip them in salt water and *haroset?*
On all other nights we eat without special festivities, Why, on this night, do we hold this *seder* service?[1]

What follows in many ways epitomises Judaism. On the one hand, the evening's ceremonies follow a familiar rhythm as the text of the *haggadah*, the book that sets out the order for the *seder* service, is worked through. In different lands and epochs, participants rehearse the story of how the children of Israel were 'passed over' or spared from the plague of the killing of the first-born, and then were led in the exodus to freedom and the Promised Land (Exodus 12 and 13). On the other hand, individual services (*sedarim*) are different, one from another. Many Jewish groups have produced *haggadot* to reflect their own perspectives. There are *haggadot* for students and for soldiers in the Israeli army; *haggadot* were produced during the Cold War to enable participants to remember Russian Jews who were unable to practise their religion freely; and recent years have seen the creation of feminist *haggadot*, which accentuate the role of women in Jewish history. Further variations on the theme develop within individual family celebrations. In the age of computer technology an increasing number of families write new *haggadot* each year, to reflect how the festival's message of liberation speaks to their changing condition.

In a similar but modest way, *Understanding Judaism* seeks to be both 'like' and 'different from' other introductory guides. In writing it, I have attempted to provide both reliable information for the reader who has little experience or knowledge of Judaism, and some analytical, interpretative insights that hopefully convey the reasons for my own fascination with the subject, and make some 'understanding' possible. If I have succeeded, then the result will have been a book that assumes little prior knowledge of Judaism, but does credit its readers with inquiring and intelligent minds.

I have been particularly concerned to pay attention to Jewish diversity. Many readers may already be aware that, as is the case with other 'world religions', there exist within Judaism a number of different movements. I have tried to give fair account of some of the well-known positions such as Orthodoxy and Reform, and also of some of the lesser-known ones (in Britain, at least) such as Conservatism, Reconstructionism, and the recently founded Union for Traditional Judaism. I have chosen not to discuss secular Zionism in detail: I wanted to focus as much as possible on Jewish *religious* expression. Some sociologically minded readers may, of course, want to argue that secular Zionism is 'religious', insofar as it offers its adherents a shared set of ideas ('beliefs') and activities ('rites') that integrate and mobilize them on behalf of certain goals. This possibility is briefly touched upon in chapter six, but it remains a controversial one, not least from the perspective of many Jews.

Cultural and religious pluralism go hand in hand in Jewish experience (see chapters three and five) and whilst it is impossible to produce a study that is free from (in my case Eurocentric) bias, I have tried to take account of and compensate for this where possible. Most English language guides to Judaism focus on the religious life and history of Ashkenazi Jewry, those Jews (approximately eighty per cent of the world Jewish population) who trace their genealogical or spiritual origins to Germany and German influenced Jewish communities, including those of northern France, Poland, and parts of Russia. This concentration is understandable. The Jewish populations of the United States, Britain, and the Commonwealth are mainly Ashkenazi (because of the largely Polish derivation of these communities). However, their story does not provide a complete account of Jewish religion and culture. The Middle East was the birthplace of and principal home to Jews for over two-thirds of documented history. Accordingly, this book offers some account of the traditions of the million or so 'Oriental' Jews from Asia and North Africa. It also attends to Sephardi Judaism, a tradition that spread from the Iberian Peninsula to the Balkans, and to parts of Africa and the Middle East. A knowledge of Sephardi and Oriental tradition is not only necessary for a full picture of, say, the situation in Israel, where these groups form about fifty per cent of the Jewish population. It is also vital to an understanding of Judaism in the West. The first Jews in the Americas were Sephardim, as were the first Jews to settle in England following readmission in the 1650s.[2]

In addition to an inevitable (but, I hope, restrained) Eurocentric bias, I write this book as a non-Jew who has for the majority of her life engaged with, studied, and then taught Judaism and Jewish-Christian Relations. Readers will be able to judge for themselves whether or not this precludes me from understanding Judaism: that is, from gaining and communicating a grasp of Judaism which is in some way both informed and intuitive. Within the field of religious studies, some practitioners argue that a religious tradition can only be comprehended by those who are themselves adherents of that tradition: there is an unbridgeable gap between the 'insider' and the 'outsider'. This position certainly requires serious consideration. Chapter five offers many examples of crude and cruel misunderstandings of Judaism that have been propagated by non-Jews over the centuries. Given such a history, it is vital that non-Jews attend carefully to how Jews experience and articulate Judaism. At a wider level, the impact of postmodernism has meant that philosophers and social theorists increasingly question the existence of any objective, describable realities. They stress the ambiguities inherent in communication, and question the extent to which any of us can authentically engage another individual's ever-changing consciousness. From this perspective, although students of religion may try to observe and write about the situation of other human beings, in reality, 'the experiences that we as scholars are able to study *are none other than our own.*'[3]

My own view is that although the processes involved in understanding are not easy or straightforward, human beings are capable of comprehending one another. If this were not in any sense the case then arguably, human cooperation, and society itself, could not exist. One particular strategic response to the limits to 'outsider' understanding is the attempt to practise what has sometimes been called the 'empathetic approach' to studying a religion. This involves deploying not just one's intellectual faculties, but also one's imagination, in order to develop sympathy with and enter into another person's feelings until one is able to defend those as if they are one's own.[4] However, the development of empathy is far from straightforward. The feelings, desires, motivations, and fears of human beings are complex and often opaque, both to subjects themselves and to others. Moreover, it is somewhat idealistic to assume that the student of religion (or one involved in the other human sciences, such as anthropology or sociology) is 'a walking miracle of empathy, tact, patience, and cosmopolitanism' who can transcend completely his or her context and presuppositions.[5]

Mindful of the problems touched on above, in offering an understanding of Judaism, this book tries to strike a compromising balance between the 'experience-near' (the 'insider' stance) and the 'experience-distant' (the 'outsider' stance). In describing his approach to anthropological research, Clifford Geertz suggests that these strategies should be married,

> to produce an interpretation of the way a people lives which is neither imprisoned within their mental horizons, an ethnography of witchcraft as written by a witch, nor systematically deaf to the distinctive tonalities of their existence, an ethnography of witchcraft as written by a geometer.[6]

Such an approach does not abandon the goal of understanding Judaism as its practitioners perceive it, but nor does it claim to abandon the 'critical distance' and conceptual frameworks that an 'outsider' may bring to his or her subject. I have not pretended to imagine myself into the position of a religious Jew (as the empathetics would advocate), but have instead tried to search out and analyse the words, images, institutions and behaviours that religious Jews individually and collectively use to represent themselves to themselves and to one another. This hybrid approach does not entail the refusal to confront differences within the tradition, nor to make judgements, but it does require attentiveness, courtesy and respect. I hope that I have been at least partly able to demonstrate these aspects in this volume, whilst at the same time offering an account of Judaism that is serious and (in the best sense of the word) critical.

In the attempt to understand Judaism I draw explicitly on a number of disciplines. Religious Studies has always practised methodological and theoretical pluralism. That is, it has used insights from a range of fields, including anthropology, economics, history, philosophy, psychology and sociology in order to further its goal of producing both an account of religious experiences and expressions, and some reflection on what gives rise to them in the first place. With respect to Judaism in particular, there are many examples of attempts to apply one or more of the human sciences to its study. For example, in the United States and Israel, writers like Liebman and Don-Yehiya, and Samuel Heilman, have employed well-established sociological tools – in Heilman's case, participant observation – to study institutions like the synagogue or groups like *Charedi* (ultra-Orthodox) Jews. This book takes account of some of the insights that such approaches can offer the attempt to understand Judaism. It also draws on approaches from cultural studies, which until recently have been less frequently applied to the study of religions. For example, the texts, practices and objects discussed have been selected on the basis of a wish to explore the realities of everyday life, rather than to concentrate exclusively on artefacts deemed to be of aesthetic or intellectual excellence. Also, several photographs showing examples of Judaism's material cultural dimension have been included alongside the text. These are intended to be regarded as equal to, rather than secondary to it. Extended captions attempt to draw out some of the meanings and the significance of the objects depicted.

Finally, it seems necessary at this point to address the book's treatment of matters theological, since some non-Jewish readers (and some Jewish ones) may be surprised by the omission of a chapter on Jewish beliefs. In some traditions, 'religion' is synonymous with 'faith' and primarily signifies 'adherence to a set of beliefs'. The decision not to have a chapter on belief should not be taken to imply that Jews do not have both private beliefs and publicly debated theologies. Nor is it implicitly a statement in favour of the view that these convictions and concerns are unimportant within Judaism. Far from it. In 1957, for example, British rabbi Louis Jacobs published a book, *We Have Reason to Believe*, in which he argued that Judaism's sacred texts were not immaculate records of divine dictation, but were partly human in origin. They were the record of revelation, products 'of the divine-human encounter in the history of our ancestors in which they reached out gropingly for God and He responded to their faltering quest'.[7] This challenge to Orthodox belief resulted in an extended and public theological controversy. Eventually the Chief Rabbi of the day vetoed Jacobs' appointment as Principal of Jews' College (now the London School of Jewish Studies, the primary training institution for Orthodox rabbis for Britain and the Commonwealth) and prevented him from being re-appointed as rabbi of the New West End Synagogue. Jacobs and his sympathisers responded with moves that led to the establishment of *Masorti*, a new movement within British Judaism. The events of what is sometimes referred to as the 'Louis Jacob affair' illustrate that issues of belief are important within Judaism. Nevertheless, explicit discussion of belief has not been the main or even one of the main modes of Jewish religious expression. Jewish beliefs are characterised by their embeddedness. To a greater extent than is the case in predominantly creedal religions such as Christianity, Jewish theology is implicit theology – theology that is manifest not in abstract treatises but in the lived faith of Jewish individuals and communities. In keeping with this characteristic, instead of discussing Jewish belief in isolation, I have addressed the subject of Jewish faithfulness in the context of other issues, be they changes in festival observance, attitudes towards the law, or relations with adherents of other religions.

I am pleased to express my appreciation of those whose diverse assistance and goodwill has made this book possible. I am grateful to my colleagues and students at the Centre for Jewish-Christian Relations, Anglia Polytechnic University and Cambridge University, and to staff of the British Library, and the Divinity Faculty and University Libraries, Cambridge. I would also like to thank the Shalom Hartman Institute, Jerusalem, for their invitation to the International Theology Conference in 2001 and consequent funding of a timely and enriching visit to Israel. Without the patience of my partner Justin Meggitt, and the dedication of Jane Doyle and all the Orchard Academic team, the project might never have come to fruition.

Finally, my thanks and greetings go to cheerful Friday-night friends: Mark Baker (who commented on parts of chapter six), Rachel Baker, Jon Gifford, John Leigh, Jerry Toner and David Woodhouse. This book is for you.

Crowle, 4th Month, 2002

All references to the Jewish Bible are drawn from the *Tanakh, a New Translation of the Holy Scriptures According to the Traditional Hebrew Text* (Philadelphia: The Jewish Publication Society, 1988). I use H. Danby's translation of *The Mishnah* (Oxford: Clarendon Press, 1933) and I. Epstein, ed., *The Babylonian Talmud*, 18 vols (Soncino, 1935-1948), although at the time of writing this it seems that the translation of the *Talmud* by Adin Steinsaltz (New York: Random House, 1989 onwards) may gain pre-eminence on completion. In the interest of accessibility, classical translations are from the *Loeb Classical Library*. All other translations and editions relied on are noted in the text.

Transliterations of Hebrew generally follow the *Encyclopedia Judaica* (Jerusalem: Keter, 1970) with modifications to avoid the use of diacritical marks. They are also italicised, with the exception of a few names and other words commonly used in English.

Notes

[1] Central Conference of American Rabbis (ed.), *The Union Haggadah. Home Service for Passover*, New York: Central Conference of American Rabbis, 1923, p. 18.

[2] Jews were expelled from England in 1290; see chapter five.

[3] R. T. McCutcheon, 'General Introduction', in *The Insider/Outsider Problem in the Study of Religion*, Cassell, 1999, p. 8.

[4] I. Markham (ed.), *A World Religions Reader*, Oxford: Blackwell, 1996, pp. 10-11.

[5] C. Geertz, '"From the Native's Point of View": On the Nature of Anthropological Understanding', in McCutcheon, *The Insider/Outsider Problem*, p. 50.

[6] Ibid., p. 52.

[7] L. Jacobs, *We Have Reason to Believe*, third edition, Vallentine Mitchell, 1965, p. 139.

1

What is Judaism?

There is a certain people (Esther 3:8)

What is Judaism? According to the *doyenne* of popular reference works, the *Pears Cyclopedia*, the answer is obvious. Judaism is 'the religion of the Jews'.[1] But is the definition really so straightforward? For many pious Jews the suggestion that Judaism is simply one of a wider category of phenomena collectively describable as religions would be bizarre, even blasphemous. From their standpoint, Judaism is *sui generis*. Unlike other things conventionally labelled as 'religions' (for example Buddhism, Hinduism) Judaism is the embodiment of divinely revealed teaching, mediated to the Jewish people (the people Israel) through a covenant with the one God.[2] For those who perhaps do not share the traditional religious perspective, other evidence also seems to argue against the easy definition of Judaism as religion. Until fairly recently, the very terms 'Judaism' and 'religion' were strikingly absent from Judaism's core texts, and even from the Hebrew language itself.

Etymology is not always a helpful starting point in attempting to determine current meanings of a term, but in the case of the English word 'Judaism' an investigation of origins may yield some worthwhile clues. 'Judaism' derives from a Greek term *Judaismos*, which emerged in the context of the Jewish encounter with Greek-speaking or Hellenistic culture, described in chapter five of this book. In extra-canonical (non-Biblical) texts like 2 Maccabees 2:21; 8:1 and 14:38, *Judaismos* refers generally to Jewish identity (distinguished from Hellenism or Greek identity) or to 'the state of being a Jew'. It was only in the Middle Ages, when rabbis and others began to engage seriously in discussion and polemic with Christianity and Islam, that Jews began to consider Judaism as a religion – something similar to but also different from the traditions followed by their neighbours. The term used in Medieval Hebrew discourse was *dat*, derived from a Persian word found in some later Biblical books, such as Esther. Originally referring to 'law' in the sense of particular prescriptions for behaviour in given circumstances, it came to denote 'religion' in a more abstract sense. From the perspective of figures like Judah ha-Levi (see chapters five and six), Judaism possessed many of the same characteristics as other 'religions' (*datot*) but it was the only true religion revealed by God.

The histories of the words 'Judaism' and '*dat*' reveal several things fundamental to the task of this book. Firstly, it is clear that Jewish self-understanding and expression is not static, but dynamic. Secondly, it has developed to a significant extent in response to the encounter with non-Jewish cultures. (This is explored in more depth in chapter five.) Definition is *negotiated*. Moreover, the phenomenon 'Judaism' is profoundly associated with a group of people: the 'Jewish people'.

The difficulties entailed in describing Judaism as a religion can be over-stated. Most practitioners of religious studies no longer share the traditional and overly-restrictive (Christian) assumption that a religion is first and foremost a set of beliefs. Some scholars prefer a functionalist analysis, focusing on the contribution religions make to meeting the essential prerequisites of society (for example, looking at the ways they help to foster value consensus and group solidarity). This approach typically defines as religious any activity that celebrates the collective, and promotes social cohesion through the articulation of commonly agreed values, roles and obligations. So, speaking about Judaism as a 'religion' does not necessarily imply that an unhelpfully narrowing or inappropriately Christianizing approach will be taken to the subject matter. Nor does it imply a lack of willingness to attend to what Jews themselves say about how they perceive their tradition.

Alternatively, critics may speak of religions as a group of phenomena possessing certain core dimensions. This approach is attractive because the kind of functionalist perspective outlined above can appear reductionist. In his well-known dimensional account, Frank Whaling suggests that all the major world religions contain eight key elements: Religious Community; Ritual and Worship; Ethics; Social and Political Involvement; Scripture/Myth; Concept; Aesthetics; and Spirituality. For the religious adherent, a transcendent reality lies beyond and is mediated or brought closer by these interacting dimensions.

Interior of the Kahal Shalom Synagogue, Rhodes, demonstrating how Whaling's dimensions are embodied in Jewish material culture.

Nine-branched candlesticks evoke the seven-branched *menorah*, which stood in the Jerusalem Temple. Their modified design expresses both continuity with and distance from Jewish worship in ancient times. The six pointed star of David has strong historical and political associations and is also found on the modern Israeli flag. But the interior of the synagogue (which dates from 1577), is dominated by the *bimah* or reading table, reflecting the extent to which Jews have found their spiritual and aesthetic outlets in the written word, particularly exposition of the *Torah* (see chapter two).

As will emerge in this book, Judaism possesses each of Whaling's dimensions. It would generally be termed a religion by both adherents and academic specialists. Perhaps, then, the problem with viewing Judaism as a religion is that it is necessary to specify what definition of religion is being used. If 'religion' is regarded as a family term, embracing a range of phenomena, which each possess their own personalities and characteristics, but nevertheless also share some broad characteristics or 'family resemblances', then Judaism *is* a religion, as are Islam, Sikhism and so on.

Whaling did not intend his eight dimensions of the religious life to serve as a rigid test or check-list against which 'potential religions' should be measured. He also accepted that within the range of phenomena termed religions, particular examples would emphasise different things:

> All the major religious traditions of the world contain eight inter-linked elements. The major religions are dynamic organisms within which there are eight inter-acting dimensions; they are historical chains within which there are eight connecting links. . . .these elements are present in separate traditions with different weights and different emphases. Because all religions have these elements this does not mean that they are all the same.[3]

So what are the particular emphases of the religion which constitutes the subject of this study? What *type* of religion is Judaism?

As was touched on earlier, Christianity is a type of religion which is strongly oriented towards belief and doctrine. Most Christians belong to denominations which place high value on the profession of assent to sets of beliefs, or creeds. In the preface, I suggested that historically speaking, Judaism has not tended to engage in abstract theological discussion and that it cannot be reduced to a system of beliefs or concepts. Another strategy might be to speak of Judaism as based on a particular set of practices, Whaling's ritual dimension. At first sight, such an approach has merit. For many Jews the clothes they wear, foods they eat, and *how* they eat and wear these thing, are fundamental to their sense of Jewishness. Yet even here it is difficult to find a particular set of practices that is uncontested and universal. Jews in some countries will eat animals or birds which others do not regard as kosher, or fit for consumption. Similarly, some regard the wearing of ritual clothing like the *tallit* or prayer shawl as a male preserve, whilst others permit or even require its adoption by women performing certain tasks in the synagogue (see chapter four).

Finally, it is worth considering whether Judaism is a religion which is based on race. This is important to address because in popular discourse, Jews are sometimes referred to as a 'race'. I also mentioned earlier that some ancient definitions associated Judaism with allegiance to a group of people, 'the Jews'. However, the definition of who constitutes that people is flexible and open to contest, particularly in the modern world (see this book's Afterword). Jews do not constitute a race - in simple terms, a group of people distinguished from others by genetically transmitted physical characteristics. Conversion, or more accurately, proselytisation into Judaism has always been possible (although sometimes subjected to greater or lesser restriction) and carries with it both adoption of a religious tradition and peoplehood: 'Your people shall be my people, and your God my God' (Ruth 1:16). Likewise, Jews who convert to another religion whilst perhaps remaining emotionally related to the people (*am*) of Israel are often regarded as having left the Jewish community. Through conversion (and increasingly through adoption and inter-marriage) Jews have become a multicultural community, which transcends the categories of nationality and ethnicity.

Some insight into what kind of religion Judaism *is* may be found in two early twentieth century attempts at definition-writing. In 1937, rabbis in the American Reform movement described Judaism as 'the historical religious experience of the Jewish people'. A few years earlier, the founder of Reconstructionist Judaism, Mordecai Kaplan, defined Judaism as the 'evolving religious civilisation' of the Jewish people. As is explored in chapter three, neither of these interpretations is uncontested. Yet both are helpful, because they recognise the significance of history and group experience. Judaism cannot be reduced to history, particularly if this entails a value judgement: Judaism is not a 'living fossil', characterised by *stasis*. But history is important. As Nicholas de Lange has tellingly observed, Judaism is a religious tradition in which the sense of tradition is unusually strong.[4] Moreover, as the emphasis on experience and civilisation in these two twentieth century definitions implies, the ideas and beliefs, and the practices of Judaism, all in some sense flow out of continuing historical experience. This interplay between tradition and event is particularly evident in the development of Judaism's legal tradition, and so it is to this aspect that *Understanding Judaism* must now turn.

Notes

[1] C. Cook (ed.), *Pears Cyclopedia 2000-2001*, Harmondsworth: Penguin Books, 2000, s. J28.

[2] There are several names for God in the *Tanakh*. One represented by the Hebrew letters YHWH is often vocalised as Yahweh by biblical scholars, but is not used by most religious Jews, either verbally or in print, following Exodus 20:7. The most common substitute is *Adonai*, 'my Lord'. 'Jehovah', used in the King James Version of the Christian Bible, is derived from a conflation of the consonants in YHWH and the vowels of *Adonai*, but is unsound, historically and linguistically speaking.

[3] F. Whaling, *Christian Theology and World Religions*, Marshall Pickering, 1986, pp. 37-48.

[4] N. R. M. de Lange, *Judaism*, Oxford: Oxford University Press, 1986, p. 69.

2

Jewish Law

Living in accordance with the Halakhah... is this the ultimate end of the religious life? The answer is both yes and no. (Yeshayahu Leibowitz)

'Law' as commonly understood by many non-Jews is a problematic rendering of the Hebrew terms with which it is most closely associated, *Torah* and *halakhah*. *Torah* means more properly 'instruction' and may be used in a specific way, to refer to a teaching or law on a specific subject (e.g. the *torah* of the Nazirite in Numbers 6:21) or more frequently in a general sense, to refer to a collection of such teachings. In particular, the Pentateuch or first five books of the Hebrew Bible, and even the entire Hebrew Bible (or *Tanakh*) is described as *Torah*. Similarly, *halakhah*[1] may be applied either to particular rules or decisions or to the whole system of religious regulations that have shaped and guided the lives of the many generations of Jews who have lived since the Biblical era.

If there are (at least) two terms associated with Judaism's legal aspects, what is their relation? How do *Torah* and *halakhah* combine? For the Orthodox rabbi and scholar Eliezer Berkovits, the two are essentially complementary. *Torah* is the eternal, unchanging aspect of Jewish law, divinely revealed to Moses at Mount Sinai (described in the Bible from Exodus 20 onwards). On the other hand, '*Halakhah* is not the Law [*Torah*] but the Law applied - and by the manner of its application rendered meaningful - in a given situation'. It is the body of post-Sinai attempts to apply the *Torah* in concrete situations.[2] These subtleties and concerns over English terminology aside, however, the phrase 'Jewish law' is usable for the purposes of this chapter, provided that it is remembered that the phrase be understood in broad, rather than narrow and restrictive terms.

This chapter briefly sketches out the basic structure and sources of Jewish law. As will be seen, the all-embracing nature of the law is such that the studies in later chapters of Jewish festival celebration, rites of passage, and even responses to the Holocaust, will inevitably be studies of Jewish law, too. Conversely, lest this sound off-putting to readers for whom 'law' still carries negative connotations, the study of law will also give insight into key themes in the history of Jewish meaning and value, including self-definition, gender relations, and interaction between Jews and non-Jews. The *halakhah* represents Judaism in its fullest vitality.

Tanakh

Supreme in authority within the Jewish legal system - in theory, if not, perhaps, in terms of *de facto* impact on Jewish life today - is the religious law found in the Hebrew Bible or *Tanakh*. For readers shaped by Christian culture, it is important to recognise that the name 'Old Testament' which is often applied to this body of literature, is essentially alien to Jewish thought. It reflects the traditional Christian view that the Jewish scriptures have been added to by a 'New Testament'. For this reason, '*Tanakh*' and 'Hebrew Bible' are used throughout this book.

There is a wealth of critical literature surrounding the formation and history of the *Tanakh*, which is a composite work of twenty-four books. According to Jewish tradition, the first five books were revealed to Moses at Sinai (see Exodus 20 following), but the people sinned and neglected God's law, leading to their military conquest and expulsion from the lands of Israel and Judah by other nations. It was on return from exile (following the conquest of the Babylonian Empire by the Persians in 539 BCE[3]) that another prophetic figure, Ezra, restored the scriptures to the people and made them accessible through public reading and interpretation (Nehemiah 8:1-8). As David Halivni has noted, setting aside the notion of revelation to Moses (which ultimately cannot be scientifically verified or disproved), there is some sympathy between this traditional account and the findings of modern Biblical scholarship, which identify a number of sources behind the final text, and date them from approximately 1000BCE to the Maccabean era (160s BCE). There is also a general scholarly consensus today that the traditional threefold division of the *Tanakh* into Law (*Torah* – the five books of Moses), Prophets (*Nevi'im* – divided into 'former prophets' and 'latter prophets') and Writings (*Ketuvim* – Psalms, Proverbs, Job, the Five *Megillot*, Daniel, Ezra-Nehemiah and

Chronicles) provides a rough guide to the relative dates at which these collections were regarded as canonical scripture. There is far less agreement, however, as to the date at which the canon of the Hebrew Bible was finally closed. It is likely that the text did not exist in the form known today until a century or more into the Common Era, although some individual books were seen as authoritative from very early times.[4]

The Books of the *Tanakh* or Hebrew Bible

Torah – the five books of Moses
Genesis; Exodus; Leviticus; Numbers; Deuteronomy

Nevi'im – the prophets
Joshua; Judges; (1 and 2) Samuel; (1 and 2) Kings; Isaiah; Jeremiah; Ezekiel; Hosea*; Joel; Amos; Obadiah; Jonah; Micah; Nahum; Habakkuk; Zephaniah; Haggai; Zechariah; Malachi

* Judaism traditionally groups together the books Hosea-Malachi, and refers to them collectively as 'The Twelve Prophets'. According to the *Talmud*, the twelve were grouped together because some were so small, that they might otherwise be lost.

Ketuvim – the writings
Psalms; Proverbs; Job; The Song of Songs; Ruth; Lamentations; Ecclesiastes; Esther; Daniel; Ezra; Nehemiah; (1 and 2) Chronicles.

The word *Tanakh* is derived from the initial letters of *Torah*, *Nevi'im*, and *Ketuvim*.

Within the *Tanakh* the *Torah* is the main source of implicit and explicit *halakhah*. The most famous laws found in these books are the Ten Commandments (Exodus 20:1-14 and Deuteronomy 5:6-18). However, the Commandments' general nature, and the lack of reference to sanctions for those who disregard them, means that they are perhaps more aptly characterised as ethical or moral exhortations than as laws *per se*. More recognisable as typical laws are the statutes outlined in passages like Deuteronomy 21:15–25:13 (which attends to the regulation of the household, including wives and servants) and the priestly code in Leviticus 17-26, so called because it relates to the sacrificial system of worship conducted by priests in the Jerusalem Temple, and surrounding purity regulations:

> Any person, whether citizen or stranger, who eats what has died or has been torn by beasts shall wash his clothes, bathe in water, and remain unclean until evening; then he shall be clean. But if he does not wash [his clothes] and bathe his body, he shall bear his guilt (17:15-16).

> You shall not render an unfair decision: do not favour the poor or show deference to the rich; judge your kinsman fairly. Do not deal basely with your countrymen. Love your fellow as yourself: I am the LORD (19:15-16).

In addition to collections of laws, some general features of Jewish jurisprudence may be traced in embryonic form in the *Tanakh*. For example, precedent is established as a source of law (see Jeremiah 26:16-19). More significantly, the enduring concept of the *Torah* as sacrament is established in the Bible. It is through the law that God and God's will are known. It is no accident that in setting the scene for the promulgation of law in Exodus, the Biblical narrator describes how 'Moses led the people out of the camp toward God' (Exodus 19:17). Just as in later periods legal experts were sometimes regarded as divinely inspired or authorised to make rulings, so in the Bible legal activity cannot be divorced from a sense of the divine presence (2 Chronicles 19:4-7; Ezra 7: 9-10, 25).

The *Tanakh* is regarded as pivotal to the Jewish legal tradition and later generations of scholars established their teachings as normative by linking themselves to scripture and particularly to Moses' receipt of law on Sinai. However, despite the foundational authority accorded to the *Tanakh* in much Jewish legal discourse, in practical terms, later Jewish literature is often the more direct, immediate source of instruction for those who seek to live their lives according to *Torah*. The distinctive literary forms that will be examined in the remainder of this chapter include *Mishnah*, *Talmud*, codes and *responsa* (in Hebrew, *she'elot u-teshuvot*, 'questions and answers').

Mishnah

Like all legal traditions, Jewish law has never been able to remain static. As new situations arise, societies develop, technologies advance, the *Torah's* meaning for new contexts has to be clarified. And as has already been noted, this process probably began in the earliest of times. The Hebrew Bible says that Ezra imparted both written text and oral instruction to the people in the sixth century BCE. Inconsistencies in the text (for example, compare Numbers 18:26 and Leviticus 27:30, or Leviticus 12:1-13 and Deuteronomy 16:2) also make it highly likely that although the notion of a perfect and eternal *Torah* has served as a crucial symbol of Israel's relationship with God, its actual content has never been sufficient as a basis for the carefully observant life.

During the Second Temple period[5] the *halakhah's* development took two main forms. *Halakhic midrashim* (collections of legally oriented exegeses or interpretations of Scripture) more closely defined the Biblical commandments or *mitzvot*. They also derived scriptural support for local *minhag* or custom. On the other hand, *aggadic midrashim* (if *halakhah* is Jewish *law*, then in very simple terms *aggadah* is Jewish *lore*, or non-legal material) like *Midrash Rabbah* offered more homiletic interpretations of the Pentateuch and the five *Megillot* - Biblical books read at festival times (Lamentations, Song of Songs, Ruth, Ecclesiastes, and Esther). However, halakhic development, like other aspects of Jewish life, experienced a revolutionary challenge in the late first century. A Jewish revolt against the Roman occupation of Israel failed and the Jerusalem Temple, generally regarded as the only site of legitimate sacrificial worship, was destroyed by Titus in 70 CE (see chapter five). The traditional *locus* of Jewish sanctity, and the existing structures of religious authority, were overturned. How, in such a context, was Judaism to be sustained for the future?

According to Jewish tradition, a group of rabbis led by Yohanan ben Zakkai negotiated with the Roman Emperor Vespasian to gain safe haven for themselves in Yavneh, a village on the coastal plain west of Jerusalem. There they established an academy and set about reconstituting Judaism for the new age. They canonized the *Tanakh*, inserted the *birkat ha-minim* (see chapter four) into the liturgy to frustrate sectarians in the synagogue and also began debating and codifying the *Oral Torah*, a body of material that had grown up around the Biblical text as new generations needed to clarify its relevance to their lives. The nature of the stories surrounding the Yavnean period is such that it is impossible to construct a reliable historical account of the events. We now know that, for example, the canonization of the Biblical text was a *process* that occurred gradually over a period of many years, rather than a one-off 'event'. It is also clear that the early rabbis did not have the authority to impose changes on scattered and diverse communities of Jews. However, what is more certain is that the late first and early second centuries witnessed a vital stage in the history of Judaism. A discernible change of emphasis in Jewish religion occurred in the early part of the Common Era. In the absence of priestly sacrifice in the Temple, the sphere of Jewish holiness was extended. God was no longer seen as tied to a geographical location but could be found wherever the people Israel were faithfully present (a development of ideas already found in earlier traditions like Ezekiel 1). In a sense, Judaism was also democratized: now that the priestly class had lost their special function, the way was open for all Jews to live priest-like lives of divine service. Prayer, study of *Torah* and observance of the *mitzvot* (commandments) were sufficient to ensure a right relationship with God. From now on, normative Judaism would regard sacrifice as unnecessary, for, 'If two sit together and words of the Law [are spoken] between them, the Divine Presence rests between them' (*m. Avot* 3:2).

The halakhic text associated most closely with the aftermath of the destruction of the Temple and reconceptualisation of Judaism is the *Mishnah*, a compendium of traditions normally attributed to the editorship of Rabbi Judah Ha-Nasi (135-220 CE), known in many texts simply as 'Rabbi'. The term *Mishnah* comes from a Hebrew verb *shanah*, 'to repeat', and the *Mishnah's* origins lie in the so-called *oral*, and hence memorised or repeated, *Torah*. For traditional Judaism these beginnings in oral culture do not diminish the status of the *Mishnah*. Whereas in the Biblical account of Ezra's work the *Tanakh* presents much of its content as recovered teaching (that is, as revelation which has been subjected to human fallibility and creativity), the later medieval practice was to seek to ground all Jewish religious activity in revelation.[6] This tendency may have been bolstered by polemical engagement with Christianity and Islam. The Spanish Talmudist and Kabbalist Nachmanides (1194-1270) and the Maharal of Prague (a Talmudist and mystical theologian, died 1609) were amongst those who attributed *both* written and oral *Torah* to God and Sinai, with limited scope for human intervention in the process. In a similar vein, whilst the following text may have originally spoken of the *written Torah's* transmission, it has subsequently been most commonly understood to assert the authenticity of *oral* law:

> Moses received the Law from Sinai and committed it to Joshua, and Joshua to the elders, and the elders to the Prophets; and the Prophets committed it to the men of the Great Synagogue. They said three things: Be deliberate in judgement, raise up many disciples, and make a fence around the Law (*m. Avot* 1:1).

This passage may be read by subsequent generations as presenting the *Mishnah* as directly linked to Judaism's foundational moment at Sinai. The role of the *tannaim* or 'men of the Great Synagogue' is one of conservation. Their task is to build 'a fence around the Law', to clarify and extend the body of *halakhah* in order to ensure that the divine will for Israel will not be accidentally infringed.

However, as the earlier discussion has hinted, the *Mishnah's* history is not so straightforward as the rabbinic tradition suggests. Modern scholars have applied to the *Mishnah* and other legal texts the techniques of Biblical scholarship, such as form and redaction criticism. The results of these investigations into the history of the *Mishnah's* formation and development suggest that, like the *Tanakh*, its text underwent a series of revisions. It cannot be regarded as a written record of a previously unchanging, eternal oral tradition, and is the product of a number of different editors. Although it is not yet possible to replace the traditional view with a critical but equally complete account of the *Mishnah's* origins, from a religious studies perspective the former argument is no longer tenable. Not least among the objections to the traditional view is the reporting of Judah Ha-Nasi's own death in *m. Sotah* 9:15: 'When Rabbi died, humility and the shunning of sin ceased'. Other passages discuss Rabbi's views in the same manner that those of earlier deceased sages are reported elsewhere (for example *m. Naz.* 1:4). Still others mention *tannaim* or teachers who succeeded him, including his son Gamliel (*m. Avot* 2:2).

The *Mishnah* of today is written in Hebrew with a small number of Aramaic sentences. It is divided into six sections or orders, named by later scholars as: *Zeraim* ('seeds' or agricultural laws); *Moed* ('appointed time', i.e. Sabbath and festival laws); *Nashim* ('laws of marriage and divorce'); *Nezikin* ('damages', i.e. torts and jurisprudence); *Kodashim* ('holy things', laws relating to Temple sacrifice) and finally *Torohot* ('purity', dealing with laws of ritual purity). Within these orders, the text is divided into tractates or *masekhot*, chapters (*perek*), and *mishnayot*. Hence, as with *Torah* and *halakhah*, the word *mishnah* can refer to both the whole corpus and to a single unit within it.

Co-existing with this regimented structure is the discursive nature of the *Mishnah's* text. Consider this brief passage:

> From what time in the morning may the *Shema'* be recited? So soon as one can distinguish between blue and white. R. Eliezar says: Between blue and green. And it should be finished before sunrise. R. Joshua says: Before the third hour: for so it is the way of kings, to rise up at the third hour. He that recites it from that time onward suffers no loss and is like to one that reads in the Law (*m. Berakot* 1:1).

Different views on an issue are offered. There is often no clear solution given at the end of a debate. This open approach, together with the terse nature of the Hebrew text, produces a rather cryptic effect and can make the work seem impenetrable to a beginning student. However, it is unlikely that the *tannaim* and their editors were being deliberately obscure. As mentioned above, the *Mishnah's* origins lay in oral tradition. It *may* be that what has been preserved is not the full account of the rabbinic discussion on a matter but a collection of 'tags' which could be used to prompt ancient students' memorised knowledge of a debate. This possibility would fit with some other characteristics of the *Mishnah*. For example, the *Mishnah* assumes that its readership will share its presuppositions and sphere of reference. There is no introduction or conclusion to outline or assess the contents for an 'outsider'. There is also no statement of purpose or philosophy other than, perhaps, the brief remarks in *m. Avot* 1:1 (the passage quoted earlier). It is presumed that the reader will know these things, and much more concerning normative Jewish practice. In the discussion quoted above, there is no definition or explanation of what the *Shema* is, nor any account of why one should bother to recite it (see chapter four).

Despite the apparent openness and accessibility of the *Mishnah's* highly ordered structure then, it remains at other levels elusive and mysterious. What is the rationale for the order in which the material is presented?[8]

Why are some chapters apparently misplaced within the thematic orders, for example, *Avot* (which deals with ethics) in *Nezikin* ('damages')?[9] Why (if the traditional story is unreliable) was the *Mishnah* written at all? If it really was an attempt to reconstruct Judaism for a new post-Temple era, why is the majority of the *Mishnah's* content (in particular that in the orders *Moed*, *Kodashim*, and *Tohorot*) concerned with priestly purity and sacrificial procedure? All these are key questions for scholars of Jewish law during the tannaitic period. In a general guide such as this one, it is possible only to sketch out some of the contours of the current consensus on the *Mishnah*.

Perhaps the most lively area of debate relates to the purposes of the *Mishnah*. Was it intended to be a practical law manual providing a guide to the *halakhah* currently in force, or were there other reasons for its compilation? The quantity of Temple-related material has led some, notably Jacob Neusner, to suggest that other concerns are at play.[10] For Neusner, the *Mishnah* is an account of an ideal world, it offers us a picture of the early rabbis' utopia. Much of what is discussed relates to a ruined institution: in Judah Ha-Nasi's day, no priests presided at the Temple on either ordinary or festival days, and no Jews were able to bring their harvest produce to be offered at the altar. But in placing the no-longer-possible (rules about Temple cult) alongside the still-possible (rules about the conduct of agriculture, and family life and so on) the *Mishnah* asserts that, in the aftermath of the Temple's destruction, Israel's holiness persists. The covenant (agreement) between God and the Jews is eternal: historical contingencies change nothing.

Neusner's view is both interesting and affective in its depiction of a deeply spiritual group of men wrestling with compelling questions about the life of Israel and the Jewish people. But other more mundane explanations for the inclusion of the Temple-related material are also possible. Given that years had intervened between the destruction of the *First* Temple and its successor, it was perhaps only evident from a vantage point of several centuries after Judah ha-Nasi that the *Second* Temple would never be rebuilt. Rabbi, his contemporaries and pupils, may have seen their exile as a temporary state of affairs. Alternatively, it *may* be that even at this early date, the study of the law was regarded as a *mitzvah* or religious duty. If this were the case then the *Mishnah* can be seen as an example of *Torah* study for its own sake, unconnected to solving the practical problems of everyday life.

Although preeminent within the halakhic output of its day, the *Mishnah* is not the only significant collection of oral law. The *Tosefta* is another book of laws from the tannaitic period. However, the *Tosefta* should not be regarded as a true 'rival' to the *Mishnah*. It implicitly presents itself as a supplementary work (it follows the *Mishnah's* structure, provides interpretations of the *Mishnah*, and adds debates from periods subsequent to the time of Rabbi) and later tradition has confirmed this secondary status, by calling the *Tosefta* and other contemporary non-Mishnaic sayings *beraitot* – 'outside' or 'external'.

Talmud

No law codes can be final. As new questions arise, interpretations are offered, so that the old summaries are inevitably supplemented or re-cast. This is true even of those codes which (like the *Mishnah*) purport to be divine in association or origin. This inherent time-sensitiveness, coupled with the Mishnaic refusal to give definite rulings on problems, meant that further additions to the corpus of Jewish religious law were inevitable. During the period 200-500 CE a new generation of scholars known as the *amoraim* or expounders applied their wisdom to the *Mishnah* and *beraitot*. These sages' conversations were conducted against a background of increasing political instability. In the fourth century Christianity became the official religion of the Roman Empire; rabbinic institutions in Galilee were closed. Already by this time alternative centres for the study and promulgation of the *halakhah* had been established in Babylonia, under heads known as *geonim*. In the medieval period, the Judaism they expounded was to be normative almost worldwide. However, even in Babylonia life was pressurized. In the early centuries CE and again in the late fifth century a number of persecutions of Jews occurred, during which communal leaders were executed and institutions dismantled.

Just as the fracturing of Jewish life brought about by the Temple's fall in 70 had created the conditions in which the *Mishnah* emerged, so this new environment gave rise to the formation of the *Talmud*, the work which still today is the main text for study in *yeshivot* and other Orthodox Jewish institutions. Similarly, just as the *Mishnah* presented itself as the end-link in a chain of faithful oral tradition going back to Sinai, so the *Talmud* presents itself as a simple addition to the antecedent tradition, a claim at once both modest and audacious. Taking the form of a running commentary on the *Mishnah*, the *Talmud* is almost never printed independently of the other work. Here, then, is further illustration of the essential character of Judaism. As suggested in chapter one, it is a tradition marked by a strong sense of tradition.

The *Talmud* builds on the *Mishnah* in several ways that generally serve to investigate and clarify the second century compilation. Sources for the *Mishnah* are investigated, and some problems settled - hence the *Talmud's* other name, *Gemara* or 'completion'. The style of the *Talmud* is oral-conversational, but actual conversations are not being reported, as in many instances the *amoraim* quoted in the same paragraph lived centuries apart. In this example, it can be seen how the Mishnaic discussion of the thirty-nine types of work prohibited on *Shabbat* is elaborated by the later text:

> *Mishnah:* The primary labours are forty less one, sowing, ploughing, reaping, binding sheaves, threshing, winnowing, selecting, grinding, sifting, kneading, baking, shearing wool, bleaching, hackling, dyeing, spinning, stretching the threads, the making of two meshes, weaving two threads, tying and untying, sewing two stitches, tearing in order to sew two stitches, capturing a deer, slaughtering, or flaying, or salting it, curing its hide, scraping it, cutting it up, writing two letters, erasing in order to write two letters, building, pulling down, extinguishing, kindling, striking with a hammer, and carrying out from one domain to another: these are the forty primary labours less one.

> *Gemara:* Why state the number? —Said R. Johanan: [To teach] that if one performs all in one state of unawareness, he is liable on account of each separately.
> Sowing and ploughing. Let us see: ploughing is done first, then let him [the Tanna] state ploughing first and then sowing?
> -The Tanna treats of Palestine, where they first sow and then plough.
> A Tanna taught: Sowing, pruning, planting, bending, and grafting are all one labour. What does this inform us? —This: that if one performs many labours of the same nature he is liable only to one [sacrifice]. R. Abba said in the name of R. Hiyya b. Ashi in R. Ammi's name: He who prunes is culpable on account of planting, while he who plants, bends [the vine], or grafts is culpable on account of sowing .... (*Shabbat* 73a-73b)

The *Gemara* tries to comprehend the *Mishnah's* ordering of the different kinds of work. For example, it attempts to explain why sowing is listed before ploughing. The comments on pruning and grafting illustrate another Talmudic tendency. Like the author(s) of *m. Avot*, the sages 'reported' in the *Gemara* want to build a fence around, or expand, the scope of the law so as to minimise the risk of its being infringed accidentally.

Similar processes of reasoning can be seen at work in this passage from *Avodah Zarah* 47a-47b. Interestingly, it also gives an insight into life in the crowded cities of the ancient world; a Jewish house and a pagan temple negotiate shared space:

> *Mishnah:* If [an Israelite] has a house adjoining an idolatrous shrine and it collapsed, he is forbidden to rebuild it. How should he act? He withdraws a distance of four cubits into his own ground and there builds. [If the wall] belonged both to him and the shrine, it is judged as being half and half'....

> *Gemara:* [But by acting as directed in the *Mishnah*], he enlarges the space for the shrine! R. Hanina of Sura said: He should use [the four cubits] for constructing a privy! – He should make a privy for use at night. But behold a Master has said: Who is modest? He who relieves himself at the same place where he relieves himself by day! And although we explain that [in that statement] the phrase 'in the same place' is to be understood as 'in the same manner', still it is necessary to safeguard modesty! – He should, then, make [a privy] for children; or let him fence in the space with thorns or shrubs.

The Mishnaic text discusses a problem raised by the commandment in Deuteronomy 7:26 to refrain from idolatry, which was interpreted as also requiring Jews to avoid either deriving a benefit from, or from offering direct or indirect support to, idolatrous worship. If the Jew rebuilds the wall he will infringe the law because he will in effect be helping in the reconstruction of the shrine. The *Gemara* identifies that the solution proposed in the *Mishnah* could also be regarded as benefiting the shrine, since room will be created for its expansion. A solution is then explored: that is, the land could be used for a night privy, i.e. one without walls. An objection to this solution is raised – it might conflict with other requirements concerning modesty. Finally, a new answer is offered, which will enable the land to be used by the Jewish family without infringing the law.

In addition to halakhic discussion exemplified by these two passages, there is much non-legal or aggadic material in the *Talmud*, including some of the best known rabbinic stories. In a debate about an oven, R. Eliezar said:

> "If the *halakhah* agrees with me, let this carob tree prove it!" Thereupon the carob-tree was torn a hundred cubits out of its place - others affirm, four hundred cubits. "No proof can be brought from a carob tree," they retorted. Again he said to them: "If the *halakhah* agrees with me, let the stream of water prove it!" Whereupon the stream of water flowed backwards. "No proof can be brought from a stream of water," they rejoined. Again he urged: "If the *halakhah* agrees with me, let the walls of the schoolhouse prove it." whereupon the walls inclined to fall. But R. Joshua rebuked them, saying: "When scholars are engaged in a halakhic dispute, what have ye to interfere?" Hence they did not fall, in honour of R. Joshua, nor did they resume the upright, in honour of R. Eliezar; and they are still standing thus inclined. Again he said to them: "If the *halakhah* agrees with me, let it be proved from Heaven!" Whereupon a heavenly voice cried out: "Why do ye dispute with R. Eliezar, seeing that in all matters the *halakhah* agrees with him!" But R. Joshua arose and exclaimed: "It is not in heaven."....R. Nathan met Elijah and asked him: What did the Holy One, Blessed be He, do in that hour? – He laughed and replied, saying, "My sons have defeated me, my sons have defeated me." (*Baba Metzia* 59b)

In this passage, significant points emerge. Like other rabbinic literature, the *Talmud* accepts the miraculous in principle. At the end of the story Nathan meets Elijah, the Biblical prophet who it was believed returned to earth to teach and discuss with the rabbis. This event is reported without any comment or hint of surprise. Moreover, the sages do not deny that the carob tree has moved, just as they would not have denied the reality of the Ten Plagues, nor the parting of the Red Sea in Exodus. But for Judaism contact with God is sought not primarily in the realm of the supernatural, through the suspension of the normal workings of nature. "'It is not in heaven'": the *halakhah* has, by Talmudic times, become a self-validating system.

Strictly speaking, there is not one *Talmud* but two, neither of which provides complete commentary on the *Mishnah*. The lengthier of the two, the *Babylonian Talmud* or *Bavli*, was compiled around 500 CE. It has *Gemara* for only thirty-six and a half of the sixty-three tractates of the *Mishnah*. In particular, two of the six orders (*Kodashim* and *Torohot*) receive scant coverage, perhaps because these applied specifically to Temple-related matters, and in the continued absence of the Temple, no new questions for clarification had been raised. The *Bavli*'s style is quite sophisticated and relatively uniform, suggesting that some coordinated editorial work was carried out by a redactor or team of redactors. Since the 1520s when the first printed copy was published in Venice, editions of the *Babylonian Talmud* have also appeared with standardised pagination. As each folio is numbered with the left and right sides designated 'a' and 'b', references conveniently need only give the tractate, folio and side. So, the reference for the story quoted above is *Baba Metzia* 59b.

The lesser *Talmud*, both in terms of length and authority, is the Jerusalem or *Yerushalmi*, a rather looser collection of teachings and discussions drawn together around 400 CE. Despite the name, the *Yerushalmi* originates not from Jerusalem but probably from Tiberias in Galilee. Like the *Bavli*, it was first printed in the sixteenth century but (perhaps in itself an indication of its lesser status) editions are less standardised and the *Yerushalmi* is therefore referenced more fully, with the reference beginning with a 'y' or 'j' prefix to designate that it is not the *Bavli* to which reference is being made.

Like the *Mishnah*, both *Talmuds* assume and operate within their own frame of reference. Much is left unexplained and what may appear to secular readers to be minute ritual matters are accorded as much respect as broader, ethical ones. In the halakhic world view things big and small are all commanded by God, and as such all merit the same careful treatment. This underlying principle guided the creation of the *Talmudim* and also meant that, with their completion, the chain of *halakhah* would continue to grow. Today, traditional editions of the *Bavli* print the *Mishnah* and *Gemara* in a main central column on each page. On either side of this text the opinions of Rashi (a great eleventh century French commentator on the *Talmud* and Bible) and various twelfth and thirteenth century French and German scholars (known collectively as *tosafot* - 'additions') are printed. Given that before the advent of the printing press medieval European Jews faced serious problems in their attempts to establish and work on accurate rabbinic texts, these commentators were of no little importance in securing the continuance of the *Talmud* as the foundation (next to the *Tanakh*) of Jewish life and thought. Writer Chaim Pearl was perhaps overstating things when he suggested that the *Talmud* needed a Rashi to ensure its survival. However, one certainly cannot study the *Talmud* without an awareness of its presence within an ongoing, and vibrant tradition.[11]

Codes

Rashi and the authors of the *tosafot* presented their contributions to the development of *halakhah* in the form of commentary on the earlier texts. However, the medieval period also saw the rise of another legal genre. The *Talmudim* and commentaries included *aggadah* and discussion of complex hypothetical halakhic problems, which did not make them readily accessible to the non-specialist reader. To remedy this, codes of law, beginning in the eighth century with collections of *she'elot* ('questions') attempted to provide more user-friendly, organised accounts of rules and regulations relating directly to the everyday lives of the carefully observant.

The codes may themselves be simply classified as either 'books of *halakhot*' (codes providing brief discussions of and conclusions on the *halakhah* currently in force) or 'books of *pesakim*' (giving decisions only). Although strictly speaking their authors often hoped to stimulate more advanced study of the law, or to provide the already learned with a handy *aide memoire*, they often attained a popularity that led to a diminishing of concern for the more difficult classical sources. This tendency is illustrated by the following discussion from the ninth century:

> Which is preferable and desirable, to delve into [the *Talmud*] or to study abridged [books of] *halakhot*? We have asked this question because a majority of the people incline to abridged *halakhot*, saying: Why should we be occupied with the complexity of the *Talmud*?! He [Rav Paltoi Gaon] answered, they are doing something undesirable...for they detract from the *Torah*....Moreover, they cause the study of the *Torah*, Heaven forbid, to be forgotten. [Books of *halakhot*] have been compiled...rather so that they may be referred to [by those who have studied] the *Talmud* and experience doubt as to the proper interpretation of anything therein.[12]

Despite the protestations of the *geonim* (the heads of the Babylonian rabbinic academies) law codes became increasingly popular, their status more elevated, and their aims more ambitious. Between the eleventh and sixteenth centuries, four of Judaism's greatest scholars, Rabbis Isaac Alfasi (also known as the Rif), Moses ben Maimon (otherwise known as Maimonides or Rambam[13]), Jacob ben Asher and Joseph Karo, all produced codes that effectively established – or sought to impose – normative observance amongst large sections of the Jewish world.

Isaac Alfasi compiled his code, *Sefer ha-Halakhot*, in the mid-eleventh century. As the name suggests, it gave brief discussions of laws currently in force. Alfasi's desire to produce a determinative text can be seen in his habit of closing the debate with an assertive, 'this is the law'. The material followed the order of the *Talmud*, earning it the name of *Talmud katan* (miniature *Talmud*) – another illustration of the strong sense of tradition in the halakhic system. Alfasi's work was accepted as binding for over a century and became one of the primary texts debated in the writings of later legal authorities. These discursive texts, stimulated by all the major Jewish codes, are known as *nosei kelim* ('arms bearers') because they battle either on behalf of or against the code in question.

Around the time of Alfasi's death in 1103, the books of *halakhot* were to some extent supplanted by the more terse collections of *pesakim* or decisions. However, the revolution was not complete and earlier codes lived on in later ones. For example, the book of *pesakim par excellence*, Maimonides' *Mishneh Torah*, drew extensively on the work of Alfasi and is rarely in disagreement with it.

Maimonides' code is a major work, such as one might expect of the man generally regarded as the greatest Jewish thinker of the Middle Ages.[14] The very name *Mishneh Torah* (loosely translatable as 'second *Torah*') is an allusion to the author's bold claims:

> I have entitled this work *Mishneh Torah* (Repetition of the Law), for the reason that a person who first reads the Written Law and then this compilation, will know from it the whole of the Oral Law, without having occasion to consult any other book between them.[15]

In consequence of this exclusive aim, Maimonides developed his work along distinctive lines. He deliberately wrote in a clear Hebrew style intended to be as accessible to as large an audience as possible. He also did not restrict himself to codifying those *halakhot* that informed contemporary Jewish behaviour. Every aspect of the law, including topics like animal sacrifice, was open for consideration: the *Mishneh Torah* was to be a guide for students as well as for everyday adherents of Judaism.

The *Mishneh Torah*'s strengths were also its weaknesses. Intending to provide a freestanding handbook, Maimonides had chosen the *pesakim* model. He gave no discussion of the Talmudic texts in question, and did not cite the sources of his rulings. Such an assertive laying down of the law inevitably prompted some acrimonious responses. Some suggested that his project was primarily one of self-aggrandisement; he wished to supersede the *Talmud* and usurp Ha-Nasi's status. But Maimonides refuted these claims, arguing that:

> My sole intention in composing this text was to clear the paths and remove the obstacles from before students of the law, so that they should not become discouraged or distressed by the overabundance of debate and argumentation, and consequently err in adjudicating the law correctly.[16]

He also expressed confidence that, although the text might be open to abuse at the hands of the wicked and the obtuse, in time it would gain acceptance from individuals of integrity who would recognise the value of what he had done.

To an extent Maimonides' confidence was borne out. In some countries the religious courts enacted statutes requiring halakhic problems to be decided in accordance with the *Mishneh Torah*'s opinion. But (particularly outside the Sephardi world) acceptance was not complete. Maimonides had apparently ignored or omitted the rulings of German and French halakhists; this was a significant problem that his *nosei kelim* sought to rationalise or remedy.

Two centuries after the *Mishneh Torah* a third major code was produced: the *Arba'ah Turim* or 'four rows' (named after the four rows of stones on the High Priest's breastplate in Exodus 28:17), so called because of its division into four sections. Just as the *Mishneh Torah* had reflected the Sephardi context of Maimonides, so the *Arba'ah Turim* (often abbreviated to *Tur*) written by Jacob ben Asher who settled in Spain, but came from a German tradition, reflects a predominantly Ashkenazi perspective. As a result the Sephardim, who were in increasing need of an updated guide to the *halakhah*, found that the *Tur* alone could not meet their requirements. Locally oriented revisions and commentaries were produced. Amongst these was the *Bet Yosef* ('House of Joseph') written by Joseph Karo, a rabbi and mystic in Safed, Israel. However, Karo's most significant contribution to the halakhic chain of tradition was the *Shulchan Arukh* ('Prepared Table', first printed in 1565) in which he distilled the *Bet Yosef* in order to arrive at a simple list of decisions. Although not intended to be such, the *Shulchan Arukh* has the distinction of being the final legal code to be widely accepted as authoritative across the observant Jewish world.

The *Shulchan Arukh* follows the *Tur* in structure but, like the *Mishneh Torah*, is a book of *pesakim*, giving no sources for its decisions. It is also predominantly Sephardi in character. It has already been shown how these two ingredients could be a recipe for controversy. However, *one* famous commentary on Karo's work emerged and helped to assure its enduring success.[17] This was the *Mappah* – or 'Tablecloth' – a collection of Ashkenazi glosses on the *Shulchan Arukh* text. Thus augmented, the *Shulchan Arukh* assumed authoritative status, to such an extent that legal authorities are sometimes named in relation to its compilation. Pre-*Shulchan Arukh* scholars are known as *rishonim* (early ones) and those afterwards as *aharonim* (later ones).

Although Orthodox Judaism accepts the *Shulchan Arukh* as binding, this does not mean that its rulings are or have been followed in a straightforward or slavish manner. In fact, acceptance of Karo's work as an authoritative code took some time. Scholars like the Polish rabbi Solomon Luria argued for a 'back to the *Talmud*' approach, remaining unconvinced of the worth of codifiers and the *nosei kelim*, whose works seemed to take Jews further and further away from the primary texts of the *halakhah*. More recently, of course, new conditions have demanded fresh decisions, and groups like the *Chasidim*, discussed in chapter three, have been happy to deviate from the *Shulchan Arukh's* norms in matters such as the timing and practice of prayer. However, there is much truth in Louis Jacobs' claim that generally speaking a strictly Orthodox Jew can be described as 'a *Shulhan Arukh* Jew'.[18]

A monumental achievement, and (thanks to the *Mappah*) the first code to be acceptable to both Western and Eastern communities, the *Shulchan Arukh* was also the final work to enjoy such status. Why, then, have there been no authoritative codes since the *Shulchan Arukh*?

The answer to this puzzle lies in the changing historical experience of Jews. Karo's code had assumed prominence in the mid-sixteenth century because it met a definite social need. Jewish communities underwent major upheavals during this period. In the 1490s a wave of expulsions of Jews from European countries (but from England in 1290) was completed with the driving out of sizeable communities from Spain and Portugal. Many of those who now found themselves fleeing the Iberian peninsula had arrived there from earlier troubles or were descendants of those who had done so. In the Middle East and North Africa, things were much better for Jews who found themselves subjects of the new Ottoman Empire (1517 onwards) but this was still a time of immense disturbance and rapid cultural change. In such a context, a code like Karo's provided a sense of stability. It reasserted norms and helped Jews to cope in both practical and psychological terms.

By the end of the seventeenth century however, Jews and Judaism were on the threshold of a new age. The Enlightenment's espousal of religious toleration sought to incorporate Jews into European culture and society, and in doing so radically transformed them. Jewish *community* was no longer assured. Newly granted civil rights meant that Jews *as individuals* were now free to make choices about their relation to the authority of the *halakhah* and the rabbinate. A secular Jewish identity became an option, as did the exposure of Jewish tradition to *Wissenschaft* or scientific criticism (see chapter three). With such diversity – even fragmentation – developing, it was impossible for any codifier to produce a work acceptable to all.

If the modern explosion of difference made codification less viable, it also generated an unprecedented number of new queries and dilemmas for those who did choose to remain to any degree observant of the *halakhah*. It is therefore now time to consider the means by which Jewish law achieves innovation – that is, to look at *responsa*.

Responsa

In the absence of a legislative body, *responsa* - in Hebrew, *she'elot u-teshuvot* ('questions and answers') - are the chief vehicle for the development of the Jewish legal tradition. As Jewish communities have found themselves in new political, economic and social contexts, different halakhic problems have been raised. *Responsa*, which are usually replies to queries that have been submitted by rabbis to more eminent colleagues, represent attempts to live carefully observant lives amidst such shifting conditions. (For example, chapter six introduces some of the recent attempts to apply *halakhah* to questions raised by environmental concerns and postwar developments in medical science.) Broadly speaking, *responsa* follow a common format. The specifics of the issue for consideration are set out. The respondent then discusses relevant legal literature, often attending to a number of analogies and previous rulings; finally, an opinion on the new issue is derived. As such, *responsa* may be characterised as the 'case

Moses Maimonides: law codes like Maimonides' *Mishneh Torah* were in part motivated by a desire to bolster Judaism against non-Jewish influences. Yet at the same time, the brilliance of Maimonides, who influenced Christian scholastics Thomas Aquinas and Duns Scotus, itself illustrates the benefits of cultural interchange.

This statue in Córdoba, Spain, depicts Maimonides wearing the turban typical of medieval Jews living under Islam. The scholar has long been depicted in this way although, given the biblical prohibition on graven images, he may not have approved of this kind of artistic tribute.

law' within the Jewish legal system - rulings on specific matters, which then enter the legal mainstream as precedent authority, or primary sources for the *halakhah*.

The *responsa's* direct link with the everyday life of carefully observant Jews means that a glance at any one of the thousands of extant collections can give fascinating insight into the development and practice of Judaism over the centuries. Whilst the more formal, ordered types of legal literature such as the *Mishnah* and Codes may sometimes deal in ideals, the *responsa* can be regarded as more reliable sources for the realities of Jewish life in various countries and periods. For example, the earliest surviving *responsa*, which date from the Geonic period, include many discussions of issues arising from Jewish contacts with their Muslim and Karaite[19] neighbours. What kinds of social and commercial relations between a Jew and a Muslim or Karaite are permissible? What is the correct Jewish attitude towards a particular point of debate or contention with a member of one of those communities?

In the modern period technological advances, together with emancipation (processes granting political and social rights to Jews, leading to increased contacts with non-Jewish culture) have led to the generation of many new *responsa*. More significantly, they have also impacted upon the status and nature of the *responsa* themselves. *Responsa* issuing from the Reform and other Progressive Jewish movements are 'not directive, but advisory' in line with those groups' views that the law is a human product (which is not to say that it is not in any sense divinely inspired).[20] This emphasis on subjectivity in relation to the *halakhah* generally and *responsa* in particular could be seen as a hallmark of a weakening of the value of law in Progressive Judaism. However, even the most radical of groups have sought to justify and develop their views with recourse to the traditional forms and sources of halakhic reflection.

The main source of *responsa* in the modern period remains the various Orthodox groups for whom careful observance of the *mitzvot* is vital to the maintenance of Jewish life in the face of a seemingly increasingly secularised environment. In particular, the founding of the State of Israel in 1948 has generated numerous legal questions. Once dormant areas of the *halakhah*, especially those relating to political and military matters, are newly awakened and have been discussed at great length. But perhaps the most poignant *responsa* from this era are those arising out of the Holocaust or, to use the Hebrew name, *Shoah*. (Because 'Holocaust' comes from a biblical word referring to a sacrifice that was 'wholly burnt', some people prefer the name *shoah* or 'destruction', since it has fewer theological connotations.) *In extremis*, Jews individually and communally sought rulings as to whether the entrusting of Jewish children to the care of non-Jews was halakhically permissible, whether slave labourers might fulfill the *mitzvah* or commandment of eating a festive meal at *Purim* (see chapter four) by consuming their regular ration of black bean soup, and even whether one could commit suicide in order to ensure burial in a Jewish cemetery. And within the constraints of their situations, rabbis prepared *responsa* which often show great compassion and sensitivity, for example in their desire to permit normally prohibited acts performed in good spirit in difficult times. The following is a *précis* of Rabbi Zvi Hirsch Meisels' postwar account of a ruling given whilst in Auschwitz, 1944.

The Nazi commander at Auschwitz had decided that only those boys between the ages of fourteen and eighteen who were strong enough to work should be kept alive; the others would be sent to the crematorium. 'Strength' in this case was measured in terms of the boys' height. Boys who did not pass the height test were imprisoned in a special cellblock and it was understood that they were to be sent to the crematorium the next night (which also happened to be *Rosh Ha-Shanah*).

Rabbi Meisels was approached by a Jew whose only son was in the cellblock. He had money to bribe the guards and save his son – but was such an act halakhically permissible given that the number of boys in the block had been strictly counted and the guards would therefore inevitably take another boy in his place to be killed?

Rabbi Meisels hesitated, unable to permit the act halakhically and unwilling to deny it. After much attempt to obtain a *responsum*, the man finally said, "Rabbi, I have done what the *Torah* has entreated me to do. I have asked a *she'elah* (question) of a *rav* (rabbi)....And if you cannot tell me that I may ransom my child, it is a sign that in your own mind, you are not certain that the *halakhah* permits it....So for me your silence is tantamount to a *pesak din* (a clear decision) that I am forbidden to do so by the *halakhah*. So my only son will lose his life according to the *Torah* and the *halakhah*. I accept God's decree with love and with joy. I will do nothing to ransom him at the cost of another life, for so the *Torah* has commanded!"[21]

In this truly awe-full account, the key tenets of normative Judaism are expressed more powerfully and with greater eloquence than any introductory study such as this book can provide: God exists and is known to Jews principally through faithful observance of the *halakhah* or religious law.

Notes

[1] The etymology of the term is unclear, but it is often thought to derive from the root *halakh* 'to go' or 'walk', and hence refers to those rules by which one 'walks' through life.

[2] E. Berkovits, 'The Centrality of Halakhah', in J. Neusner (ed.), *Understanding Rabbinic Judaism: From Talmudic to Modern Times*, New York: Ktav, 1974, p. 69.

[3] The chronological designations AD ('Anno Domini') and BC ('Before Christ') are in origin professions of Christian faith; for this reason, they have been substituted with CE ('common era') and BCE ('before common era').

[4] D. Halivni, *Revelation Restored: Divine Writ and Critical Responses*, Boulder: Westview Press 1997, pp. 5, 12-14; J. Barton, 'The Significance of a Fixed Canon of the Hebrew Bible', in M. Saebo (ed.), *Hebrew Bible/Old Testament. The History of Its Interpretation Vol. 1 From the Beginnings to the Middle Ages (Until 1300)*, Göttingen: Vandenhoeck and Ruprecht, 1996, pp. 67-83.

[5] The Temple built by Solomon (1 Kings 6:1) was destroyed in 586 BCE by the Babylonians (2 Kings 24:10). Rebuilding began in 515 BCE, but it was not until 64 CE that the Second Temple was complete.

[6] Halivni, *Revelation Restored*, p. 73.

[7] The *Shema* ('hear!' or 'listen!') consists of three Biblical passages: Deuteronomy 6:4-9 (which begins, '*Hear* O Israel, the Lord our God, the Lord is One') Deuteronomy 11: 13-21 and Numbers 15:37-41. Though not a creed, it is a declaration of fundamentals including belief in one God.

[8] The ordering of the *Mishnah's* contents seems to be on the grounds of length; longer tractates precede shorter ones. This arrangement is found elsewhere in ancient texts: the *Suras* are so organised in the *Qur'an*.

[9] The structuring of the *Mishnah* is discussed in H. L. Strack and G.

Stemberger; M. Bockmuehl trans., *Introduction to the Talmud and Midrash*, Edinburgh: T. and T. Clark, 1991, pp. 133-138. The most plausible explanation for *Avot's* placing may be that it was added circa 300 CE to the *Mishnah* which at that time was differently ordered and concluded with *Nezikin*.

[10] J. Neusner (trans.), *The Mishnah: A New Translation*, New Haven: Yale University Press, 1988.

[11] C. Pearl, *Rashi*, Peter Halban, 1988.

[12] S. Assaf, *Teshuvot haGe'onim*, Jerusalem: Darom, 1928, p. 81.

[13] Many medieval rabbis are known either by name or by a shorter acrostic. Rabbi Isaac Alfasi (born Algeria, 1013) becomes Rif; Moses Maimonides, Rabbi Moses ben Maimon becomes Rambam.

[14] Maimonides (1135–1204) was born in Córdoba, and spent his adult life in Fez and Cairo. He was physician to the Sultan of Egypt and wrote medical treatises, but is best remembered for the *Mishneh Torah*, and *Guide for the Perplexed* (Hebrew, *Moreh Nevukim*).

[15] Quoted in I. Twersky, *Introduction to the Code of Maimonides (Mishneh Torah)*, New Haven: Yale University Press, 1980, p. 30.

[16] Ibid., pp. 40-41.

[17] Another reason for the *Shulchan Arukh's* rapid dissemination was its rapid appearance in print (Venice, 1564-65).

[18] Jacobs, L., 'Shulhan Arukh', in his *The Jewish Religion: A Companion*, Oxford: Oxford University Press, 1995, p. 467.

[19] Originating in the eighth century CE, the Karaites rejected the *Talmud* and later rabbinic literature. Well into the Middle Ages, many rabbis regarded Karaites as Jews but in time the traditions grew apart, viewing each other as different religions. See N. Schur, *History of the Karaites*, Frankfurt-am-Main: Peter Lang, 1992 for a brief history.

[20] Solomon B. Freehof (1893-1990) in *Reform Responsa*, New York: Ktav, 1960, p. 22.

[21] See in I. J. Rosenbaum, *The Holocaust and Halakhah*, New York: Ktav, 1976, pp. 3-5. The other cases mentioned are in E. Oshry, *Responsa from the Holocaust*, New York: Judaica Press, 1989.

3

Jewish Diversity

Two Jews, three opinions (proverbial)

Diversity, with its pains and its pleasures, is a fact of Jewish life today. Many popular and some scholarly accounts of the problematic of contemporary Jewish difference look back to a golden age when Jewry was cohesive and unified, people shared a common commitment to a carefully observant lifestyle, and cases of assimilation and intermarriage were rare. In a recent guide to *Modern Judaism*, one writer speaks of pre-modern Judaism as 'monolithic', and of the modern age as having heralded the dissolution of 'traditional' Judaism.[1] In fact, attitudes, emotions and praxis have always varied. Throughout Jewish history, different philosophies and programmes have vied for the support of the faithful. At times, the diversity has been so great as to make it more appropriate to speak of the Judaism*s* rather than of the Judaism of a particular age.

A Jewish historian of the first century, Flavius Josephus, described several parties within early Judaism, some of which are also mentioned in the Christian New Testament and the *Mishnah*. A range of issues including belief, religious practice, and attitudes towards the Roman forces occupying the land of Israel divided groups known as Pharisees, Sadducees, Essenes and Zealots. For example, Josephus expresses the difference between Pharisees and Sadducees as follows:

> the Pharisees had passed on to the people certain regulations handed down by former generations and not recorded in the Laws of Moses [i.e. The Oral *Torah*], for which reason they are rejected by the Sadducaean group, who hold that only those regulations should be considered valid which were

written down [in Scripture] (*Antiquities*, 13.297).

The Pharisees' flexible approach to *Torah* had, of course, practical implications. When a Sadducee High Priest refused to follow the practice of making a water libation at *Sukkot* or Tabernacles (something not commanded in the *Tanakh* but a popular act defended by the Pharisees) the crowd pelted him with the citrus fruits used in the festival celebrations (an event described by Josephus and in *m. Sukkah* 4.9).

In subsequent times, commitment to *Torah* was a force for cohesion in Jewish life (see especially chapter four). But equally, the *halakhah's* practical implementation in concrete situations could be a source of debate and friction, as was suggested in chapter two. The Babylonian and Jerusalem *Talmuds* are compilations of varied opinions and rulings that often remain unresolved; moreover, they were not uniformly accepted as authoritative. Medieval *responsa* delineated appropriate relations between Jews who paid allegiance to the Oral *Torah* as preserved in the *Talmud* and the Karaites, who did not. Within 'mainstream' Jewry, other *responsa* constructed relations between those with different cultural backgrounds, the Ashkenazim and Sephardim.[2] At the mundane level then, codes and *responsa* are about what to eat, drink, wear, or do in certain contexts. Beyond that, they also have a social-psychological role in the formation and maintenance of boundaries between communities of difference *within* Judaism, as well as those between Jews and non-Jews. This chapter will concentrate on the diversity within modern Ashkenazi Jewry. Arguably, in the last two centuries the religiosity of the Ashkenazim has exhibited more variation than other modern and pre-modern forms of Judaism. But as a means of comparison, the chapter will also discuss briefly some Sephardi responses to modernity.

So far the terms 'modernity' and 'modern' have been used without comment, but their meanings are by no means fixed or self-evident. 'Modern', from the Latin *modo* ('just now') was used in the fifth century CE to distinguish the 'Christian present' from the 'pagan past'. As Jürgen Habermas has identified, it has been prominent in European discourse during periods characterised by a strong sense of change. Times labelled as modern have been those during which participants have believed themselves to be witnesses to the replacement of an older social or political order. Hence the term is linked to ideas of change, progression, and sometimes – but certainly not always – improvement. 'Modernity' has a more specific usage. Popularized in the early nineteenth century by Honoré de Balzac, it today refers specifically to the intellectual and cultural consequences of the Enlightenment, and often also to the social, economic, and political development associated with its creation and sustenance. For Balzac, instability and insecurity was a fundamental aspect of modernity: traditional sources of meaning no longer held sway, and had not been, or could not be, replaced by authoritative new ones.[3]

The forces Balzac recognised in early nineteenth century France spread across Western and much of Central Europe, profoundly affecting Jews who lived in those regions, or in other places subject to their influence or control (for example the French colonies in North Africa). On the one hand communities found themselves caught up in the intellectual challenges of the Enlightenment, the originally philosophical but later wide-ranging cultural movement characterised by a commitment to and confidence in reason, truth and progress. A distinctively Jewish Enlightenment, the *Haskalah*, emerged in Germany amongst the small number of Jews who had received both traditional Jewish and secular educations. The career of Moses Mendelssohn (1729-1786), the most prominent member of this first generation of *Maskilim* ('the intelligent', from Daniel 12:3), exemplifies that of the *Haskalah's* pioneers. Mendelssohn sought to strike a balance between commitment to Judaism and non-Jewish Enlightenment culture. In *Jerusalem, or On Religious Power and Judaism* (1783) he attempted to prove that Judaism was a system of 'revealed legislation' and that its central beliefs were capable of rational investigation and therefore not at odds with the *Zeitgeist*. To demonstrate further the compatibility of Jewishness and European culture, he also tried to produce a correct or critical Hebrew text of the *Tanakh* and translated the *Torah* and Psalms into German, partly as a means of enabling Yiddish-speaking Jews to learn the vernacular. Yet despite Mendelssohn's commitment to rationalism and the modern, he found himself the subject of unfavourable attention from the non-Jewish world. Having been immortalised by philosopher-playwright Gotthold Lessing (Mendelssohn is the thinly disguised hero of *Nathan the Wise*), he was challenged in an open letter to convert to Christianity by a Swiss pastor, Johann Kaspar Lavater. Indeed, *Jerusalem* is primarily an *apologia* prompted by such pressures.

Mendelssohn's defence of Judaism amounted to a new philosophy of the Jewish religion. However, whilst the problems (and their solutions) have often been presented as philosophical ones, the most immediate challenges facing many ordinary European Jews were practical in nature. Intellectual and theological dilemmas often became apparent only as a result of the legal and social developments brought about by the Enlightenment's thrust towards cultural hegemony founded on a 'secular' logic. Starting in France in 1789 with the publication of '*les droits de l'homme*' and continuing during the nineteenth century, West and Central European Jews experienced emancipation – not a single phenomenon uniformly repeated across different countries, but a range of legal measures which conferred on them civil and political rights in their countries of residence. In medieval Europe, the possession of full rights had usually been restricted to members of an Established Church. Jews (and members of heterodox Christian denominations) lived as a (generally) tolerated minority, subject to legal and social restrictions. The removal of these impediments meant that for the first time European Jews could experience the rights, duties and obligations incumbent on the other citizens of the states in which they lived. In the past, many Jews had been forced to live in approved areas of rural settlement or in urban ghettos. State legislation had obliged them, if they wished to live as Jews, to be subject to *halakhah* and rabbinic authority. In the nineteenth and early twentieth centuries (until the rise of National Socialism) this ceased to be the case. At least in theory, European Jews could vote and stand as candidates for public office, live where they wished and gain access to previously closed institutions. Modernity entailed the transition from 'fate' to 'choice'.

Whilst Emancipation brought many real benefits for Jewry, the attitude towards Judaism of the liberal thinkers and politicians who framed the legislation was not always positive. Voltaire's (1694–1778) attacks on the traditional beliefs of pre-Revolutionary society – the divine right of the monarchy, the infallibility of the Church, and the freedoms accorded to the nobility – did much to prepare the ground for the legal Emancipation of Jews in France. But in his opposition to established privilege, Voltaire spoke of Judaism as the debased, degenerate foundation on which Christianity (his principal target) was built: 'superstition, born in paganism, adopted by Judaism, infected the Christian Church from the earliest times.'[4] Some modern analysts trace a line from Voltaire's ascerbity to secular antisemitism and the Holocaust or *Shoah*.[5] This is too simplistic. In his *Philosophical Dictionary*, Voltaire sometimes uses Jewish tradition to critique Christianity: he also pokes fun at Christian anti-Judaism. However, in places he does appear to move from opposition to the Jewish religion to criticism of Jews as a people. Throughout the *Dictionary*, Jews are characterised as a coarse people, who lack creativity and have plagiarised their culture from that of their host nations. In a discussion of the story of Jephthah's daughter, Voltaire's text also echoes some of the blood libels (see chapter 5) that had such dangerous consequences for medieval Jews: 'Human blood sacrifices were thus clearly established. No historical detail is better attested. A nation can be judged only by its archives and by what it tells about itself'.[6]

Less vehement than Voltaire, but equally (in)famous was the Comte deClermont-Tonnerre's statement that 'the Jews should be denied everything as a nation, but granted everything as individuals. They must be citizens'.[7] This remark does not necessarily imply that Clermont-Tonnerre expected emancipated Jews to disavow their heritage. Like some of Voltaire's comments, it may be better interpreted as part of the French National Assembly's wider project to dismantle the *ancien régime*. This entailed the destruction of previous relationships between the king and the corporate or guild structures (like the Jewish community) and the contracting of new ones between individual citizens and the state. Nevertheless, emancipation was often motivated at least in part by a desire to 'normalise' Jews, in the hope that forms of Jewish separateness and distinctiveness – in effect, that Jews *as Jews* – would wane and ultimately disappear.

Modern forms of Jewish religious diversity are largely responses to the difficult freedom brought about by the twin forces of Enlightenment and emancipation. A proportion of Jews, recognising perhaps that legal measures alone did not secure equality and acceptance, converted to Christianity. German poet Heinrich Heine took this route in 1825 in the hope of gaining a career as an academic or civil servant. He famously described the baptismal certificate as 'the ticket of admission to European culture'. However, contrary to many legislators' wishes, most Jews did not wish to assimilate totally. Even Heine would later write, 'I make no secret of my Judaism, to which I have not returned, because I never left it'.[8] As Mendelssohn's heirs, modern Jews have instead grappled with the challenges of reconciling or striking a balance between Jewish and non-Jewish cultures.

Charedim

Despite the undeniable influence of the Enlightenment on the lived experience and intellectual activity of Ashkenazi communities it would be a mistake to regard pre-modern Judaism as a cohesive community which then suddenly fractured under pressure from external factors. As a precursor to an examination of modern forms of Jewish diversity, we will first examine the *Charedi* movement.

Out of a total Jewish world population of approximately twelve million, there are between five and six hundred thousand *Charedim* – carefully observant Jews who by and large eschew the kind of negotiation and compromise with modernity exemplified by Mendelssohn. Particularly in the anglophone world, the *Charedim* (literally, 'those who tremble [before God]', as in Ezra 10:3 or Isaiah 66:5) are often described as 'ultra-orthodox'. However, I have tried to avoid that term in this book. It is often used in a way that unfairly implies a cold, rigid approach to observance. (Moreover, ortho*doxy* or 'right belief' is in origin a Christian category and as such is a slightly inept way of talking about Judaism.) As an intrinsically Jewish term, *Charedim* seems a more appropriate and sympathetic designation for this group. Within the ranks of the *Charedim* are many different Jewish movements, including all the Chasidic groups, of which the most famous today are the Lubavich, the Ger, the Belz and the Satmar Chasidim; other Ashkenazi groups who try to preserve intact the way of life followed in pre-modern Eastern Europe; and various Oriental and Sephardi groups who are similarly committed to the patterns of Jewish life in the pre-modern East.

Alone among these groupings, the chasidim, who combine strict observance of the *halakhah* with an intense pietism and mysticism, trace their origins directly to a named individual, one Israel ben Eliezer (1669–1761) also known as the Baal Shem Tov or Besht. In fact there is considerable evidence to demonstrate that before the advent of its 'progenitor', small circles of Jews already existed who sought to marry acceptance of the entirety of Jewish tradition with an emphasis on deep piety and mystical exercises intended to enable the adherent to achieve *devekut*, a cleaving to or intense being-with-God. *In Praise of the Baal Shem Tov*, a hagiographic account produced some fifty years after the Besht's death, admits as much. It recounts tales of his confirmation as leader by circles of men learned in *Talmud* and rabbinics, and renowned for their expertise in the mysteries of kabbalah, Jewish mysticism.[9] However, if not strictly speaking its originator, then ben Eliezar was certainly chasidism's most charismatic early leader. Born in Tluste, on the then Polish-Turkish border, in early life he earned a reputation as an itinerant *baal shem*, a 'master of the holy Name' or 'wonder worker' who could use prayers and mystical practices to achieve healings and other miraculous ends. Whilst medieval rabbis, like contemporary scholars of religion, tended to view such professions with disdain, the *baal shem* was an important functionary in later medieval Jewish life. As Simon Dubnow points out:

> The *baalei shem* exerted a tremendous religious influence among the folk masses who believed implicitly in their remedies and their "miracles". There were many who exploited this blind faith for their own profit, but the best ones considered their work a sacred calling. The healing they performed was not done merely for the sake of their own livelihood, but primarily as a means of redeeming the souls of those who approached them for help, or of disseminating knowledge of the revealed Torah.[10]

The Besht was amongst the most successful of these *baalei shem*, requiring the services of a scribe who answered letters from believers across Poland and Ukraine, and wrote amulets for therapeutic and apotrophaic purposes. (Later chasidic leaders have had similar intermediaries to handle written queries and financial donations.) It was the Besht's blending of these popular instrumental techniques with a life of intense prayer and reliance on the teachings of the *Zohar*, the most important work of Jewish mysticism, that placed him at the forefront of the emergent chasidic movement.[11] Ben Eliezar challenged existing religious aspirations, replacing the traditional rabbinic ideal with that of the chasid or pious person who, without the privilege of a lifetime's textual studies, could achieve intimate knowledge of and association with the divine. Moreover, this intimacy was not simply for the individual chasid's gain. Earlier Jewish mysticism (in the *Zohar* and the work of Isaac Luria Ashkenazi of Safed) had taught that, as a necessary aspect of creation, elements of God, the 'divine sparks', had become embedded or exiled in the universe: in God's attempt to communicate something of God's own perfect essence to the world, fracture and disruption of the God-head had occurred. Earthly and cosmic redemption or *tikkun* (repair) would be achieved only when these sparks were enabled to be united once again with their ultimate source. The new movement regarded the chasid as a vital figure in this restorative process. Everything done in terms of prayer, observance, and mystical discipline could serve to free the trapped sparks and reunite them with the unknowable, ultimate aspect of the divine, the *Ein Sof*. Far from being dryly 'ultra orthodox', the chasid is, then, almost a kind of co-redeemer of the universe, a participant in an on-going cosmic drama. Concomitant with this understanding of the human role is the implicit notion that, being in need of human help, God is not, as classically conceived, omnipotent – a radical development in Jewish theology, and one which has been of particular appeal in the contemporary, post-*Shoah* world.

In the generations immediately following the Besht's death, chasidism became dominant throughout Eastern Europe, but it was never uniform. The polygenesis of the movement was reflected in the later, still current, division of chasidim into different groups or courts, each following their own *rebbe* or *tzaddik* who took his name from the region in which he asserted his authority (Lubavich in Belarus, Satmar in Hungary, and so on). The *rebbe* was (and still is) mystically believed to function as a kind of conduit between heaven and earth, as well as a teacher and model of the right life. So, chasidim regarded their *rebbe* as much more than an expert in *halakhah*. Drawing near to the *rebbe*, consulting him on personal and business matters, eating with him (even eating his *shirayim*, leftovers), and helping to meet his financial needs, were means of achieving intimacy with the divine.

The emphasis on group intimacy and cohesion centred around the strong charismatic authority of the *rebbe* undoubtedly contributed to the success of chasidism. Not long before the emergence of the Besht, Eastern European Jewry had been traumatised by the horrors of the Chmielnicki massacres of 1648, during which thousands of individual Jews died and hundreds of communities were wiped out. Jewry was also in religious turmoil, as is illustrated well by the rapid success and decline of Shabbateanism, a messianic movement named after its leader, Shabbatai Tzvi (from Smyrna), who eventually converted to Islam, leaving his many followers in disarray.[12] In such an environment, the teaching of the Besht and his followers, and the structures which chasidism developed, were of strong appeal. In a world where many ordinary Jews lacked the right to political and economic self-determination, the movement gave them a cosmic role of ultimate importance. However, innovative practices (especially the outwardly visible ones such as the use of ecstatic techniques during prayer, and changes to the knives used for *shechitah*, the ritual slaughter of animals for food) and the non-halakhic basis of the *rebbe's* authority, invoked the opposition of many Jews who remained committed to the view that an attachment to *halakhah* constituted real Judaism, and that scholarship, not dynastic ties or mysticism, was the source of leadership. Anti-chasidic literature appeared. In 1772 one of the greatest rabbinic authorities, the Vilna Gaon, Elijah ben Solomon Zalman (1720–1797) excommunicated the chasidim. But despite the Gaon's protestations against those who in his view belittled the study of *Torah*, made false prayers and regarded every day as a festival, chasidism won the day, numerically at least. Its opponents were known as just that, *mitnaggedim*, a title that in itself attests to their increasingly non-normative status.

With the dawning of the *Haskalah*, the once opposed chasidim and *mitnaggedim* encountered a common enemy. From the late nineteenth century onwards, whilst not completely accepting each other's praxis as authentic, their shared desire to maintain a thoroughly observant life has prompted the groups to form alliances and work together to prevent Judaism's 'decline'. Samuel Heilman describes this on-going process as one whereby in the post-Enlightenment, post-emancipation world both chasidim and *mitnaggedim* have 'become' *Charedim* - a shared designation which illustrates the extent to which older disputes have been superseded.[13] Indicative of this trend is the constitution of *Agudat Israel* (League of Israel) formed in 1912 to defend 'Torah-true' Jews from assimilation and secularisation. Whilst primarily a chasidic body, its Council of Sages includes the leaders of other *Charedi* groups.

The conservationist, introversionist response of *Agudat Israel* in particular, and the *Charedi* emphasis on traditionalism more generally, often means that the *Charedim* are perceived simply as the embodiment of the Jewish past, evocative of so many faded sepia photographs from pre-*Shoah* Poland. However, whilst not a modern Jewish grouping, in the sense that they believe Jewish faith can be externalised only through the *halakhah*, the *Charedim* are very much part of the contemporary Jewish picture.

In recent years they have undergone something of a resurgence. Whilst all but a small proportion were slaughtered during the Nazi era, the attendant dispersal of refugees and survivors enabled *Charedi* communities to establish themselves successfully in new locations, especially in Israel (particularly in the Me'ah She'arim district of Jerusalem, and Bene Barak, near Tel Aviv), the United States (including Crown Heights, Williamsburg, and other Brooklyn neighbourhoods), and Western Europe (for example, Stamford Hill in north London, and Gateshead, north-east England). In

Gateshead Talmudical College. Amongst Orthodox Jews, this centre in the north-east of England is considered one of the most important training institutions in Europe.

these new contexts, *Charedi* Judaism has adapted in order to survive and flourish.

Pre-war *Charedi* communities operated chiefly in contexts in which (despite formal emancipation) they were largely separate from the wider non-*haredi* population. Today the majority live in urban environments, in societies that are open to them, both *de jure* and *de facto*. Nowhere is this more clearly the case than in the modern state of Israel where legislation not only recognises the *Charedim* but also goes some way towards facilitating their lifestyle, exempting *Charedi* girls and women from military service, and tolerating the existence of the Orthodox Community with its own *bet din* and militant, campaigning wing *Neturei Karta* ('guardians of the city'). In return, *Charedi* responses to Israel have been mixed. *Neturei Karta* (dominated by non-chasidic groups and the Satmar chasidim) regards the existence of the state as an abomination, on the grounds that God alone can redeem or re-establish Israel. In this vein, the most famous recent Satmar rebbe, Joel Teitelbaum (1888-1979) described the State of Israel as satanic, and maintained that, even if its inhabitants were to observe the *halakhah* fully (a feat traditionally held to prompt the dawning of the messianic age), they would have forfeited a share in the divine promises because they had established a state before the advent of the Messiah.[14] Others have disowned the activities of *Neturei Karta* and try to work with the modern state and its secular power structures, typically seeking to secure legislation that promotes religious observance. Amongst these groups are those represented by *Agudat Israel* and *Yahadut Ha-Torah Ha-Me'uchedet* (United Torah Judaism). In 1983 the *Shas* party (Sephardi Torah guardians) was founded in an attempt to secure a distinctively Sephardi *Charedi* voice and to counter the perceived Ashkenazification of much Israeli religious and secular life. Its success led to unprecedented media exposure for founder Eliezer Shach (born 1894), whose burial in 2001 was attended by a crowd of 250,000 people.

Outside Israel the *Charedim* have been less directly involved in national politics, but have played an increasingly prominent role in Jewish communal affairs: *Charedim* are not Amish. Perhaps the most successful of *Charedi* groups in *Diaspora* is the Lubavich movement, founded in Belarus by Shneur Zalman of Lyady in the late eighteenth century. Zalman's ideas were distinct from those of his contemporaries. He stressed the importance of wisdom, understanding and knowledge, and hence emphasised *Torah* study, far more than did other chasidic leaders. In recent years, Lubavich chasidism has played a key role in the *Baal Teshuvah* phenomenon, encouraging people with little or no previous Jewish education to return to or adopt a carefully observant lifestyle. Its combination of traditionally chasidic and non-chasidic traits (mysticism *and* rabbinic study) and acceptance of modern technologies, if not of modernity, has allowed it to flourish in the late twentieth and early twenty-first centuries. Today the Lubavich are the least geographically confined of all *Charedi* groups. Despite recent controversies concerning the possible messianic identity of the late leader, Rabbi Menachem Mendel Schneerson (died 1994) the group seems likely to increase numerically and in profile.

Reform Judaism

In spite of the visible successes of the Lubavich and other *Charedi* groups, the seventeenth century was the last in which Rabbinic tradition founded on *Talmud Torah* truly prevailed in Jewish society. A century before chasidism spread across Eastern Europe, Baruch Spinoza's (1632–1677) historical criticism of the Jewish Scriptures, whilst earning him a ban of excommunication (*Cherem*) from the Amsterdam community, foreshadowed the rationalist tradition with which future Judaisms would have to make peace or war.[15] In the early nineteenth century some German Jewish communities began to articulate and rationalise their decision to make friends with modernity, downplay the distinctive features of Jewish life, and reform Judaism in order to create an expression of Jewish religiosity that (they felt) was more in keeping with their status as citizens of a new Europe.

In 1818, following previous short-lived attempts in Amsterdam, Westphalia, and Berlin, the Hamburg Reform Temple was opened. Its express intention was to offer the predominantly middle class membership a more dignified form of worship than that found in the traditional synagogue or *shool*. Services were shortened, largely because they omitted *piyyutim*, decorative liturgical poems that had proliferated during the Middle Ages. They included sermons and some prayers in the vernacular, a choir accompanied by an organ, and gave young people opportunities to receive 'an enlightened Jewish education', in which a balance or synthesis between Judaism and non-Jewish *mores* would be fostered. Moreover, although there were (as traditionally) men's and women's sections in the temple, there was no partition or *mechitzah* to obscure the latter's view of the service. Similar measures to those in Hamburg were instituted elsewhere, not only in continental Europe but also in the United States and England, where the first Reform congregation met in 1840 (the West London Synagogue of British Jews) and another was established in Manchester a decade or so later. The motivations for these practical changes to the forms of Jewish worship were not explicitly theoretical or theological but pragmatic. Anxious to demonstrate to the countries of which they were now citizens that 'Jew' no longer signified an attachment to a culture that was frequently perceived as alien, foreign and inherently impoverished, early reformers wanted to develop a style of worship – of public, corporate Jewish expression – that was in sympathy with the modern aesthetic. In doing so they were moving towards the legislators' assimilationist ideals. But, at the same time, their adaptive work was seeking to ensure the survival of Judaism, and therefore a form of Jewish difference, in the modern world.

Despite the popular success of the Hamburg Temple the congregation and its worship style aroused considerable controversy. Traditionalists declared the use of German, shortening of services, and the playing of musical instruments in synagogue on the Sabbath and festival days, as contrary to *halakhah*.[16] It was such conflicts with groups wishing to preserve what began to be known as 'Orthodoxy' that eventually led the reformers to develop a philosophical rationale for the changes being made. Whilst many of those who had joined or attended the Hamburg Temples had done so for personal or social reasons, the new Reform Judaism needed a theoretical justification. It also required a set of principles and procedures if it were to survive in the long-term, and not merely be a staging post between *shtetl* and secularisation.

This second stage in the development of Reform Judaism is best illustrated by the career of Abraham Geiger (1810–1874) who in the early nineteenth century was one of the few thinkers who truly sought to apply modern ideas to Judaism. Together with Leopold Zunz, he was a founder of the *Wissenschaft des Judentums* movement, advocating that Judaism be subjected to rigorous investigation. Scientific rather than religious truth was for him paramount, and this led him to question established Jewish norms: 'The Talmud must go, the Bible, that collection of mostly so beautiful and exalted – perhaps the most exalted – *human* books, as a divine work must also go'.[17] In a sense Geiger's remarks, whilst going farther than many would wish today, encapsulate the questioning stance towards the Sinai revelation which characterises Reform Judaism. Whilst the Sinai event is recognised as being of great importance to Israel, the *Torah* is understood as something inspired by God but written down by humans according to their appreciation of God's will – and hence not infallible, but open to challenge and revision. However, it was not one of Geiger's many scholarly works on language or *halakhah* but his prospective appointment as assistant rabbi of Breslau (then in Prussia), which led directly to his involvement in the most significant controversy of the early Reform movement. The chief rabbi of Breslau, Solomon Abraham Tiktin, was a staunch traditionalist. His refusal to preach sermons and institute other moderate reforms had frustrated the town's relatively

well-to-do Jewish community. In 1838 they decided to force Tiktin's
hand by engaging Geiger as a second rabbi, with special responsibility for
religious education. But Tiktin and his supporters refused to recognise
Geiger and a prolonged clash ensued, taking the form of harsh exchanges
between the two factions, and occasionally spilling over into physical
violence. On the one hand the Tiktinites stressed the eternal validity of
Jewish law and the halakhic, non-pastoral, nature of the rabbinic office.
On the other, Geiger emphasised the practical need for reforms in liturgy
and law, and his desire to use historical criticism of sacred texts as a basis
for the construction of a Judaism relevant for the nineteenth century.
Eventually the controversy came to an end with Tiktin's death in 1843,
but in the process both factions had been forced to articulate reasons for
their differing approaches to Judaism. They could no longer function
effectively as a single Jewish community. The final outcome of the Geiger-
Tiktin affair, indicative of what was to come elsewhere in following
decades, was a clear division of Breslau Jews into two separate religious
societies. Whilst reformers and traditionalists came together for some
practical and social welfare purposes, functionally, they were distinct
denominations. Reform had emerged as a new form of Jewish diversity.

As Reform Judaism came of age, various associations and other
structures necessarily emerged to give it a greater degree of coherence. In
the 1840s three rabbinical assemblies were held. These meetings in
Brunswick, Frankfurt-am-Main, and Breslau, were followed by further
European conferences in the 1860s. Ostensibly, those gathered did so in
order to formulate shared statements on principles and goals. This they
did, but the prominence given to participating rabbis and other religious
specialists was also of great significance. Whereas early liturgical changes
had been prompted by congregational concerns over aesthetic matters,
the rabbinate had now resumed the driving seat within Reform Judaism.

Whilst the 1840s witnessed much discussion of Reform in Europe,
the same decade also saw the emigration of a large number of German
Jews, amongst them some Reform rabbis, to the United States. An
American Reform community had been established as early as 1824 when
members of the *Beth Elohim* congregation in South Carolina gave assent
to Judaism's truth, but requested prayers and a sermon in English, and
numerous other changes in order to create a more respectful atmosphere
and counter the tendency of their fellow Jews to lose 'those strong ties
which bind every pious man to the faith of his fathers'.[18] As the nineteenth

century was succeeded by the twentieth, America became increasingly dominant within Reform Judaism, and a number of conferences held there issued platforms or programmatic statements on the religious life. These platforms are of central importance within Reform. Although not binding, they illustrate well its changing concerns and emphases.[19]

The first platform, adopted at Pittsburgh in 1885, witnesses to the very great extent to which Enlightenment concerns infused the early reformers. The omnipotent, omnipresent God of traditional Jewish thought is conspicuously absent from its text. Rationalism and a confident belief in the reality and goodness of human progress are to the fore. Judaism is affirmed as 'the highest conception of the God-idea as taught in our holy Scriptures and developed and spiritualised by the Jewish teachers in accordance with the moral and philosophical progress of their respective ages'. This association between development and spiritualisation also led the reformers to assert that the observance of laws relating to diet, dress and purity 'is apt rather to obstruct than to further modern spiritual elevation'. Only those moral laws thought capable of elevating the modern Jew were regarded as binding. Above all, the Pittsburgh participants, under the leadership of Kaufmann Kohler, stressed that in line with the modern universalist spirit of the age they considered themselves 'no longer a nation but a religious community'.

By the time that the Columbus Platform (drafted by Samuel Cohon) was issued in 1937 many Jews and non-Jews alike were no longer as confident in the inevitably of human progress as their nineteenth century predecessors had been. World War I had scarred much of Europe, including many areas of Jewish population. This impacted on America, too. Like other Jewish movements Reform ranks there were swelled by the arrival of Eastern European immigrants, many of whom had only recently encountered the twin forces of Enlightenment and emancipation and were more traditional in orientation than their German predecessors. Moreover, in Europe political forces including secular Zionism and Nazism were becoming increasingly powerful. All this forced Reform Judaism to address issues such as Jewish particularism and its hallmarks with a new sense of urgency. Hence the Columbus platform affirms belief in a providential God, and attitudes towards *Torah*, phrased negatively at Pittsburgh, are voiced in different terms. 'Revelation is a continuous process' of which the Bible is a product. As 'a product of historical processes, certain of its laws have lost their binding force with the passing of the conditions that called them forth', but 'as a depository of permanent spiritual ideals, the *Torah* remains the dynamic source of the life of Israel'. Perhaps most poignantly in an age of race politics, the Columbus Platform also asserts the bonds of sympathy between religious and non-religious Jews and 'urges organized international action for disarmament, collective security and world peace'.

Fully one third of the Columbus Platform was concerned with Jewish life in home, synagogue, and school. These concerns were foregrounded again in 1976 when the movement issued the San Francisco Platform to commemorate the centenary of the Union of American Hebrew Congregations (UAHC) and Hebrew Union College (HUC), American Reform's primary organisational bodies. At the same time, this third platform also reflects the theological tensions inherent within post-war Reform Judaism. It acknowledges that 'the trials of our own time and the challenges of modern culture have made steady belief and clear understanding difficult for some', but adds that 'we...remain open to new experiences and conceptions of the Divine.' The State of Israel is presented as a demonstration of what 'a united people can accomplish in history' but 'a genuine Jewish life is possible in any land'. Tension between universalism and particularism is also evident and regarded as intrinsic to the Jewish experience: 'In recent years we have become freshly conscious of the virtues of pluralism and the values of particularlsm'. The San Francisco Platform is an admirable effort at fostering a sense of unity whilst also upholding the reality of ongoing diversity within the Reform movement, and the Jewish community at large.

Just over a century after the first platform was issued, the Central Conference of American Rabbis returned to Pittsburgh to formulate 'a set of principles that define Reform Judaism in our own time'. The 1999 platform, structured around the three pillars (*m. Avot* 1:2) of God, *Torah* and Israel, addresses familiar themes. Whilst the first platform recognised 'in every religion an attempt to grasp the Infinite', the new statement advocates that Reform Jews 'seek dialogue and joint action with people of other faiths in the hope that together we can bring peace, freedom and justice to our world'. However, some of the platform's planks reflect shifts within Reform Judaism with which some progressive Jews are less at ease:

We are committed to the ongoing study of the whole of [the] *mitzvot* and to the fulfilment of those that address us as individuals and as a community. Some of these…have long been observed by Reform Jews; others, both ancient and modern, demand renewed attention as the result of the unique context of our own times.

Reform Judaism has always seen itself as a dynamic, evolving body, but for some the comments on the renewed importance of *mitzvot* imply a creeping conservatism within the movement – the result of the increasing professionalisation of the rabbinate, perhaps, or of a failure of nerve and a giving in to the Orthodox definition of the Jewish way of being. Earlier drafts of the Platform had discussed specific practices like wearing *tefillin* and visiting the *mikveh* (see chapter four) but these references had proved controversial and were deleted from the final version. The section on 'Israel' has also proved difficult for some and seemingly represents a realignment with more traditional approaches. The first Pittsburgh Platform associated 'national life in Palestine' with the Jewish past. Later statements affirmed the importance of a Jewish homeland but also maintained that 'a genuine Jewish life is possible in any land' and 'the foundation of Jewish life is the synagogue' (not the state). In 1999, however, the Conference adopted the statement that:

> We are committed to…the State of Israel, and rejoice in its accomplishments. We affirm the unique qualities of living in…the land of Israel, and encourage…immigration to Israel.

Whilst the same passage went on to say that 'Israeli Jews have much to learn from the religious life of *Diaspora* Jewish communities' and that 'both Israeli and *Diaspora* Jewry should remain vibrant and interdependent communities', this wording has been interpreted negatively by some critics to imply a retreat from the universalism of Kohler and his peers, and a return to the notion of *Diaspora* life as *galut* (exile) and what the San Francisco platform called the 'dangerously parochial goals' of nationalism.

Viewed collectively, the Reform platforms highlight many of the features that have attracted upwards of a million Jews to the movement in North America alone. (According to a 1996 survey, in Britain there are 17,614 households affiliated to Reform synagogues and 7,971 affiliated to the historically more radical Union of Liberal and Progressive Synagogues, in comparison to the 56,895 'mainstream orthodox households'.[20]) In the modern and contemporary age, Reform's emphasis on personal autonomy in spiritual matters, and its characterisation of Judaism as a religion offering social justice and equality to all regardless of affiliation or gender, has proved appealing for many. Moreover, in a context of increasing intermarriage its willingness to accept Jews married to non-Jews, and a general flexibility in matters of personal status law, has also meant that Reform Judaism offers a Jewish home to those whom more traditional groupings often exclude (see chapter four and Afterword).

The four platforms also attest the extent to which, in an age of doubt, Reform Judaism has maintained a lively discussion of belief. More so than Orthodoxy or the *Charedi* groups, Reform has acknowledged that people conceive of the 'God-idea' (as the 1885 platform phrased it) in different ways, and that traditional conceptions of the Divine have been profoundly challenged by events like the *Shoah*; unlike Conservativism and Reconstructionism, it has not seen this difference as a reason to downplay or devalue the role of belief and theology in Jewish life. This willingness to explore belief publicly resonates with many for whom renewed interest in Judaism is prompted by a personal quest for meaning and contact with the transcendent.

At the same time, the real tensions within Reform Judaism are undeniable. I have already highlighted the ways in which the platforms chart changing attitudes towards the commandments or *mitzvot*. In the last thirty years or so, there has been a return to observance, not so much of detailed dietary and purity laws, as of festivals and *Shabbat*. There is also typically more enthusiasm for the teaching of Hebrew to synagogue members and their children, and for its increased use in worship. Viewed pessimistically, such shifts could be appraised as symptomatic of a crisis of confidence on the part of the movement, or as implying that its early leaders were misguided in their approach to the outward expression of Jewish faith. Alternatively, the return to observance could be seen as a positive response to the contemporary context. In an age when the majority, non-Jewish society no longer requires Jews to maintain outward manifestations of difference such as special types of clothing or names, Jewish difference (and with it Jewish identity) could disappear completely unless a concerted effort were made to ensure its survival. Revival of Hebrew and the observance of at least some *mitzvot* meet this need for modes of positive Jewish identification. (Of course, from a *Charedi* perspective, such partial renewal of observance for pragmatic or aesthetic reasons is misguided, perhaps even dangerous, for it results in people

48

living 'Jew-*ish*' rather than truly Jewish lives). Eugene Borowitz outlines this kind of progressive approach to ritual as follows:

> Rituals have no magic power. They may not change us and they cannot coerce God. Doing them does not excuse abusing our freedom by doing evil, and they do not win us God's favor despite how badly we have behaved. But they can provide us with a means of trying to maintain a personal, Jewish contact with the Holy. In a world where so many other influences work to demean us, religious ritual must be considered a therapeutic necessity and a life-affirming activity.[21]

Modern Orthodoxy

In many non-Jewish minds (and to some Jewish ones) the term 'Orthodox' conjures up an image of a position within Judaism that is the majority or normative one, and carries connotations of inflexibility and centralised, unyielding authority. This image is, however, misleading. Orthodox Judaism is by no means monolithic. Arguably, it exhibits greater internal diversity than any of the other modern forms of Judaism discussed in this chapter. There is no single mode of belief or practice to which all Orthodox Jews must assent, and as mentioned in chapter two, there is no centralised authority structure or ultimate hierarchy of power which can make universally applicable rulings on matters, or mobilise groups to make common cause. Moreover, as incidents like the Geiger-Tiktin affair illustrate, Orthodox Judaism was forged partly in response to early experiments at reform. Indeed, 'Orthodoxy' was first employed in Jewish discourse by reformers who applied it to their traditionalist interlocutors as a derogatory term. Strictly speaking, then, Orthodoxy does not enjoy historical precedence over Progressive (non-Orthodox) Judaisms. Nor is it numerically dominant in the United States (which currently has a larger Jewish population than the state of Israel).

If Abraham Geiger can be regarded as the figure who gave theoretical support to early reform attempts, Samson Raphael Hirsch (1808–1888) a student-friend of Geiger's at Bonn, is the genius of modern Orthodoxy. Whereas Geiger shared the Enlightenment's commitment to the 'universals' of reason, science, and progress, and believed that Judaism as traditionally based on *Talmud Torah* must eventually decline, Hirsch sought, 'to show…that full and authentic Judaism does not belong to an antiquated past but to the living, pulsating present; nay, that the whole future…belongs to Judaism, the full and unabridged Judaism'.[22] In 1836, whilst serving as the chief rabbi of Oldenburg, he pseudonymously published *Nineteen Letters About Judaism*. Ostensibly a written dialogue between Benjamin, a young Jew inclined to abandon Judaism, and Naftali, who dissuades him from such a plan, the *Letters* argue for a revitalisation of traditional Judaism, informed by a study of its sources – *Tanakh*, *Talmud* and *Midrash*. Hirsch intended that his readers would be encouraged to reject both the position of those who observed the *mitzvot* faithfully but unthinkingly, and of those whose very advocacy of reform constituted an abandonment of Israel's 'lifeblood' – the letter and spirit of the law. Instead Hirsch championed an approach summarised by the motto of the traditional congregation in Frankfurt-am-Main which he later served, *excellent is the study of the Torah with the ways of the land*. Jews might rejoice in emancipation as it offered new opportunities for true and voluntary commitment to the Jewish mission, the observance of *mitzvot* and fulfilment of the divine will. (For example, in 1848, Hirsch campaigned for Jewish emancipation in Austria.) However, the emphasis in Jewish life was to be on *Torah*, which (Hirsch maintained) must be conceived of as divine, despite the fact that it contained some material which human reason struggles to appreciate as such. If this *Torah*-centredness were abandoned or curtailed, emancipation and the opportunity to participate in society should be regarded as regrettable.

Since Hirsch's day modern Orthodoxy has been characterised by the attempt to balance involvement in the wider world with commitment to the norms and values of *Torah*. In practice, this means that an Orthodox Jew who attempts to live a *halakhic* life typically also has the benefit of a secular education (and in many cases also a secular career, as opposed to a distinctively Jewish one), adopts the vernacular and the customs of dress of the country in which he or she lives, and participates in a modified form of worship (probably not employing medieval *piyyotim*, but still reserving Hebrew as the language of prayer). At least in theory, an Orthodox Jew maintains his or her identity as a Jew whilst also taking the best of what secular culture has to offer, insofar as that does not challenge the validity and ultimately binding character of the *halakhah*. Jonathan Sacks, the Chief Rabbi of the United Hebrew Congregations of the British Commonwealth, expresses it thus:

The religious imperative at any age is born at the intersection of the timeless and the time-bound. We must not lose our ability to hear, across the generations, the transcendent voice of revelation: that is the argument against liberalism. But neither may we apply the texts of revelation as if nothing significant had changed in the human situation in the intervening years: that is the argument against extremism.[23]

This goal of *Torah im derekh eretz*, or *Torah* 'with the ways of the land,' is demanding. For much of the late nineteenth and early twentieth centuries it seemed that whilst Reform and Conservative Judaism gathered in momentum, Orthodoxy was under threat. Whilst Hirsch believed that some innovations could legitimately be introduced (including the holding of weddings in synagogue, rather than out of doors; delivering sermons in the vernacular, and the wearing of clerical-style robes by rabbis) without abrogating the authority of *Torah*, it has not always been as clear to his successors that such details can be changed without undermining Judaism's essentials, too. As a result some modern Orthodox leaders have approached *Charedi* positions in their refusal to countenance any innovation, and have thereby alienated many Jews who are religiously committed, but also seek acceptance in non-Jewish society and share some of its goals and values. Focusing on the American context, Marshall Sklare's 1955 book, *Conservative Judaism*, presented Orthodox Judaism as a case study in decline. As recently as 1983, Reuven Bulka defined Orthodox as 'referring to any individual or group religiously to the right of the Conservative movement', a description which is in itself a testimony to the powerful challenges to Orthodoxy's claims to normative status in the contemporary era.[24]

Despite predictions of impending demise, Orthodox Judaism is today in a place of relative strength when compared with its position of a few decades ago. Why is this? At the right-wing, more religiously conservative end of the Orthodox spectrum, the belief that the halakhic life is divinely ordained for Jews persists. Exponents of this view are unlikely to abandon their commitment to *Torah* even where this represents a minority position. The slightest tampering with the *status quo* is condemned; Orthodoxy must remain the authentic bearer of religious Jewish tradition. But other factors are also involved in the revival. Ironically, the forces of postmodernism and multiculturalism (which, with their denial of the existence of the normative and the overarching metanarrative, are radically opposed to the spirit that animates Orthodoxy) have worked to create societies in which Orthodox life can survive. Whereas some Enlightenment thinkers hoped to speed the assimilation of Jews, western societies today are willing to tolerate – even to celebrate – difference. For example, teachers, health service workers, and other public sector employees are trained to be sensitive to the customs and philosophies of ethnic and religious groupings other than their own. Where there are no economic obstacles to doing so, major supermarket chains will stock ready-prepared kosher foods, making it easier to lead an observant life and implicitly validating such a 'lifestyle choice'. At the same time the very openness which leads to this acceptance of the Orthodox form of difference has also allowed lifestyles and philosophies that Orthodoxy has been roused to counter, and about which many Jews who strictly speaking are non-Orthodox, are also concerned. Non-observant parents today are more willing to send their child to an Orthodox Jewish day school or to regular *cheder* classes on a Sunday, perhaps because they fear that the alternative may be that he or she 'marries out', takes drugs, joins a non-Jewish religious movement, or simply grows up ignorant of Jewish history and culture.

This is not to say that the reasons for Orthodoxy's survival are entirely external. The movement's revitalisation also owes much to the contribution of a number of distinguished leaders such as Rabbi Joseph D. Soloveitchik (1903–1992). Soloveitchik departed from the position of most twentieth century *charedi yeshivah* heads and re-asserted the principle of *Torah im derekh eretz*. In classic neo-Orthodox style, Soloveitchik received both a traditional Jewish education and gained a secular Doctorate in Philosophy at the University of Berlin. Having moved to the United States in 1932, he became a central figure in the Union of Jewish Orthodox Congregations (commonly referred to as the Orthodox Union or OU). His teachings urged Orthodox Jews to combine commitment to the *mitzvot* with worthwhile participation in secular society, arguing that the *ish ha-Halakhah* ('halakhic man') could creatively reconcile both a scientific, rational drive and a sense of religious pathos and yearning for God. This characterisation of the religious Jew found favour with those who felt unhappy with the tendency within 'right-wing' Orthodoxy to withdraw from the world, and gave the observant Jewish life an air of creativity and romance which it was commonly felt to lack.[25]

In spite of the new impetus given by changing social trends and thinkers like Soloveitchik, Orthodoxy faces its own dilemmas at the start of the twenty-first century. One of the challenges is to address the relation of the carefully observant and orthoprax minority to the residual or nominally Orthodox. Perhaps more than other modern Jewish groupings, Orthodoxy has associated with it a sizeable body of people (characterised by Sklare as the 'non-observant Orthodox') who identify as Orthodox but may not share belief in the divinely revealed *Torah* and do not observe even those *halakhot* that pertain to the Sabbath, food and family purity. This nominally Orthodox group, when occasionally joining in public worship, prefers to do so in accordance with traditional patterns, perhaps because, for nostalgic or sentimental reasons, this 'feels right' in the way that progressive practice would not. Yet at the same time many such families are touched by intermarriage and conversion, and are pained by the Orthodox hierarchy's perceived lack of willingness to reach out to the wider Jewish and non-Jewish community. This image of insularity needs to be countered, particularly as the nominally Orthodox constitute a significant source of financial and political support for Orthodoxy, and are 'true' Orthodoxy's most likely future members.

The place of women in Orthodox Judaism is also a source of contention. Today the Reform, Conservative, Liberal and Reconstructionist movements within Judaism all ordain women as rabbis. Most Orthodox Jews would not want to take such a step, arguing that the genders have means of serving God which differ but are of divine origin and comparable importance. However, many would like to see greater opportunities for girls to receive religious education, and for the public recognition of the worth of women (for example, birth ceremonies for daughters as well as sons; healing rituals to acknowledge events like miscarriage or rape). A crucial issue of controversy here is the plight of the *agunah*, the woman who remains 'anchored' in marriage to a missing or recalcitrant husband, because in traditional Jewish law only he may initiate the divorce that would enable her to re-marry (*Gittin* 20a; see chapter four). In the last twenty years changes have been made on these issues. For example, among Orthodox Jews there are groups of women who meet separately for prayer. Nevertheless, the sense that in Orthodoxy women's voices are diminished, and their contributions undervalued, persists amongst those who would like to create a Judaism which is willing to subordinate itself to the *Zeitgeist*, at least in the area of gender equality. Modern Orthodoxy may have to find a way to address these concerns creatively within a *halakhic* framework. If it does not, then it may lose the sympathies of many young Jewish women, and with them, their future offspring. This is a real possibility, as some other modern Judaisms have made progressive changes whilst still retaining much of the 'feel' of Orthodoxy. Chief amongst these groups is Conservative Judaism, to which the discussion will now turn.

Conservative Judaism

For many early nineteenth century Jews, what they perceived to be the unprincipled assimilationist tendencies of Reform, and the relative inflexibility of Orthodoxy, were equally problematic. Beginning in the United States under heavy influence from Continental European leaders, a final major grouping within modern Judaism emerged. Known in America (where it claims the allegiance of about one and a half million people) as Conservative Judaism, and in Britain and Israel as *Masorti* ('Traditional') it has aimed to occupy the middle ground between the Orthodox and Reform positions on the Judaism-modernity encounter.

In 1840s Germany it was already apparent that a range of positions on Jewish life and observance existed within the ranks of the non-Orthodox. Some groups were willing to jettison all particularist practices deemed to be at odds with the professed spirit of Enlightenment. Others wanted only moderate change. They accepted the implications of historical study and the need to ensure Judaism's ongoing relevance, but also wished to conserve that which was best in Jewish tradition – those distinctive religious practices that characterised Jewish life and gave even mundane activities a sacramental character. Amongst the ranks of the latter party was Zachariah Frankel, a rabbi in Dresden. Frankel (1801-1875) dramatically quitted the 1845 Frankfurt assembly when a majority of the more radical participants voted that it was not obligatory to use Hebrew in worship. Abraham Geiger, whose place in the history of Reform Judaism was noted earlier, had argued that, as Jews were now fully citizens of the countries in which they lived, they needed a more universally applicable religion, free of the narrow, national ties implied by a commitment to Hebrew. Frankel, whilst accepting that there was no legal obligation to use Hebrew, held that it had attained a kind of normative or sacred status by virtue of its historic use by previous generations of Jews. In this argument lies the kernel of what Frankel called Positive Historical Judaism. Unlike the more radical reformers, Frankel took a positive approach towards both *minhag* (custom) and *halakhah*, but his rationale for valuing the law differed from that traditionally offered. Whereas Orthodoxy emphasised divine origins, Frankel argued that it was Judaism as practised by the people committed to it that ultimately had authority. This emphasis on the Jewish people as a kind of living organism inevitably meant that, whilst traditional forms were generally to be treasured and conserved, change was inevitable as the community responded creatively to new spiritual and practical challenges:

> There are those who would think that we have but two alternatives, to reject or to accept the law, but in either case to treat it as a dead letter. Both of these alternatives are repugnant to the whole tradition of Judaism….Jewish law must be preserved but…it is subject to interpretation by those who have mastered it, and…the interpretation placed upon it by duly authorized masters *in every generation* must be accepted with as much reverence as those which were given in previous generations.[26]

For more than forty years Frankel's successors did not found a separate religious movement. In Europe and the Americas they tried to work within Orthodoxy to modernise and, in doing so, to counter assimilation and the drift towards Reform. Isaac Leeser (1806-1868) employed as *chazan* to an Orthodox congregation in Philadelphia, even attempted to find common ground with Reform leader Isaac Mayer Wise (1819-1900); together they planned to create a unified American Jewish religious body. However, as Reform moved from relatively minor alterations to the style and decorum of synagogue services to a broader project of challenging the validity of the halakhic system *per se*, it became clear that scope for co-operation was limited.

Conservatism's final break from both Reform and Orthodoxy came in the wake of the 1885 Pittsburgh Platform. Just as Frankel had withdrawn from the Frankfurt assembly, so his successors in the next generation did not accept the Platform's rejection of *kashrut* (see chapter four). Perhaps unsurprisingly for a movement that has always emphasised history and culture, the response was to found a new centre of learning, the Jewish Theological Seminary of America, dedicated to the 'preservation in America of the knowledge and practice of historical Judaism as ordained in the law of Moses expounded by the prophets and sages in Israel in Biblical and Talmudic writings'. Other institutions (the Rabbinical Assembly and the United Synagogue of Conservative Judaism) followed, so that by 1914 Conservative Judaism had emerged as a discrete denomination.

Although Conservative Judaism remains primarily an American movement, many of the early founders and teachers in the Jewish Theological Seminary were European.[27] Most famous is Solomon Schechter, who left a post at Cambridge University to lead the Seminary and establish it as an internationally renowned centre of academic excellence. In addition to his considerable organisational talents, Schechter gave to Conservatism a new articulation of its approach. He popularised the concept of *klal yisroel* ('Catholic Israel') as a source of authority in Judaism, emphasising that *halakhah* and *minhag* be seen not as eternal and unchanging entities divinely gifted at Sinai, but as the dynamic embodiment of Jewish responses to God.

The Conservative emphasis on Judaism as a dynamic, developing tradition has meant that unlike Reform it has hesitated to issue platform statements. The movement's 1988 publication, *Emet ve-'Emunah: Statement of Principles of Conservative Judaism* is a consensus document (the Reform platforms are drafted by individuals and then debated, primarily by rabbis) stressing the broad parameters of belief and praxis within the movement. Moreover, it has also been more reluctant to issue collections of responsa; perhaps the nearest thing to such a work is Isaac Klein's posthumously published *A Guide to Jewish Religious Practice*, but it is not binding on those affiliated to Conservative synagogues.[28] As a result, Conservative Jews exhibit a wide range of religious attitudes and practices. For some, the label 'Conservative' implies a position close to that of Modern Orthodoxy. For others, the emphasis on Israel as the source of its own authority entails a de-emphasis on God and permits quite radical, atheistic positions.

Conservatism's attempt to occupy the Jewish middle path has been popular, particularly in North America. Immigrants from a variety of religious and cultural backgrounds have found its 'broad church' approach to Judaism welcoming (although this is perhaps less true of Sephardim than of Ashkenazim). Conservatism has also developed institutional forms that support religious life in the suburban context. Chief amongst these is the Synagogue Center, which houses not only worship but also a range of other activities (such as Hebrew and Judaism classes, men's and women's groups, charity events, and speaker meetings) and facilities (libraries, swimming pools, cafeterias) designed to foster feelings of 'social togetherness' amongst Jews who might live and work at some distance from one another. At the same time Frankel and Schechter have been succeeded in later generations by figures such as Abraham Joshua Heschel

(1907-1972). Heschel's books covered a wide range of topics including the Bible and mysticism-influenced theology, and his writings on the evocative, ultimately mysterious character of *Torah* and *mitzvot* captured well the spirit that animates Conservatism. He was also a prominent civil rights campaigner and a leading figure in Jewish-Christian relations who played an important role behind the scenes during the Second Vatican Council.[29]

At the same time, Conservatism's emphasis on community and consensus has always made it vulnerable. The movement's philosophy implicitly validates groups who wish to break from the Conservative fold and develop their own interpretations of tradition; this has already happened on two notable occasions. Reconstructionism (discussed below) is now a separate Jewish denomination in its own right. In 1990 a further group of members suspended their affiliation to Conservatism and formed the Union for Traditional Judaism, which aims 'to bring the greatest possible number of Jews closer to an open-minded observant Jewish lifestyle'. (David Halivni, who was mentioned in chapter two, heads the Union's Institute which is in Teaneck, New Jersey.) The UTJ's cautious approach to modernity is reflected clearly in its 'Declaration of the Principles of the Union for Traditional Judaism', which asserts that the dual *Torah* 'authoritatively expresses the will of God for the Jewish people' and that 'Jewish law alone is the final arbiter of Jewish practice.' A distinctively Conservative impulse is felt, however, in the assertion that the UTJ seeks to:

> relate lovingly and respectfully to all Jews regardless of their level of commitment to traditional Jewish beliefs and observance of Halakhah. We must co-operate, to the fullest extent possible within the parameters of Halakhah, with other Jewish groups and their leaders, without regard to the political boundaries of denominational affiliation. Shared history and common destiny are sufficient reason for making far-reaching efforts to preserve the unity of kelal yisrael (the entire Jewish people).[30]

Unlike Modern Orthodoxy and Reform, Conservative Judaism arguably needs to find a new rationale for its existence, to clarify its mission or ideology more successfully for the twenty-first century. Some Conservative writers like Simon Greenberg have resisted calls for a clear enunciation of what the movement stands for, arguing that 'Conservative Judaism is writing its own definition of itself....as does every living thing, through the institutions it is creating. ...It will thus continue to define and redefine itself'.[31] But it seems increasingly expedient that some kind of statement be produced. Reform Judaism's return to the *mitzvot* has meant that Conservatism is less distinctive than it used to be. At the same time, whereas many early exponents of Conservatism regarded the movement as the sole vehicle for the preservation of traditional Jewish religion in the modern age, this has clearly not been the case. Orthodox Judaism has persisted and even flourished. Meanwhile, Conservatism has failed to develop a large body of distinctively Conservative Jews who are halakhically committed. Most members have broken with the *halakhah* as a system, in a way that its early advocates did not intend. Just as much as Reform Judaism, Conservative practice is subject to personal taste and preference. Traditionally minor observances, like candle-lighting at *Chanukah*, have become more widespread than once major ones such as the lighting of Sabbath candles. How to continue in the light of such realities is a problem which Conservative Judaism, perhaps more than any other group, will have to address in the twenty-first century.

Reconstructionism

If Conservatism is now undergoing retrenchment following a period of numerical dominance in North America, Reconstructionism continues to grow and command the sympathies of many Jews not formally associated with the movement. Outside the United States, most Jews have probably never even heard the term Reconstructionism, but those who would describe their attachment to Judaism as cultural rather than religious would likely find much in its philosophy with which they could concur.

Reconstructionism is the youngest of the movements discussed in this chapter. Unlike other modern Judaisms, it owes its origins to the teachings of an individual, Rabbi Mordecai M. Kaplan (1881–1983). In *Judaism as a Civilisation* (1934) Kaplan applied the term 'reconstruction' to the programme he regarded it as necessary for Judaism to adopt if it were to meet the demands of the modern age.[32] His project rested on a radical redefinition of Judaism itself. Judaism should not be defined narrowly as a religion, or an ethnic grouping, but as the *evolving religious civilisation of the Jewish people*. By looking more closely at each of the key words in this

definition, a fair impression is gained of the concerns of Reconstructionism today.

The deliberate classification of Judaism as *civilisation* rather than religion
implies that Judaism is wider or more comprehensive than other
phenomena traditionally identified as religions. (But compare what follows
with Whaling's dimensional account of religion discussed in Chapter one.)
It identifies Judaism as something *total* which embraces 'all the elements
of group life: art, culture, philosophy, language, law, ethics, celebrations,
patterns of eating and dressing, sancta (holy things, times, events, and
places)'.[33] Controversially, for Kaplan the total nature of Judaism meant
that only in the land of Israel (or outside it, but in a *Diaspora* community
with strong links to Israel) would it be possible to enjoy a fully Jewish life.
He argued that 'Judaism is unlikely to survive either as an ancillary or as a
co-ordinate civilisation, unless it thrives as a primary civilisation in
Palestine'.[34] Kaplan's initial programme for Reconstructionism was
developed at the peak of Zionist hopes and designed in part to conserve
Judaism in anticipation of a future return to the Promised Land.
Contemporary Reconstructionists, whilst they are generally Zionists like
Kaplan, also stress the historic role played by *diverse* communities in
constructing Jewish identity. The claim that Israel is the only possible means
of Jewish survival is rejected by many today.

In characterising Judaism as a civilisation Kaplan was *not* somehow
fulfilling the dreams of those Enlightenment thinkers and politicians who
granted improved legal rights only in order to regularise Jewry and hasten
its disappearance. Reconstructionists do not believe that Judaism is identical
to other cultures and polities. Rather, it is distinctively a *religious* civilisation.
Of course, this then prompts the question, what is religion? The
traditionalist or modern Orthodox Jew might speak of religion in terms
of theistic belief in one God who communicates God's will for the
Jewish people through the *Torah miSinai* or *min ha-Shamayim* (Torah 'from
Sinai' or 'from the Heavens'). For Reconstructionists, such supernatural
beliefs are no longer tenable and cannot provide adequate rationale for
the observance of the commandments. There is no deity at the heart of
Judaism, although there may be a 'divine' and Jews may bring 'godliness'
into the world when they act with compassion, kindness and justice. For
Reconstructionism, religion is understood in sociological terms, as that
which functions to make meaning and purpose in our lives. Religion is,

the search to discover what is ultimately meaningful in life and to find ways of expressing the resulting visions of the ultimate in behaviours and ideas....a religion is the aspect of a culture with which we structure reality, separating the significant from the insignificant, interpreting the apparently chaotic events of our lives in a meaningful and ordinary way.[35]

The implication of the idea that there is no God, but that the religious dimension is still a vital part of Jewish civilisation, is clear for Reconstructionists. Whilst unhelpful convictions such as the belief in an interventionist God who acts on prayer are to be abandoned, meaning-making acts like communal worship are still of great value. Liturgies express shared hopes, pains, and aspirations, foster a sense of group identity and continuity with the Jewish past, and satisfy the aesthetic faculties. To borrow another essential phrase from Kaplan's *epitomé*, if the *mitzvot* do not connect Jews with a transcendent God, they do define and strengthen the *Jewish people*.

Finally, any consideration of Reconstructionism must attend to the word *evolving*. Kaplan's stress on civilisation was a deliberate critique of what he saw as Reform's overemphasis on Judaism as a philosophy. This stance would, he argued, inevitably lead to the diminishing of Jewish community and religion. Similarly, the emphasis on evolution signals opposition to the traditionalists' claim that Jewish religious principles and forms may be traced directly to revelation at Sinai. Reconstructionists argue that, like other civilisations, Judaism adapted to changing circumstances. It has undergone periods of decline, advancement, and alteration. This is not to say that Jewish civilisation is seen to be undergoing a steady progression from 'primitive' to 'sophisticated' or from 'lower' to 'higher' forms. Alpert and Staub summarise 'evolution' as follows:

> In the evolution of species, one form survives because it is better adapted to new environmental conditions. It is not superior except with reference to the current conditions in which it lives.... Our position does not require a belief that in all or even most respects twentieth-century Jews know more or are more ethical than previous generations of Jews.[36]

Given the practical overtones of the very name 'Reconstructionism' (and its roots in Conservatism), it is perhaps not surprising that, from the outset, this movement has regarded the building of communal structures as a priority. Following the publication of *Judaism as a Civilisation* in 1934, the Jewish Reconstructionist Foundation was established in 1954 to co-ordinate the activities of *chavurot* and a number of congregations who had declared themselves to be in sympathy with the new programme. The *chavurah* remains one of the central institutions within Reconstructionism. Meaning 'fellowship', the *chavurah* is a small group of people who support each other in their Jewish lives – worshipping, studying and celebrating together. The characteristics of the *chavurot* mean that a new understanding of the rabbinic role has necessarily developed within Reconstructionism, too. In such a setting, with its emphasis on intimacy and open, equal participation, the Orthodox model of the rabbi as halakhic authority, and the progressive model of rabbi as preacher and exhorter, are both equally inappropriate. Hence in 1968 the Reconstructionist Rabbinical College was opened to train rabbis to be educators – Jews with specialist knowledge of Jewish civilisation that equips them to serve their contemporaries as guides and facilitators as the group struggles together to build Jewish lives. In theory at least then, the Reconstructionist rabbi wants to help other Jews assume as many of the traditional rabbinic functions as possible, and teaches as many people as are willing to do the things that he or she has learned to do previously.

As indicated earlier, although Reconstructionism remains relatively small and largely restricted to North America, much of its programme is attractive to Jews who are linked formally to other movements or who are unaffiliated. In particular, the non-theism and emphasis on culture resonates with those who feel an attachment to art, music and other primarily secular forms of Jewish expression. The willingness not simply to evolve, but to celebrate change and development in accordance with wider societal norms, appeals also to those who, for example, dislike the perceived patriarchy of other Judaisms and would like to see women included more fully in public religious life. Finally, the attractions of the *chavurot* should not be underestimated. In what is an increasingly transient, fragmented society, they can function as extended families, providing many Jews with the mutual support networks they might otherwise lack.

The same features that necessitate the creation of *chavurot* also present Reconstructionism with difficulties. The newness of the State of Israel and the increased social and geographical mobility of Jews there and in *Diaspora* make it very hard to reconstruct Jewish community in the way Kaplan described. People may simply not be present in a city or country for the time needed to establish deep connections with the local population and build the kind of interconnected Jewish life he advocated. Reconstructionism's greatest problem, however, is internal. Given that most forms of difference, Judaism included, carry with them penalties as well as pleasures (one may be subject to negative stereotyping or discrimination, or simply to embarrassment and misunderstanding) why perpetuate a different, distinctive, identity as a Jew? Traditionally, Judaism's rationale has been the belief that God commanded such difference, as recounted in passages like Exodus 19:5f.: 'If you obey my voice and keep my covenant, you shall be my treasured possession out of all the peoples'. Reconstructionism takes away the traditional rationale but argues that difference, in the form of observance of Jewish religious norms, should be perpetuated. It is sometimes hard to see just *why* this is the case, and indeed it remains to be seen whether the grandchildren and great-grandchildren of first-generation Reconstructionists will feel motivated to carry on the tradition. Conceivably, a sense of common ethnicity and ethical heritage could prompt future generations to desire to live distinctively Jewish lives, but less than a century after Reconstructionism's founding, it is too early to predict with confidence the future life of the movement.

Sephardi and Oriental Responses to Modernity

The Sephardi and Oriental Jews (also known as *Adot ha-Mizrach*, 'communities of the East') living in the Middle East, the Balkans, and North Africa, have had a quite different encounter with modernity, which in turn has had distinctive consequences for their Judaism. Modernity arose in Western Europe, both philosophically and technologically speaking. Sephardi and Oriental Jews, like the majority Muslim populations of the countries in which they lived, generally encountered modernity at a later date than their Ashkenazi counterparts did (sometimes only from the mid-twentieth century onwards) and usually as a result of the expansion of Western influence.

Of itself, Eastern Jewry has produced no modern religious movements of the type found in the West. There is no Modern Orthodox or Reform Sephardi Judaism, nor is there a Sephardi Reconstructionist movement. This is not to say that there are not or have not been reform-minded individuals in the Eastern Jewish world, or that there have ever been periods when Eastern and Western Jewries were totally isolated one from another. (Spinoza, for example, was a product of the Sephardi community in Amsterdam.) What has distinguished Sephardi Judaism has been its ability to maintain a greater degree of equilibrium than Western European Jewry generally managed to preserve. This is due more to historical contingencies rather than to any inherent characteristics of Sephardi tradition. In Western Europe, Jews sought to adapt to the promise and expectations of secularizing societies which pressed them to shed their medieval heritage. In contrast, many Eastern Jews were introduced to European *mores* by other Jews. For example, the leaders of French Jewry encouraged Algerian Jews to modernise and campaigned for them to be granted French citizenship (1870). Because European culture was presented to them by other Jews, North African Jews were perhaps motivated more by considerations of social mobility than by considerations of national identity. They also felt less pressure to assimilate to the surrounding context which, being Muslim, did not regard the publicly religious life as outmoded and redundant. At the same time, although Sephardim in the Middle East and Africa were affected by European phenomena like the virulent antisemitism of the late nineteenth century, geographical distance meant that modernity was introduced or imposed on them by the West in an often piecemeal fashion. Rather than desiring to adapt wholly to the *Zeitgeist*, or to reject it outright, these Jews were able to take a pragmatic approach to new challenges. Hence when Egyptian men adopted European style dress fashioned from fabric containing *shaatnez*, the Biblically prohibited mixture of linen and wool (Deuteronomy 22:11), the Hakham Bashi Raphael Aaron Ben Simeon issued a *responsum* enabling Jewish tailors to remain within the boundaries of the *halakhah* and preserve their livelihoods. To make such a suit for a Gentile (non-Jew) was acceptable; Jewish customers should be warned of the situation, and if they still wished to proceed with the purchase, then the tailor might avoid infringing the law by asking the customer or a non-Jewish colleague to fit the garment. In another instance, Ben Simeon positively welcomed the potential of new technologies for solving old halakhic problems. He hoped that French plumbing expertise might be copied in order to facilitate the creation of *mikvaot*, ritual baths that were difficult to establish in regions with low, erratic rainfall.[37]

Inevitably, however, just as Eastern Jews encountered modernity as a result of Western influence, so their responses to it have been influenced by the Ashkenazim. Important Sephardi communities in Greece and the Balkans were virtually wiped out during the *Shoah*, and in the latter half of the twentieth century elsewhere in the Arabian peninsula, Turkey, Iran, and North Africa, communities dwindled in the face of political oppression or harsh economic circumstances. Despite the fact that it was a European import – modern nationalism – that sounded the death-knell for many of these Eastern communities, most of the emigrants moved to Western and Western-influenced locations, particularly France (where African Jews now constitute the majority of Jews in the country) and Israel, where Sephardim today constitute around fifty per cent of the Jewish population.

In Israel, Sephardi and Oriental Judaism has been transformed as a result of increased contacts with the Ashkenazi groupings until recently dominant. For many years the Ashkenazim dominated the Israeli establishment (if one can speak of an 'establishment' in a state of just fifty-odd years) and saw themselves as absorbing and assimilating Sephardi and Oriental 'newcomers'. Non-Western Jews were too often regarded as backward and somehow inferior; their distinctive practices as superstitions or mere 'folk religion'. The Ashkenazification of Eastern Jewry accelerated. Pressures for traditionally religious Jews from East or West to think, behave, and act alike have grown as a secular Israeli culture develops and becomes increasingly confident. As was discussed earlier, this has led amongst other things to the development of *Charedi* forms of Sephardi Judaism (built around Western models) and the *Shas* party. However, distinctively Sephardi and Oriental forms of Jewish religiosity have reasserted themselves in more recent years. This is particularly true of Moroccan Jews in Israel.

The Moroccan Jewish community was established as early as the sixth century BCE; in the late medieval period its numbers grew as a result of the influx of Jewish refugees from the Iberian peninsula, and there were over a quarter of a million Moroccan Jews by the mid twentieth century. Two distinctive forms of religious expression developed – the festival *Mimouna*, and the widespread veneration of saints or holy men (less frequently, holy women), figures revered for their piety and miracle-working capacities both in life and after death.

Many Moroccan Jews emigrated to Israel in the 1960s, and in this new location saint-veneration has both continued along largely traditional lines and found new channels of expression. Social anthropologist Ben-Ami notes that, there is a prevalent belief that [like their devotees] the saints themselves moved to Israel, leaving behind in Morocco only the edifices built in their names….patron saints…reveal their presence in Israel by communicating in dreams with their disciples.[38]

In many cases then, the old subjects of devotion, and the practices associated with their honour (such as an annual pilgrimage marking the saint's death) are transplanted to a new context. At the same time, Jews of Moroccan origin are the major practitioners of cult rituals in many older established holy sites in Israel, and are responsible for the 'rediscovery' and decoration of the burial sites of *tannaim* (sages from the Mishnaic era). Moreover, religious Israelis of non-Moroccan origin increasingly participate in saint veneration and pilgrimage, indicating that whilst shaped by their experiences of emigration, Moroccan Jewish practices are in turn exerting a growing influence on Israeli folklore and religiosity.

Even more widespread in Israel is the attraction to the Moroccan festival of *Mimouna* (on the night after *Pesach*) which has re-emerged as a time when families meet at home or at picnics and celebrate with food, music and colourful costumes. *Mimouna's* precise origins are unclear, but its customs are connected with the desire for good fortune in the coming year. In some Moroccan communities it is the tradition for Jews and Muslims to exchange gifts and other favours, and to wish one another luck; other practices include waking early (thought to prevent one from becoming lazy during the year). *Mimouna* is also traditionally the time of the year when Moroccan Jews are encouraged to initiate friendships leading to marriage, with older relatives wishing younger people 'a wedding within the year'.[39]

Jewish Diversity - an Evaluation

This chapter has discussed a series of what have been presented as relatively distinct, clear-cut groupings within contemporary Judaism. Such an approach makes for clarity but at the same time leaves unanswered some important questions about Jewish diversity. Firstly, how far does reality match the model that has been offered? Do the different labels, Orthodox, Reform, Conservative (and so on) really refer to people who take distinctive approaches to Jewish religion and culture? That the answer to this question must at least sometimes be 'no' is already clear. For example, the discussion has touched on the case of the non-observant Orthodox who, whilst maintaining an affiliation to an Orthodox synagogue, do not share the beliefs or live the thoroughly halakhic lives that are commonly thought to define Orthodoxy. Many members of the United Synagogue, the largest Orthodox body in Britain, would fall into this category today. Moreover, amongst carefully observant Jews, there are moves to reformulate doctrines like *Torah min ha-Shamayim*. Some choose to retain the theological aspects of this concept (beliefs about the continuing authority of Scripture for Jews) whilst abandoning the historical claims that became intertwined with them (belief in *Torah* as a piece of 'divine dictation').[40] 'Orthodox' and many of the other designations that have been used in this chapter may, therefore, be best understood as family terms. Like the members of a family, those who call themselves (for example) Reform or Conservative Jews may share certain resemblances of attitude, appearance and behaviour. At the same time, each family member also has his or her own individual characteristics. Not all Smiths or Cohens are identical, nor are all Orthodox or Reform Jews.

Many factors combine to ensure that each Jewish family or religious movement exhibits internal diversity. Jonathan Magonet, a Reform rabbi, summarises the current situation in Britain as follows:

> if we look at what people do, as opposed to which side of the line they identify with, the boundary between them becomes somewhat fuzzy....when research has been conducted as to why people join a particular synagogue, it is rarely the ideological reason that is prominent in the first instance. Instead people tend to join if they have friends who are members. Only afterwards do they ask about the particular facilities available or ideology.[41]

Similarly, in his study of synagogue or 'shul shopping' in Palm Beach County, Florida (home to over 200,000 Jews), Joel Levine found that newcomers to the district would typically visit a different synagogue each week, their decision to join one rather than an other eventually being made on the grounds of such factors as 'the quality of the rabbi' (how he or she conducts the service, explains the *Torah*-reading or delivers a sermon), the friendliness of the congregation, the costs of membership and the vocal talents of the cantor.[42] In short, a host of pragmatic and personal reasons may influence an individual's chosen affiliation just as much – or more than – matters of ideology or theology. Moreover, such mixed motivation is not an exclusively contemporary phenomenon. Writing in the 1920's philosopher Franz Rosenzweig argued that historically Jews observed the *mitzvot* not 'because God imposed it upon Israel at Sinai' but largely because their social reality compelled and made sense of it.[43] What is different about life in the modern and contemporary eras is that Jewish social reality is less cohesive than was the case pre-emancipation. A male (or female) may today decide to wear a *kippah* (skullcap) out of a desire to adhere to the traditional acknowledgement that 'the *Shechinah* [Divine Presence] is above my head' (*kiddushin* 31a). Alternatively, he or she may wish to assert a Jewish identity in a predominantly non-Jewish society, perhaps to appear exotic, subversive, or just different. (Jews today have greater freedom to act in a range of ways and more opportunities to debate or reflect on their reasons for doing 'a' rather than 'b', 'c' or 'd', but of course this does not mean that in earlier centuries Jews did not make other choices for equally varied reasons, albeit within a more circumscribed range of options.)

Finally, it is important to consider how Jewish diversity is evaluated by Jews today. Is it regarded as a problem, or as a sign of creativity and vibrancy in religious life? From a more intellectual viewpoint, was modernity good for Jews, or was emancipation a 'mistake'? Radical as they may seem – who now, outside some *Charedi* circles, would advocate a return to the enforced seclusion of the ghetto – these questions have a lengthy history.[44]

From a non-Orthodox perspective, the encounter with Enlightenment and emancipation, and all that has followed, is primarily a positive one, although without doubt the general democratization of government that aided European Jewry also gave rise to new hazards for Jews, including a revival in antisemitism, as politicians tried to woo the new mass electorates.[45] Progressive Judaisms (Reform, Liberal, and Reconstructionist in particular) have embraced modernity's emphasis on rationality, progress and the right to self-determination. They have also accepted the fundamentally postmodern concept of religious pluralism – the view that different, or contradictory forms of Jewish (and non-Jewish) belief and practice can (or even should) coexist. Accordingly, whilst difficulties may exist where one particular tradition is dominant and uses that position to marginalise others (as in Israel, where Orthodoxy has been able to block full recognition of Progressive conversions, marriages and divorces) Jewish diversity itself is not to be problematised. Culturally and religiously different groups of Jews can live peaceably alongside one another and work collectively for the good of Jewry as a whole.

Some evidence can be found to support this optimism. There is, for example, a fair degree of co-operation between *Masorti*, the Union of Liberal and Progressive Synagogues (ULPS), and the Reform Synagogues of Great Britain (RSGB) in Britain, due partly to the relatively small size of these bodies, but also because of their recognition of common goals and interests. Whilst contemporary Orthodox Jews remain divided about the propriety of co-operation with these groups, contacts are not without precedent. As described earlier, the Geiger-Tiktin affair resulted in the creation of two separate communities that nevertheless collaborated on issues of social welfare. Going further back in Jewish history, it is clear from *responsa* that contacts and even marriages occurred between Jews of very different cultural (Ashkenazi-Sephardi) and religious (Rabbinic-Karaite) backgrounds.

Despite theses precedents, the 'right wing' of Orthodoxy sees some modern forms of Jewish diversity as problematic and a threat to Jewish continuity itself. In the past, one was either a faithful or conforming member of *the* Jewish community, or one left it – perhaps by converting to Christianity or Islam, or by being excommunicated for behaviours deemed intolerable by the Jewish authorities. Excommunication did not eliminate difference (the Vilna Gaon's ban on chasidism did not crush it; Spinozism commanded the sympathies of Enlightenment philosophers and many Romantics), but it did establish boundaries and act as a deterrent. Once Jews as individuals gained emancipation and joined the wider non-Jewish society, the self-governing capacity of communities disintegrated, perhaps inevitably leading to a decline in intellectual and emotional commitment to, and practice of, the Jewish religion. Gifted individuals who, in the past, would have necessarily channelled their energies down Jewish avenues, giving worthwhile service in positions of communal leadership, are now able to find other outlets for their talents, with the result that the rabbinate, and the many other institutions that used to be a part of Jewish life (such as the *chevra kadisha* or burial society) have declined in status and prestige.

Many commentators have shared this pessimistic assessment of diversity as synonymous with decline. It is easy to idealise the *shtetl* of the past and equate today's lack of unity with a lack of Jewish commitment. This is, however, too simplistic. It is more appropriate to speak of the Enlightenment and its aftermath as an age of the reconfiguration, rather than of the destruction, of Judaism. From a study of religions viewpoint, it is certainly problematic to see past forms of religious expression as the only worthwhile or 'true' ones; the founders of Modern Orthodoxy and Chasidism themselves recognised that this is the case. Each new epoch and context carries with it new trials and opportunities for Judaism. From the sixteenth to the nineteenth centuries the ghetto forced many Jews to live lives that were overcrowded, unhealthy, and oppressed. At the same time, it provided opportunities for Jewish scholarship to develop with relatively little outside interference. The ghetto's regulation according to *halakhah* also ensured the survival and vitality of Jewish civil law, which might otherwise have withered. Likewise, the nineteenth, twentieth and twenty-first centuries have witnessed the loss of cohesion and the rise of potent new dangers to Jewish continuity. Yet, at the same time, new opportunities and vistas opened. For example, in the 1870s Jews across Europe successfully deployed the very rhetoric and ideology of modernism in lobbying the Congress of Berlin for the religious freedom of Romanian Jews.[46] More generally, the Western trend towards voluntaryism (the right not just to freedom of religion, but also to freedom *from* religion) has led possibly to a decline in religious commitment, certainly to a positive emphasis on personal responsibility and integrity in matters of belief and practice.

Notes

[1] D. Cohn-Sherbok, *Modern Judaism*, Macmillan, 1996, p. 1.

[2] See H. J. Zimmels, *Ashkenazim and Sephardim: Their Relations, Differences, and Problems as Reflected in the Rabbinical Responsa*, Hoboken: Ktav, 1996.

[3] J. Habermas, 'Modernity and postmodernity', *New German Critique* 22 (1981); C. Affron, 'Honoré de Balzac (1799-1850)' in J. Barzun and G. Stade (eds), *European Writers. The Romantic Century. Volume 5: Johann Wolfgang von Goethe to Alexander Pushkin*, New York: Charles Scribner's Sons, 1985, pp. 635-657.

[4] Voltaire; T. Besterman (trans.), *Philosophical Dictionary*, Harmondsworth: Penguin, 1971, p. 383.

[5] A. Hertzberg, *The French Enlightenment and the Jews*, New York: Columbia University Press, 1968, p. 313.

[6] Voltaire, *Dictionary*, p. 257.

[7] See D. Sorkin, 'Jewish Emancipation in Central and Western Europe in the Eighteenth and Nineteenth Centuries', in D. Englander (ed.), *The Jewish Enigma*, Open University, 1992, p. 92.

[8] P. Mendes-Flohr and J. Reinharz, (eds), *The Jew in the Modern World. A Documentary History*, second edition, Oxford: Oxford University Press, 1995, p. 259.

[9] B. Dinur, 'The Origins of Hasidism', in G. D. Hundert (ed.), *Essential Papers on Chasidism: Origins to Present*, New York: New York University Press, 1991, p. 159.

[10] S. Dubnow, 'The Beginnings: The Baal Shem Tov (Besht) and the Center in Podolia', in Hundert, *Essential Papers*, p. 31.

[11] *Sefer ha-Zohar*, 'Book of Splendour' (or 'Illumination') is the most famous example of Jewish mystical literature. Formally a commentary on the Pentateuch, its ultimate concern is with the investigation of God's nature – the limitless, unknowable *Ein Sof*, and the *Sefirot* (powers or emanations), those aspects of God which are active in the universe and knowable by humans.

[12] G. Scholem, 'Sabbatai Sevi: The Mystical Messiah', in M. Saperstein

(ed.), *Essential Papers on Messianic Movements and Personalities in Jewish History*, New York: New York University Press, 1992, pp. 289-334.

[13] Heilman, *Defenders of the Faith*, p. 26.

[14] H. Rabinowicz, *Hasidism and the State of Israel*, Rutherford: Fairleigh Dickinson University Press, 1982, p. 237.

[15] R. H. Popkin, 'Spinoza and Bible scholarship', in D. Garrett (ed.), *The Cambridge Companion to Spinoza*, Cambridge: Cambridge University Press, 1996, p. 383.

[16] M. A. Meyer, *Response to Modernity. A History of the Reform Movement in Judaism*, Oxford: Oxford University Press, 1988, pp. 54, 58.

[17] Ibid., p. 91.

[18] Ibid., pp. 228–229.

[19] For the early platforms see Meyer, *Response to Modernity*. The 1999 *Statement of Principles* is available at, http://ccarnet.org/platforms/principles.html (current on 10/11/2000).

[20] M. Schmool and F. Cohen, *British Synagogue Membership in 1996*, Board of Deputies of British Jews, 1997.

[21] E. B. Borowitz, *Liberal Judaism*, New York: Union of American Hebrew Congregations Press, 1984, p. 418

[22] Comment from the journal in *Yeshurun*, 1861, in S. R. Hirsch; J. Elias (trans.), *The Nineteen Letters*, Jerusalem: Feldheim, 1995, p. xxi.

[23] J. Sacks, *The Persistence of Faith: Religion, Morality and Society in a Secular Age*, Weidenfeld and Nicolson, 1991, p. 105.

[24] M. Sklare, *Conservative Judaism. An American Religious Movement*, New York: Schocken Books, 1955; R. Bulka, 'Orthodoxy Today,' p. 14.

[25] J. D. Soloveitchik; L. Kaplan (trans.), *Halakhic Man*, Philadelphia: JPS, 1983.

[26] Former Jewish Theological Seminary chancellor Louis Finkelstein in I. Klein, *A Guide to Jewish Religious Practice*, New York: JTS, 1979, p. xxii.

[27] Today there are Conservative congregations throughout the Americas and in Britain and other European countries. See D. J. Elazar and R. M. Geffen (eds), *The Conservative Movement in Judaism: Dilemmas and Opportunities*, New York: SUNY Press, 2000, p. 130.

[28] I. Klein, *A Guide to Jewish Religious Practice*, New York: JTS, 1979.

[29] See A.J. Heschel, *The Prophets*, New York: Harper and Row, 1962 and *God in Search of Man. A Philosophy of Judaism*, John Calder, 1956, and also H. Kasimov, *No Religion is an Island: Abraham Joshua Heschel and Interreligious Dialogue*, Maryknoll: Orbis, 1991.

[30] Declaration at, http://www.utj.org (current on 10/11/2000).

[31] Sklare, *Conservative Judaism*, p. 225.

[32] M. M. Kaplan, *Judaism as a Civilisation: Toward a Reconstruction of American-Jewish Life*, New York: Thomas Yoseloff, 1934.

[33] R. T. Alpert and J. J. Staub, *Exploring Judaism: A Reconstructionist Approach*, Wyncote: The Reconstructionist Press, 1997, p. 10.

[34] Kaplan, *Judaism as a Civilisation*, p. 273.

[35] Alpert and Staub, *Exploring Judaism*, p. 11.

[36] Alpert and Staub, *Exploring Judaism*, pp. 14 – 15.

[37] N. A. Stillman, *Sephardi Religious Responses to Modernity*, Harwood Academic Publishers, 1995, pp. 22, 27.

[38] I. Ben-Ami, *Saint Veneration Among the Jews in Morocco*, Detroit: Wayne State University Press, 1998, p. 177.

[39] H. C. Dobrinsky, *A Treasury of Sefardic Laws and Customs: The Ritual Practices of Syrian, Moroccan, Judeo-Spanish and Spanish and Portuguese Jews of North America*, revised edition, New York: Yeshiva University Press, 1998, pp. 264-270.

[40] N. Solomon, 'Jewish Fundamentalism', in *The Newsletter of the International Interfaith Centre at Oxford*, Number 12 (December 2000), p. 6.

[41] J. Magonet, *Manna*, Number 60 (Summer 1998) insert.

[42] J. L. Levine, 'Why People in the Sunbelt Join a Synagogue', in D. E. Kaplan (ed.), *Contemporary Debates in American Reform Judaism: Conflicting Visions*, London: Routledge, 2001, pp. 56-65.

[43] F. Rosenzweig, 'Teaching and Law', in N. N. Glatzer (ed.), *Franz Rosenzweig: His Life and Thought*, New York: Schocken, 1961, p. 238.

[44] D. Feldman, 'Was Modernity Good for the Jews?', in B. Cheyette and L. Marcus (eds), *Modernity, Culture and 'the Jew'*, Cambridge: Polity Press, 1998, pp. 171-187.

[45] Ibid., p. 180ff.

[46] Ibid., p. 179.

4

Common Ground

Without our traditions, our lives would be as shaky as a fiddler on the roof!
(*Fiddler on the Roof*, Bock and Harnick, from stories by Sholem
Aleichem)

Much of the discussion so far has focused on Jewish diversity, but it
would be wrong to regard the Jewish story as one of overwhelming
fracture and dissolution. This chapter will concentrate on some of the
most popularly observed private and public rituals within Judaism. A
strikingly common approach to life-cycle events, the religious calendar,
food, and worship, has persisted during the centuries. This patterning of
individual and public behaviours creates a kind of 'symbolic universe',
which strengthens and promotes Jewish community. Practices like the use
of a shared language (Hebrew) for prayer, and male circumcision, foster
a sense of religious unity based on people-hood. They also reinforce
awareness of common history and heritage. Without these expressions
of identity and faith, Judaism might not have survived the pressures to
diversify which were imposed upon it by repeated geographical dispersion
and political change. But it must also be stressed that Jewish ritual life is
not characterised by *stasis*: flexibility is necessary for survival. The givens
of tradition themselves provide a framework within which change and
innovation are managed to ensure Judaism's continued viability.

Shabbat

Many Jews would agree with Zionist Ahad Ha-Am's judgement that
'far more than Israel has kept the Sabbath, it is the Sabbath that has kept
Israel'.[1] *Shabbat*, the Sabbath, is a sacred or set-apart time, a period of

spiritual and physical refreshment delineated from the rest of the week by candle-lighting and *kiddush* on Friday night and the ceremony of *havdalah* or 'separation' as the first stars appear on the following Saturday evening. (In the Jewish calendar, day follows night.) Not all Jews observe *Shabbat* in the manner envisaged by the classic rabbinic texts, but for religious Jews of all kinds the day remains special, a time for joy or delight (Isaiah 58:13) as much as for rest. In short, it is a true holy-day, or time-outside-time.

The historical origins of *Shabbat* are hard to determine. Many ancient Near Eastern societies had a ritual year punctuated like the Jewish one by regular, frequent days on which work was prohibited. There is some common ground here with the weekly Jewish holiday referred to in Biblical texts (for example, Jeremiah 17:22) which indicate that the characteristic means of observing *Shabbat* was to refrain from work. The word *Shabbat* possibly comes from the root *shavat*, 'to rest'. However, these ancient non-Jewish rest days were regarded by their observers as inauspicious, the opposite of what the Sabbath seems to be. Moreover, Jewish tradition from the *Tanakh* onwards stresses the distinctiveness of *Shabbat*. It is associated with experiences which are foundational for Judaism, the creation of the world, and slavery and the exodus from Egypt:

> Gen. 2:2-3: On the seventh day God finished the work that He had been doing, and He ceased on the seventh day from all the work that He had done. And God blessed the seventh day and declared it holy, because on it God ceased from all the work of creation that He had done.

> Exod. 20:8: "Remember the sabbath day and keep it holy...."

> Deut. 5:12-15: "Observe the sabbath day and keep it holy, as the LORD your God has commanded you. Six days you shall labour, and do all your work, but the seventh day is a sabbath of the LORD your God; you shall not do any work – you, your son or your daughter, your male or female slave, your ox or your ass, or any of your cattle, or the stranger in your settlements, so that your male and female slave may rest as you do. Remember that you were a slave in the land of Egypt and the LORD your God freed you from there with a mighty hand and an outstretched arm; therefore the LORD your God has commanded you to observe the sabbath day."

In these extracts *Shabbat* emerges as an affirmation of the Jews as God's chosen or 'set apart' people. It is in this sense, perhaps, that the Sabbath has preserved Israel. (Rabbinic Judaism understood this to mean that the non-Jew may not keep the Sabbath, and proselytes to Judaism traditionally do not fully observe the day until after the conversion process is complete.) But like the environmental teachings mentioned in chapter six, it is also crucially a celebration of, and reminder that, the world ultimately belongs to God, not to humanity.

As noted above, arrival of *Shabbat* at sunset each Friday evening is traditionally marked by two ceremonies, candle-lighting and *kiddush*. The lighting of (at least two) candles is performed at home by a woman, often the mother of the family. Rabbinic texts specify the blessing to be recited, 'Blessed art thou, Lord our God, King of the Universe, who has commanded us to kindle the Sabbath lights', and also offer a two-fold rationale for the ritual. Candle-lighting is mandatory for Jews who accept the authority of the *Talmud* and subsequent rabbinic interpretation, in order to distinguish them from the Karaites, who rejected the oral *Torah* and (initially, at least) interpreted Exodus 35:3 as prohibiting the practice. Particularly clear here is the role that ritual plays in constructing Jewish community. At the same time, for some ancient authorities, candle-lighting by women makes amends for Eve's having 'put out the light of the world'. It is also appropriate because women are connected with home-making, and with bringing Sabbath-like peace and happiness into the domestic sphere. Despite the ambiguous picture of women offered by these teachings, for many Orthodox women candle-lighting is *the* paradigmatic Jewish women's ritual. Some feminists have stressed the sense of empowerment gained in performing a ritual which 'makes' the Sabbath.[2]

In contrast to candle-lighting, the Friday night *kiddush* or 'sanctification [of the Sabbath]' is an historically male preserve. A glass of wine is held and a series of blessings (*berakhot*) recited, praising God for wine, and for giving the Sabbath to Israel. After the drinking of the wine, the blessing over bread is said and the first meal of *Shabbat* is eaten. (A shorter version is said before lunch on Saturday.) Strictly speaking, *kiddush* is also a home ritual. But the medieval practice of reciting it additionally at the synagogue (on behalf of visitors) has persisted in many congregations.

There are and have been many different attitudes to Sabbath rest and refreshment. The Bible does little to define the 'work' which is prohibited, although prior to the description of the building of the tabernacle in the wilderness (the moveable tent of meeting [with God] on which the Jerusalem Temple was later modeled) Exodus 35:2 says of the Sabbath that 'whoever does any work on it shall be put to death'. It was in fact to the account of the building of the tabernacle that early rabbis turned in their attempts to clarify the definition of prohibited work. Studying the tasks required to build the structure, they produced a list of *melakhot*, thirty-nine kinds of work prohibited on *Shabbat*. The list appears in the *Mishnah* and was reproduced in chapter two.

The investigation of Jewish law in chapter two highlighted the dynamic nature of the *halakhah*. On the one hand, there is a rabbinic tendency to build a fence around the law in order to guard against its accidental infringement. At the same time, despite its claim to be a self-authenticating system which does not require external sanction, halakhic Judaism has always developed in dialogue (to a greater or lesser extent) with the spirit of the times. Sometimes this has lead to the outlawing of previously sanctioned practices. For example, circa 1000CE, Rabbi Gershom of Mainz declared a *herem* (excommunicatory ban) against polygamists, a decree that has been accepted as permanently binding on Ashkenazi men. In the case of *Shabbat*, technological and other developments have meant that since Mishnaic times, the definition of prohibited *melakhot* is subject to review and adjustment.

The application of the ancient prohibition against the kindling and use of fire (Exodus 35:3) to electricity provides a handy case study in the modern day application of Sabbath law. In the early days of electricity, some rabbis argued that electric lights could be switched on during *Shabbat*. Their reasoning was that since no combustion occurred in the filament, and since electricity is already present in the circuit, the switching-on of the light was only an act of indirect kindling.[3] However, Orthodox Judaism today rejects these arguments and does not permit the direct use of electricity on *Shabbat*. Lights and other appliances may not be turned on or off. The strict avoidance of such work requires careful preparation. The sensor-catch on a refrigerator light may need to be covered with tape, for example, so that one does not switch on the light when opening the door. In an apartment block or hotel that has been approved for the use of Orthodox Jewish guests by a rabbinic court or *bet din*, the electrically powered elevator will need to be switched off, or set to operate automatically, calling at each floor in turn continuously throughout the night and day. Similar time switches are frequently used to operate lights at home or in the synagogue. These developments illustrate not just the demands made on traditional Jews by careful Sabbath observance, but also the constructive approach taken to the responsible exploitation of new technologies, and the extent to which Orthodox and even *Charedi* Jews have increasingly adopted the values of consumerism. According to the *Talmud* the joy of the Sabbath is a sixtieth part of that reserved for the righteous in *olam ha-ba*, the World to Come (*Berakhot* 57b). It is therefore appropriate to make use of legitimate opportunities to enhance one's enjoyment of the day.

In much popular parlance, the very term, 'Sabbath', conjures up images of passivism and *stasis*. Artist Marc Chagall suggested similar sentiments in his painting *Sabbath* (1910) which depicted his family as frozen in time, symbolised by the clock on the wall of their simple Vitebsk home. From the standpoint of Judaism, however, *Shabbat* is a time of sweetness, the passing of which has to be made less painful by the ceremony of *havdalah* (separation) when blessings are said over wine, a box of scented spices, and a plaited candle. The weekly period of abstention from work frees time for the pursuit of pleasurable or elevating activities. These include the holy task of studying *Torah* (each Sabbath takes the name of its designated *Torah* reading) and also prayer and worship.

The Friday evening service (*maariv*) is traditionally short; the home is the primary location in which *Shabbat* is welcomed. But its liturgy contains one of the most well loved hymns, *Lekhah Dodi*, 'Come my friend', which was originally a kabbalistic piece, composed by Solomon Alkabetz of Safed to accompany an elaborate mystical ritual in which *Shabbat* was hailed as Israel's bride. When the final stanza is sung, it is a custom for the congregation to turn towards the door and bow, to welcome the Sabbath:

> Come, my friend, to greet the bride; let us welcome the Sabbath day.

> To meet the Sabbath let us go, the fount of blessing from of old; when time began, it was enthroned; last in creation, but first in God's thought....[4]

On Friday afternoon generally, but especially after the service, it is common to wish friends *gut Shabbos* (Yiddish, 'good Sabbath') or *Shabbat Shalom*, 'a peaceful Sabbath'.

The remaining Sabbath services (Saturday morning and afternoon) are lengthier than their weekday counterparts, but in keeping with the day their mood is one of thanks and praise. Worship on Saturday morning is for many the main service of the week. In Orthodox circles, it consists of *shacharit* (morning prayer) followed by *musaf* (additional prayer) and extends across two full hours, as the liturgy includes lengthy readings from the *Torah* and Prophets, a second *amidah* (see below) and a sermon. After the conclusion of the service, when *kiddush* is recited, it is common practice for people celebrating a family event such as a wedding or *bar mitzvah* to provide refreshments. In his 1976 study of an Orthodox synagogue in urban North America, Samuel Heilman identified these festive additions to *kiddushim* as key moments in the building and definition of community. Observing that, 'the drink and its accompanying benediction are often of the least social consequence', Heilman suggested that what was at stake in these events was the transformation of sacred space into 'an array of sociability spots; tables, corners, stairwells, niches and books become demarcated by the sociable assembly taking place in them'. As much as the services themselves, the time before and after Sabbath prayers is vital for congregants to create and sustain emotional unity with one another.[5] Heilman's remarks serve as a reminder that observance of *Shabbat* operates at a variety of levels to shape Jewish life. For many the wine and *challot* (plaited loaves) used for *kiddush*, like the ubiquitous *cholent* eaten at Saturday lunchtime (a stew of meat, potatoes and beans which is prepared before *Shabbat* and left cooking on a low heat overnight) are a fundamental part of what it means to be Jewish, even if they are enjoyed with decreasing frequency today. Whilst it would be a travesty to claim to understand a religion through its cuisine, it would also be a mistake to ignore the extra-halakhic dimension – the rich detail of Judaism's cultural aspects, and the dramas inherent in the everyday.

Conservative, Reform and other Progressive movements have always openly acknowledged the importance of non-halakhic factors in defining Jewish life. In relation to *Shabbat*, this has tended to result in an explicit emphasis on the Sabbath as a day of joy. Most non-Orthodox Jews will seek to cultivate the distinctiveness of the day and avoid or minimise involvement in work-like activities (for example, paid employment, shopping and other commercial transactions) whilst at the same time not attending to most of the traditional regulations. For instance, Progressive Judaism sanctions driving to attend synagogue on *Shabbat*, placing regular attendance at services above the halakhic definition of the internal combustion engine as a form of prohibited fire. Some congregations have also replaced variable service timings, governed for Orthodox Jews by the changing hour of sunset, with standardised times to suit the preferences and needs of members. Perhaps most radically, Reconstructionism will in certain circumstances condone career-related work, placing the individual's right to pursue legitimate ambition over Sabbath observance. But it also advocates family activities such as the *Shabbat seder* (a Friday night meal followed, Passover-style, by four questions and answers on some Jewish theme). These initiatives aim to bring together small groups of Jews for intimate experience of celebration and study. For Reconstructionists Alpert and Staub:

> Comfort within Jewish ritual comes only with practice....Whatever the lighting of the Shabbat candles …is supposed to mean according to rabbis, philosophers, and mystics, its true meaning to an individual is discovered at the moment when the flickering of those candles and the resonance of the accompanying *berakhah* (blessing) make sense, signifying a real, internal transformation from workday concerns to the peace of Shabbat.[6]

Festivals

In addition to the weekly *Shabbat*, a number of festivals punctuate the religious year. The Preface to this book introduced one of most well known ones, *Pesach* or Passover, which celebrates the exodus from Egypt. As the weeks pass, *Pesach* is succeeded by the four other major (or Biblically ordained) festivals of *Shavuot* (Weeks or Pentecost, like *Pesach* a pilgrim festival when people were historically expected to visit the Temple), the High Holy Days of *Rosh Ha-Shanah* (New Year) and *Yom Kippur* (Day of Atonement), and *Sukkot* (Tabernacles, also a pilgrim festival). There are also two minor festivals, *Chanukah* (Dedication) and *Purim* (Lots), which are popularly celebrated, and a number of other special days including *Tu Bi-Shevat* (New Year for Trees), *Yom Ha-Shoah* (Holocaust Remembrance Day) and *Yom Ha-Atzma'ut* (Israeli Independence Day) which will be discussed in chapter six.

Collectively, these festivals are fundamental to the experience of being Jewish. Whether generally observant or not, most Jews will participate in some kind of *Pesach* ritual, or have memories of having done so as a child. Most will also attend synagogue at *Rosh Ha-Shanah* and *Yom Kippur*. That these activities are engaged in by even largely secularised Jews means that they warrant serious consideration. Studying how a people orders its time – how it keeps its calendar – provides a way into its value system and its sense of self. So, in looking briefly at the Jewish festival calendar an effort will be made to balance detail about *what* is done, with an account of *why* it is done, and in particular why certain festivals have been observed in different ways and have assumed greater or lesser prominence in different times and places.

The Jewish calendar is essentially a lunar one. (Dates in the religious calendar for 2003-2004 are listed in an appendix at the back of this book.) Each month begins with the new moon and lasts twenty-nine or thirty days. In the Biblical period the appearance of the new moon (*Rosh Chodesh*) was marked by a festival comparable to *Shabbat* in importance (2 Kings 4:23). In later centuries, however, it declined in prominence and is typically marked by an announcement in synagogues on the preceding *Shabbat*, and additional prayers on the day itself. In some medieval communities women abstained from work at *Rosh Chodesh*, and in recent years Jewish feminists have used this tradition as a basis on which to construct new moon rituals reflecting women's experience of monthly menstruation.[7]

Whilst the months of the Jewish year are lunar, the ritual year is solar, with festivals linked to agricultural seasons determined by the position of the sun. According to Deuteronomy 16:1 *Pesach* must fall in the spring month of *Aviv*, *Sukkot* around harvest-time, and so on. This dual system creates a problem. Since the lunar year takes eleven fewer days than the solar one, adjustments must be made to avoid *Pesach* (for example) moving through the solar year to fall outside the spring month. To ensure that this does not happen an extra lunar month (a second *Adar* or *Adar Sheni*) is added to seven years out of every nineteen lunar ones. This calendar is accepted by all Jews except Karaites. Difference does exist, however, concerning the observance of so-called 'second days' of *Pesach*, *Sukkot* and *Shavuot*.

According to the *Mishnah* (*m. Rosh Ha-Shanah* 1:1-3:1) the arrival of the new moon was declared by the *Sanhedrin* (the ancient supreme court in Jerusalem) on the testimony of reliable witnesses. Probably because of the delay in communicating this to *Diaspora* Jews, communities outside Israel adopted the custom of observing an extra day at *Rosh Chodesh* and other festivals, in order to ensure that they kept the feasts at the right time. When Roman policy led to the destruction of the Temple and the abolition of the role of *Nasi* or High Priest, the *Sanhedrin* was lost and no institution existed with the authority to announce the new moon. The fixed calendar in use today was instituted, but the *Talmud* advised *Diaspora* Jews to continue celebrating extra days (*Betzah* 4b). Whilst Orthodox and *Charedi* communities preserve this custom, seeing it as both vital for careful observance and an acknowledgement that the land of Israel possesses a distinctive holiness, many Progressive Jews have abolished the second day, arguing that it is anomalous, and that its underlying assumption (that a life outside Israel is an inferior one of *galut* or exile) is no longer valid.

Pesach

Like *Shabbat*, *Pesach* is predominantly a home-based festival. Before the week-long season, the home is cleaned, to remove leaven or *chametz*. In many cases, this disposal of leaven is not simply functional, but becomes something of a game. For example, young children may be encouraged to search for bread-crumbs deliberately left to be swept up and burnt on the eve of the festival. Amongst some Moroccan Jews, pieces of bread with slices of grilled liver are left for the male members of the household to search out.[8] These practices of placing *chametz* in key places are probably traditional ways of ensuring that, when the blessing for the search for leaven is recited, the divine name is not taken in vain. The removal of leaven itself is in response to the commandments, in Exodus 23:15 and Leviticus 23:6, which prohibit the use of *chametz* during 'the Festival of Unleavened Bread'. The high-point of the festival is without doubt, however, the *seder* meal held on the eve of Passover. This too generally takes place at home, although in Temple times the arrival of the Festival of the Passover was marked by the slaughtering of a lamb marking God's 'passing over' the Children of Israel when the Egyptian first-born were killed (Exodus 12).

So far I have spoken about 'Passover' and the 'Festival of Unleavened Bread'. Many critics believe that the contemporary Passover festival is the product of a long process of the assimilation and transformation of a number of rites practised in the ancient Near East. The Hebrews adopted a spring agricultural festival which involved the sacrifice or consumption of a lamb, retaining the agrarian aspects and adding to it another dimension, so that it also commemorated the exodus from Egypt. Orthodox Judaism

81

would of course disagree with any approach to Scripture which denies the doctrine of *Min ha-Shamayim*, and sees the two names as referring to the same divinely instituted feast.

Whatever one's view of its origins, Passover's ability to accommodate historical and theological change within the structured framework of its rituals means that it in many ways epitomises Judaism. The existence of unity alongside diversity, tradition without stagnation, is vital to Jewish religious expression. The *seder* meal follows a unique, often beautifully reproduced text called the *haggadah*. At the core of the *haggadah* is a proto-*seder* described in the *Mishnah* (*m. Pesachim* 10) but the present liturgy includes poems and songs, ostensibly introduced to keep children awake during the long evening celebrations. It has also been transformed in ways that reflect Jews' changing understanding of the key exodus themes of bondage and liberation.

At the centre of the rituals outlined in the *haggadah* is the *seder* table, typically decorated with a white cloth and candles, and the *seder* plate or tray, on which are placed a variety of symbolic foods. These include three *matzot* (pieces of unleavened bread); *maror* (bitter herbs, often horseradish) said to symbolise the bitter lot of the slaves in Egypt (Exodus 1:14); *charoset* (a sweet paste made from almonds, apples and wine) symbolising both the mortar used by the slaves and the sweetness of their redemption; salt water (symbolising tears); parsley (for dipping in salt water) and a roasted bone and egg, reminders of the festival sacrifice brought in Temple times (and not consumed during the *seder*).

The key rituals associated with the recital of the *haggadah* are the drinking of four cups of wine (recalling the fourfold promise of redemption in Exodus 6:6-8); the eating of parsley dipped in salt water; the four questions (reproduced in the Preface to this book) and the reply they elicit; the chanting of psalms; the eating of *matzah* (including a piece known as the *afikoman*, which in many traditions, is hidden by the leader of the *seder*, to be found later by the children and consumed as 'dessert') and *maror* (bitter herbs).

At first sight, much of the thrust of the *seder* appears to be historical-commemorative. In response to the four questions, the reply begins:

> We were once slaves to the Pharaohs of Egypt, and God in all his glory and power caused the shackles of slavery to be broken. He redeemed us and brought us forth into freedom. And had this great miracle of history not

been bestowed upon us, we, to this day, and our children after us, might still be subjects of the Pharaohs of Egypt. We therefore consider it a sacred duty and obligation to keep this miracle of salvation ever alive in our memories. And it matters not how wise or learned we are or how well versed we are in the teachings of Torah. The duty of retelling the story of our deliverance from slavery is important and compelling; it must be retold each year at this time. And the more we repeat the story and dwell upon its message of freedom, the more praiseworthy are we.[9]

However, the *seder* is not simply a memorialisation of ancient deliverance. Each generation of participants is encouraged to regard itself as standing on the edge of redemption, emphasising the important links between the sense of history and contemporary identity with the Jewish people. The *haggadah* exhorts individuals to regard themselves as if they personally had come out of Egypt. Moreover, at the end of the meal a cup of wine is filled, and the door of the house momentarily opened. Both of these actions are marks of hospitality extended to the prophet Elijah, whom tradition holds will visit each Jewish home on *seder* night, and who is also the forerunner of the *Messiah*, God's anointed one, who will usher in a future age of redemption and peace.

In the preface to this book, the flexibility of the *seder* was emphasised. There are distinctive Israeli *haggadot* for example, produced for use by the Israeli Defence Forces, or by *kibbutz* residents. Their contents reflect the view that Jews have left '*diaspora* wandering' and are now back in their homeland. In contrast to the traditional proclamation, 'Next year in Jerusalem!', the hope is for 'Next year in rebuilt /reunited Jerusalem!' Similarly, feminist *haggadot* include *midrash* on female characters from Jewish history, especially Miriam, and recall not just the oppressions of Egypt, but the diversity of ways in which women have been subjugated.[10] And many communities now hold group services in synagogues and hotels, to cater for those who would not otherwise have a *seder*, or for those for whom wider ethnic or cultural solidarity ranks above immediate family ties.

What does this variation in Passover observance indicate? On the one hand it reflects a conscious desire for each generation and group to make the festival relevant and meaningful. But, to an even greater extent, the changing *seder* is a product of the impulse to subsume new events and concerns within Judaism's metanarrative. The exodus from Egypt and entry into the Promised Land are fundamental to Jewish religious consciousness, they are the types of suffering and liberation in relation to which other experiences can be made sense of. Within the framework of the *seder*, tradition and change are held in creative tension. But this in turn raises a further question, for arguably, 'exodus' and 'entry' are not the only Jewish fundamentals. Others include the making of the covenant at Sinai (Exodus 19:4-6) and the *Torah* itself. Festivals celebrate Sinai (*Shavuot*) and *Torah* (*Simchat Torah*), yet neither of these has assumed the status of *Pesach*. Is there then something intrinsic to the *seder* which has led it to acquire its status as the most celebrated and well-loved of Jewish festivals?

Arnold Eisen suggests a number of reasons for the unique status of the *seder* within modern Judaism. In addition to the *haggadah*'s combination of tradition and plasticity, he argues that the timing and location of the *seder* are crucial. Because the meal is held in the evening (outside normal working hours) and at home (in the private sphere) it allows participants to express their distinctiveness in a way that does not require social isolation. For Jews who live in societies shaped by Christianity, *Pesach* also falls close to and diffuses pressures generated by the wider religious culture. Functionally (especially for young children and for the assimilated or largely non-observant) the festival provides a Jewish alternative to the Easter celebrations in the wider community. Finally, Eisen suggests two further ways in which Passover meets the needs of modern Jewry. The orientation of much of the *seder* to children provides nostalgic and nominally observant adults with justification for their participation. And, last of all, the infrequent performance of the *seder* means that the boundaries which it implicitly establishes between Jews and non-Jews are limited, permeable and relatively non-problematic.[11] Not everyone would agree with Eisen's reading of *Pesach*. The *seder* is less firmly a domestic event than was once the case, and where extended families do meet together this can understandably be an occasion for tension and stress as much as for nostalgia. And rather than setting boundaries, some contemporary *haggadot* identify non-Jews (for example, African Americans or Tibetan Buddhists) as falling within the extended scope of Jewish concerns. *The Concise Family Seder* includes the following universalizing passage:

> We speak
> Of the tyranny of poverty
> And the tyranny of privation,
> Of the tyranny of wealth

And the tyranny of war,
Of the tyranny of power
And the tyranny of despair,
Of the tyranny of disease
And the tyranny of time,
Of the tyranny of ignorance
And the tyranny of color.

To all these tyrannies do we address ourselves this evening. Passover brands them all as abominations in the sight of God.[12]

Shavuot

In Temple times, a sheaf of wheat (an *omer*) was presented as a harvest offering on the second day of *Pesach*. A further commandment stipulated that from that day a period of seven weeks was to be counted, and on the fiftieth day a festival celebrated (Leviticus 23:9-21). This festival became known as *Shavuot*, or Weeks (Exodus 34:22). Like *Pesach*, *Shavuot* appears to be an originally agricultural observance which has acquired historical associations. In the first century CE, the Alexandrian Jew Philo described it as being a festival for the corn harvest and the fruits of the lowlands (*Special Laws* 1:183). But the rabbis understood it to commemorate the giving of the *Torah* at Mount Sinai.

In contrast to *Pesach*, *Shavuot* is not marked by a service in the house. One explanation or rationalisation for this is that the day does not celebrate one aspect of the *Torah*, but the *Torah* as a whole, and is therefore incapable of being articulated by any one specific rite. However, it is forbidden to work on *Shavuot* (as on other pilgrim festivals) and a number of customs have attached to the day over the centuries. In his introduction to Joseph Karo's *Maggid Mesharim*, Solomon Alkabetz (composer of *Lekhah Dodi*, quoted earlier in this chapter) describes an all-night vigil held by mystics in Safed in the fifteenth century. Some *Charedim* continue to emulate this practice, by remaining awake to study *Torah*. It is also traditional to decorate home and synagogue with foliage and flowers, and to eat dairy foods. These practices are sometimes associated with qualities attributed to the *Torah* – sweetness, beauty, and an ability to nourish the faithful (see for example *m. Avot* 1:2), although it may be that they are vestiges of *Shavuot's* earlier links with the harvest.

Finally, it is also customary to read the book of Ruth at *Shavuot*. Ruth's voluntary declaration of allegiance to the God of Israel makes her paradigmatic of the responsibly observant adherent of Judaism (Ruth 1:16), a 'successor' of the generation which first received the *Torah*. For this reason, some Progressive communities which have replaced or supplemented *bar* and *bat mitzvah* with Confirmation hold that ceremony at *Shavuot*, too.

Rosh Ha-Shanah and Yom Kippur

There are two points at which the Jewish year could be said to begin. In the *Tanakh*, *Nisan*, the month during which Passover falls, is described as the first month of the year (Exodus 12:2) but in the *Talmud* (*Rosh HaShanah* 16b) an early autumn festival is known as *Rosh Ha-Shanah*, literally 'the Head of the Year'. *Rosh Ha-Shanah* is certainly a time for new beginnings, as it ushers in the annual season of *teshuvah* (returning, or repentance) known as the *Yamim Noraim* or 'Days of Awe'. At the end of this ten day period is *Yom Kippur*, a 'Day of Atonement' when the Jewish people stands before God as a collectivity. Sins are confessed, unfulfilled vows cancelled and, tradition says, God makes final judgement on one's fate for the coming year. *Yom Kippur* is the high point of the Jewish year, from the viewpoint of rabbinic tradition and also in popular consciousness. Attendance at synagogue on this day is the minimal annual effort expected of even the most nominally observant Jews, who are for this reason sometimes jokingly referred to as '*Yom Kippur* Jews'.

Rosh Ha-Shanah is a mixture of celebration and solemnity. As the beginning of the year, it celebrates God's creation of the world: synagogue liturgy depicts God as King of the Universe. But Jews are also pictured as God's subjects, passing before God to receive judgement on their conduct in the previous year. Popular piety captures the ambiguity of the period. Special foods are eaten, especially apples with honey, to symbolise the desire for a good and sweet year. Yet the custom is to greet family and friends with a wish that they be 'written and sealed for a good year', reflecting the idea that God's judgement on one's fate is recorded and sealed in a heavenly book. Many traditional communities also observe *tashlikh*, visiting the seaside or river to hurl their sins symbolically into the water (compare Micah 7:19). Although this is a later medieval Ashkenazi custom, it has spread amongst the Sephardim and Oriental Jews.

Extended services mean that for observant Jews, the majority of *Rosh Ha-Shanah* will be spent in the synagogue. The story of the *akedah* or binding of Isaac (Genesis 22) is read. This is understood as paradigmatic of Jewish readiness to obey God, even to the point of martyrdom. A traditional hymn chanted by the congregation begins:

> At the time that the gates of favour are about to be opened; on this day I spread forth my hands to thee, O God. On this day of judgement, remember in my favour Abraham who bound, Isaac who was bound, and the altar.[13]

Parts of the *musaf* refer to the blowing of the *shofar*, the horn which gives the new year period a distinctive and evocative sound. Numbers 29:1 commands that *Rosh Ha-Shanah* be a day of horn-blowing; in some congregations this extends to a melody of around a hundred notes in different combinations of long and short sounds. The *Talmud* allows the use of the horn of any kosher animal except the cow, but preference is given to the ram's horn, in commemoration of the substitution of the ram for Isaac at Genesis 22:13.

By the time that *Yom Kippur* arrives, Jews are expected to have undertaken a period of soul-searching reflection and reparation. In Jewish thought, where one party wrongs another, that sin must be forgiven by the individual directly affected, before God will do likewise. Some people use the Days of Awe as an opportunity to ask forgiveness of one another for offences committed during the past year. At the same time, prayers inserted into the regular liturgy emphasise *teshuvah*, repentance or turning back to God, and there is a general attempt to practise stricter standards of ritual purity during this period. In *Charedi* circles, and in some Oriental communities, preparation for *Yom Kippur* takes additional symbolic forms. For example, the pious may visit the *mikveh* or ritual bath. In the unusual rite known as *kapparot*, a white chicken is swung around the head, slaughtered and then given to the poor. Some people find the practice repugnant, either on animal welfare grounds, or because it is open to being misconstrued as a kind of magical attempt to transfer one's sins onto an animal. But *kapparot* has persisted into the twenty-first century. In certain contexts it has been (or still is) a valuable source of income for the otherwise relatively poor *shochet* or ritual slaughterer. However, most people prefer to give charity in the form of money, or to offer hospitality to those who are not able to provide themselves with adequate food before the *Yom Kippur* fast.

The *Yom Kippur* fast, from which young children and the sick are exempt, consists of a complete abstention from food and drink, and begins just before sunset. Its roots lie in the Biblical purification ceremony outlined in Leviticus, as do the other forms of ritual purity to be observed: no washing, no anointing, no wearing of leather shoes, and no sexual intercourse. As on *Shabbat*, all types of work are also prohibited (Leviticus 16; 23:29). These measures are not ends in themselves: the need to fast on *Yom Kippur* is formally derived from the Biblical text, which advocates self-denial on this day. It is associated with penance, self-discipline, and the need to focus the mind on the spiritual rather than the material realm: 'You shall practice self-denial ... for on this day atonement shall be made for you to cleanse you of all your sins' (Leviticus 16:29-30).

In the synagogue, the ark, scrolls and reading desk (see below, synagogue and prayer) are all draped in white and many male Jews (in some Progressive congregations, male and female) will wear a white tunic known as a *kittel*, as some do at the *Seder*. In Judaism, white is the colour of purity (Isaiah 1:18). But other connotations are attached to the garment, too. Many Jews will ultimately be buried in their *kittel*, so its use at this time also heightens the sense of humility and an awareness of the transience of individual human life.

The first service on the eve of *Yom Kippur* effectively begins with the *Kol Nidrei* (literally, 'all vows') prayer:

> All vows, renunciations, promises, obligations, oaths, taken rashly, from this Day of Atonement till the next, may we attain it in peace, we regret them in advance. May we be absolved of them, may we be released from them, may they be null and void and of no effect....Such vows shall not be considered vows; such renunciations, no renunciations; and such oaths, no oaths.[14]

In effect, *Kol Nidrei* cancels vows or oaths that Jews are not able to fulfil. In the medieval period, the antisemitism prevailing in wider European culture encouraged non-Jews to mis-interpret the prayer as a proof of the unreliability of Jews in business and other matters – allegedly, their religious tradition itself offered them a means of reneging on a deal. In a number of places Jews appearing in state courts were required to swear the *More Judaica* in consequence. This special oath forced Jews to recite the punishments that would befall them should they fail to respect Christian jurisprudence, and was sometimes accompanied by humiliating rites, such as standing on a pigskin. In fact, the *Kol Nidrei* only relates to those vows or promises made to God, and also to vows which have proved impossible, rather than ones that one has simply failed to honour. The success of Zechariah Frankel (introduced in chapter three) and his contemporaries in explaining the prayer to non-Jews in nineteenth century Germany, and the famous traditional melody to which it is sung, have ensured its survival and popularity in the modern period.

During the next day, long services continue. The liturgy emphasises the reasons for the ritual fasting as this reading from the morning service illustrates:

> This is the fast I desire:
> To unlock fetters of wickedness,
> And untie the cords of the yoke
> To let the oppressed go free;
> To break off every yoke. (Isaiah 58:6)

It is solemn but generally not mournful. Amongst the distinctive features of the day is a part of the *musaf* known as the *avodah* (Temple service). It recounts the observance of *Yom Kippur* rituals in Temple times, and at various points the congregation kneel and prostrate themselves in imitation of the practices recounted. The Biblical book of Jonah is also read during the afternoon service, emphasising the conviction that whilst it is impossible to hide from God, God will accept genuine repentance – from the pagan Ninevites as much as from Jews.

The end of *Yom Kippur* is marked by the unique service of *neilah* or 'closing'; the name refers to the closing of the Temple gates, which happened at around this time. As the sun begins to set, a hopeful dimension is introduced into the prayers. The liturgy expresses a yearning for a better future, and triumph over sin. Finally, the whole congregation recite the first sentence of the *Shema*, 'Hear O Israel, the Lord our God, the Lord is One!', and then three times, 'Blessed be the name of His glorious reign for ever and ever' and finally, seven times, 'The Lord alone is God.' This latter phrase echoes the words of those who witnessed the prophet Elijah's defeat of the prophets of Baal on Mount Carmel (1 Kings 18:39). In this way *Yom Kippur* ends with a declaration of renewed loyalty to God.

Sukkot

Just a few days after *Yom Kippur*, the festival of *Sukkot* or tabernacles begins. It lasts for seven days and is followed immediately by *Shemini Atzeret* ('eighth day of assembly', the end of the new year festival cycle) and *Simchat Torah*, 'rejoicing in the law' (in Israel the two observances are conflated). During *Sukkot* a *sukkah* or tabernacle (booth) is constructed, using branches from trees and plants. This is in compliance with the commandment to construct and dwell in booths as a reminder of the structures in which the people Israel sheltered when they fled from slavery in Egypt (Leviticus 23:42-3). Like *Pesach* and *Shavuot* then, *Sukkot* is a pilgrimage festival, connected in the *Tanakh* with the exodus. But it also has strong agricultural connotations. Jews are commanded to take 'the product of goodly trees, branches of palm trees, boughs of leafy trees, and willows of the brook' (Leviticus 23:40), and this has been interpreted to require the waving of an *etrog* (citrus fruit) and a bundle consisting of a palm branch, myrtle and willow sprigs, during the recital of the *hallel* psalms during the synagogue.

Traditional Jews will strive to fulfil the commandment to construct and live in the booth, eating and sleeping there for the duration of the festival. However, such observance has sometimes been difficult. In many *diaspora* contexts (for example, in Britain) the autumn climate does not favour outdoor living. In the past, it was also difficult to obtain the required four species, and the *sukkah* presented hostile non-Jews with a vulnerable and highly visible target. As a result, in many communities it has become customary to build a *sukkah* in the synagogue grounds, rather than in individual families' homes. Not all Jewish congregations own suitable land, however. They may meet and worship in a school hall or other suitable public place, and where this is the case, similarly creative steps must be taken to find space for a *sukkah*. The photograph opposite shows the *sukkah* constructed by members of a Progressive Jewish community. It is located in the grounds of a training college for Methodist ministers, which also provides space for the community's High Holy Day services. The construction of the *sukkah* in the college garden is not simply about the fulfilment of the commandments in Leviticus.

Sukkah of a Progressive Jewish community. The sukkah has been built in the grounds of a Methodist seminary.

It also illustrates the two communities' recognition of one another, and constitutes what might be termed an interreligious dialogue of life.

In Israel today the family *sukkah* has undergone a revival. Many balconies of apartment blocks and hotels are constructed to allow residents to build a booth, which fulfils the halakhic requirement that it be open to the sky. At the end of the festival, *Shemini Atzeret* introduces a liturgical change, as words acknowledging God who causes wind and rain are inserted into the *amidah* (see below, 'synagogue and prayer'). But the culmination of the ritual season is *Simchat Torah* – the day on which, in Orthodox circles, the annual reading of the *Torah* is completed, and immediately resumed. The *Torah* scrolls are processed around the synagogue, usually accompanied by singing, dancing, and general celebration. The seventeenth century diarist Samuel Pepys attended the celebration of the festival in the Creechurch Lane synagogue in London (the synagogue of the Spanish and Portuguese community, replaced by the Bevis Marks synagogue in 1701) and found the experience a puzzling one:

> Their service is all in a singing way, and in Hebrew. And anon their Law…is carried by several men…and they do relieve one another, or whether it is that everyone desires to have the carrying of it, I cannot tell…. But Lord, to see the disorder, laughing, sporting, and no attention, but confusion in all their service, more like Brutes than people knowing the true God, would make a man forswear ever seeing more; and indeed, I never did see so much, or could have imagined there had been any religion in the whole world so absurdly performed as this.[15]

Pepys was writing in 1663, not long after the readmission of Jews to England (in 1655). His account reflects both supercessionist theology and a conception of Jews as exotic, alien Others. The Creechurch Lane synagogue, opened in 1657, was something of a tourist attraction in Restoration London. Nevertheless, visitors to an Orthodox or *Charedi* service today could reasonably expect to find similar exuberance. Setting aside Pepys' prejudices, his account attests to a powerful demonstration of the *Torah*'s status within Judaism. Joy at *Simchat Torah* reflects the blending of intimacy and respect that characterises traditional approaches to the law.

Chanukah

Unlike the other festivals mentioned so far, *Chanukah* ('dedication') is a post-Biblical addition to the Jewish ritual calendar. Celebrated for eight days during the month of *kislev*, it was instituted following the second century BCE victory of the Maccabees (see chapter five) over the Seleucids, as recounted in the non-canonical books of 1 and 2 Maccabees. According to legend, when the Maccabees recaptured Jerusalem, they found only a day's worth of halakhically fit oil with which to fuel the *menorah* (seven-branched candelabrum) in the rededicated Temple (*Shabbat* 21b).

Miraculously, the oil lasted for eight days. *Chanukah* celebrates this wonder by lighting candles or lamps (accompanied by special *berakhot*) – one on the first day, two on the second, and so on. An additional light, the *shammash* or 'servant' is used to kindle the main lights, so the special candle-holder (*Chanukiyah*) used by many Jews is nine-branched.

Like other Jewish festivals, the observance of and meanings applied to *Chanukah* have exhibited considerable diversity over time. Whilst early Jewish texts are generally marked by their discursiveness, the Talmudic rabbis asked, 'What is *Chanukah*?' (*Shabbat* 21b), suggesting that in the early centuries of the Common Era, the festival was undergoing a period of neglect, or perhaps that the reasons for its distinctive ritual were not widely grasped. Throughout the medieval era, *Chanukah* observance was relatively low-key and centred around the lighting of oil lamps and the recitation of the Psalms of praise known as *hallel* (Psalms 113-118). But in the modern period, *Chanukah* has assumed new popularity and significance.

The revival of *Chanukah* perhaps stems from its internal flexibility. The emphasis on the miraculous flask of oil provided suitable reason for its observance during politically difficult times in medieval Europe and under Islam. But inextricably linked to the story of the oil-cruse is the military success of the Maccabees. In a post-Enlightenment world, where the politics of nationhood were discussed more openly than theories of the miraculous, the Judaean victory over occupying forces gave the festival a newly relevant rationale.

For early Zionists, the miracle of the flask of oil had little place in the interpretation of the holiday. Indeed, its central role in the traditional *Chanukah* observance was regarded as an illustration of the passivity of Jews living in exile or *galut*. Placing emphasis on the struggle of the Maccabees to win back control of their homeland, the Zionists recast *Chanukah* as symbolic of Jewish self-redemption. It was the historic destiny of Jews to struggle for national liberation without reliance on outside powers, either natural or supernatural.[16] These interpretations persist in Israel today, where the commemoration includes the carrying of a torch from Modiin (the burial site of the Maccabees) to other parts of the country.

Not all Jews were (or are) Zionists. Samuel Cahan, editor of the nineteenth century *Archives israélites de France*, believed that emancipation could be hastened if Jews demonstrated to their fellow citizens that Judaism and French patriotism were not in conflict. An article in the *Archives* urged that *Chanukah* be reinterpreted along these lines. The festival should not be a prayer for the restoration of a Jewish homeland, but could be recast as an example of the positive role that religions could play more generally in promoting responsible citizenship, and pride in one's *patrie*.[17]

Contemporary trends in *Chanukah* observance in the *Diaspora* suggest that, as with *Pesach*, the timing and location of *Chanukah* commemorations have been crucial factors in promoting the festival. Although candles are lit in synagogue, most people celebrate at home, and since the lighting occurs after dark (except on Friday night, when it is done before the kindling of Sabbath lights) it is, like the *seder*, a ritual celebration of Jewish identity that is also readily compatible with full membership of a largely non-Jewish society. As a winter festival, *Chanukah* also provides a Jewish alternative to the Christian festival of Christmas. Mordecai Kaplan, founder of Reconstructionism, was explicit about this in his *Judaism as a Civilisation*:

> Since *Chanukah* falls so near the Christmas season, it must be made as interesting and joyful for the Jewish child as Christmas is made for the Christian child. The *Chanukah* festival should be the season for gifts. The children should look forward to gifts from their parents, and parents from their children.....It should be the season for paying social calls, playing home games, and holding communal entertainments.[18]

Whilst such direct and obvious Christian influence worries many traditional Jews, others see an accentuation of the festival as the only means of resisting Christmas. Without such concessions, some young Jews may come to regard *Diaspora* Jewishness as an oppressive and alienating condition. Some *Charedi* groups like the Lubavitch chasidim have promoted public *Chanukah* observance for similar reasons, and pay for the erection of large candelabra in municipal parks and squares. Many North American and Western European Jews have built on the traditions of giving money (*gelt*) to children, playing games, and eating special foods (especially doughnuts and potato cakes or *latkes*) in ways that approximate Christmas celebrations and might well have pleased Kaplan. *Chanukah* cards and gifts have become more popular and elaborate. Ironically, then, this festival which commemorates resistance to a failed attempt at forced enculturation has itself become a one of the main indices of Jewish acculturation today.

Purim

Purim or 'lots' is similar in origin to *Chanukah* in that it is traditionally regarded as a minor (or humanly instituted) festival. It also recalls a crucial moment in Jewish survival – the deliverance of Jews from the Persian official Haman – who drew lots (*purim*) to determine the date on which he would exterminate the Jewish people (Esther 3:7-14). According to the Biblical story, Esther was chosen by the Persian King Ahasuerus to be his queen, and she successfully pleaded with him to avert both the marriage and the slaughter.[19] Her cousin Mordecai (the only individual to be called a Jew in the *Tanakh*) proclaimed the festival in commemoration of the escape:

> And he [Mordecai] sent dispatches to all the Jews throughout the provinces of King Ahasuerus, near and far, charging them to observe the fourteenth and fifteenth days of Adar, every year- the same days on which the Jews enjoyed relief from their foes and the same month which had been transformed for them from one of grief and mourning to one of festive joy. They were to observe them as days of feasting and merrymaking, and as an occasion for sending gifts to one another and presents to the poor (Esther 9:20-22).

The *mitzvot* or good deeds specified in this text (celebratory feasting, gifts to the poor, and gifts to one another) ensure that *Purim* is a joyful festival. The general atmosphere is one of carnival. In the synagogue, the *megillah* or scroll of Esther is read on the night of *Purim* and the next morning. In many communities, children wear fancy dress to attend the reading and, when Haman's name is mentioned in the text, worshippers may stamp their feet, and hiss. In some Oriental communities in the past, the desire to erase Haman's name was taken even further. The letters were chalked on the synagogue floor and then rubbed out by the stamping feet. Ashkenazi Jewry developed the playful theme differently, probably in dialogue with the Lenten carnivals staged by their Christian neighbours. From as early as the thirteenth century, many European Jews practised what anthropologists would term 'rituals of rebellion', briefly dropping the usual restraints on behaviour and acting in ways that inverted social norms. For example, most communities in medieval Provence elected a mock *Purim* king or *Purim* rabbi. There are also accounts of (rabbinically sanctioned) male transvestism, and associated entertainments which later developed into *Purim* plays, relating the original biblical story to contemporary events and personalities. These practices echo those of European Christians on the eve of Lent; they may also have served as a psychological safety-valve, a coping mechanism for Jews who found themselves the subject of unwelcome and often violent attention during the approaching Easter season. Although later, post-emancipation generations regarded the medieval *Purim* celebrations as irreligious and unedifying (some early Reform communities abolished the festival completely), a satirical element survives today, in the wearing of fancy dress by children and the consumption of three-cornered cakes filled with poppy seeds or date and known as *hamantaschen*, 'Haman's pockets' or 'ears'.[20]

As at other points in the ritual calendar, the classical sources enjoin the use of alcohol at *Purim*. According to the *Talmud*, a man should drink so that he can no longer distinguish between 'blessed be Mordecai' and 'cursed be Haman' (*megillah* 7b). In *Charedi* circles this much elaborated pinciple is often still taken literally; the *Chasidim* value the power of alcohol to dull one's intellect and thereby promote a mystical transcendence of everyday realities. However, celebrations in most communities are more sober, if not less joyful.

Life Cycle Rites

The sections on *Shabbat* and festivals have stressed the importance of group ritual observance in strengthening Jewish community. In fact, ritual practice has at times been a means of reconfiguring ideas about what being Jewish entails. Some Israeli *haggadot*, for example, reflect Zionist ideas about centre and periphery in Jewish life. Feminist recastings of the *Seder* service attempt to provide a corrective to what is perceived as the distorting, patriarchal focus of many Orthodox traditions. In chapter three, I described how Reform philosophy grew out of the need to articulate reasons for liturgical changes that had already been implemented in German congregations. These and other changes to outward observances reflect and shape changing notions about Judaism, Jewish peoplehood, and Jewish relations with non-Jews.

Just as the calendar has its own rhythm, established by *Shabbat* and the various fasts and holiday seasons, so an individual Jew's life is punctuated with a number of publicly observed life-cycle rites. These rituals are associated with birth, religious majority, marriage and death; in other words, with transitions from one stage in life to another. Anthropologist Arnold van Gennep termed them 'rites of passage' – through their observance the individual is helped to pass over a *limen* or threshold, into a new state or condition.[21] Like many other religious traditions, historic Jewish sources do not have a concept of rites of passage. The rituals described below are, like all others, determined by *halakhah* and *minhag*. So long as this is borne in mind, however, distinguishing rites of passage as a separate set of ritual practices is a useful approach, and it is one that some recent works by Jewish writers have employed.[22]

Birth and Naming

Judaism places great importance on procreation. The first *mitzvah* in the *Torah* is the command to 'be fertile and increase' (Genesis 1:28), and a Talmudic passage suggests that when someone refuses to do so it is as if they had shed human blood (*Yevamot* 63b). Whilst contemporary birth rates amongst Jews in the west are close to (amongst some groups, slightly lower than) those for the surrounding non-Jewish populations, amongst the *Charedim* large families are the norm. Within such carefully observant communities, gender roles are clearly boundaried in a way that places childrearing at the centre of women's lives, and sees this as a reflection of women's 'naturally' devotional character:

> It is more feminine to be devotional than to be narcissistic. It is masculine to be narcissistic. Biologically, a man does not really give of himself in any real sense to have children. A woman does. That's why there is a difference in teaching men and teaching women. When you teach a woman about devotion and marriage and selflessness and altruism, what you're really telling her is be yourself.[23]

Rituals surrounding birth and naming reflect the general importance of children within all Jewish denominations, and more particularly, the higher value which the tradition has historically placed on the birth of sons. For example, women who give birth are considered ritually unclean (and not able to engage in sexual relations) for seven days and then a further thirty-three days for a male child, and for fourteen days and a further sixty-six for a female one (Leviticus 12:1-5). As there is no physiological reason for the distinction, many modern Orthodox and non-Orthodox women see it as a manifestation of the discriminatory attitudes lying behind the *Talmud*'s assertion that, 'The world cannot exist without males and without females – happy is he whose children are males, and woe to him whose children are females' (*kiddushin* 82b).

Outside *Charedi* circles, relatively few women observe the laws of ritual purity or *niddah*, save for some feminists who regard the associated practices of prayer and immersion in a ritual bath or *mikveh* as precious, distinctively female *mitzvot*. However, the majority of Jews will observe other rituals distinguishing the birth of a son from that of a daughter.

The arrival of a baby girl is typically announced at the synagogue on the *Shabbat* following her birth. The father may be called for an *aliyah* ('going up') and make the blessing over the reading of the *Torah*. A prayer is then said for the mother and daughter and the girl is named. In most societies, naming a baby is an act at once both intensely private and subject to wider cultural and historical forces. Given names convey messages about child and parents, and their place in the flow of history, be that the history of the family, nation, or humanity. This is as true of Jewish cultures as it is of non-Jewish ones. Within Judaism, there are a variety of *minhagim* or customs on naming. In Sephardi communities the custom is to name a child after a grandparent or other honoured member of the family, whilst Ashkenazi custom tends towards naming after a recently deceased family member, whose good qualities it is hoped the child will assume. Further- more, many Jewish children are given two names – a Hebrew one, which is proclaimed at the naming ceremony and will be used for religious purposes in later life, and a secular one. Often there is a similarity of sound or meaning between the two, and in some communities there is a tradition of hyphenating or joining them together. For example, the name Djamela ('beautiful' in Arabic) has as its Hebrew equivalent Yaffa; the woman might be known as Djamela-Yaffa. Finally, in Israel today, the general trend is towards short Hebrew names like Shir or Tal, which are easily pronounced in any language, and do not have strong religious or literary connotations.

In contrast to the simple ceremony associated with the birth of a daughter, male children are circumcised on the eighth day after birth in accordance with the instruction to Abraham in Genesis 17:9-14 (see also Leviticus 12:3). Circumcision is a sign of the covenant made between God and Abraham and his descendants, hence the Hebrew name, *berit milah* or 'covenant of circumcision'. It does *not* signify entry into membership of the Jewish people or Judaism. In *halakhah* all children, whether male or female, are Jewish if born of a Jewish mother.

There is no rule regarding the place in which the circumcision is carried out. In some communities the synagogue is the usual venue. In Bevis Marks synagogue in London, for example, it is possible to see the chair in which the Victorian Prime Minister Benjamin Disraeli was circumcised (he was later baptized a Christian – and hence able to enter English political life – after his father quarreled with the synagogue). In Israel many hospitals have a room set aside for the circumcision ritual. But often the *brit*, as it is popularly known, takes place at home. An adult chosen by the parents acts as a *sandek* or patron and holds the baby during the operation, which is performed by a *mohel*, a professional circumciser (often also a qualified doctor or perhaps a ritual slaughterer). Both these roles may be fulfilled by a woman, but in Ashkenazi communities in particular they are usually male, and female participation is discouraged as immodest. Most Ashkenazi boys will however have a godfather and a godmother, who bring the child into the circumcision room. The final absent-presence in the room is the prophet Elijah, who is regarded as being present at every circumcision. A chair is set aside for him in the room, so that he may 'observe' the procedure – the removal of the foreskin accompanied by blessings, followed by the naming of the child, and a celebratory meal.

A further ceremony observed by traditional couples whose first child is a son is redemption of the first-born. Thirty days after the birth, the father symbolically buys back his son from a *kohen* (a male Jew who is believed to trace his ancestry back to Aaron and the priests or *kohanim* who ministered in the biblical Temple). This ceremony recalls a practice in Numbers 18:15-16 whereby in ancient times fathers could redeem their first-born sons, who were otherwise expected to take on the duties of Temple service.

Circumcision is not uncontroversial within the Jewish world. Early reformers like Samuel Holdheim and Abraham Geiger suggested that the Covenant of Abraham was spiritual, and that circumcision was unnecessary: in Geiger's words, 'a barbaric, gory rite which fills the infant's father with fear and subjects the new mother to harmful emotional strain.'[24] Such views are still found today, but most Progressive Jews continue to have their sons circumcised. Other objections amongst non-Orthodox Jews stem from the lack of an equally elaborate celebration of the arrival of a daughter, and the exclusion of women from the traditional *brit*. Since circumcision is a mark of entry into the Abrahamic covenant, the lack of an equivalent practice for girls can be taken to imply that males are normative Jews, and that females are somehow marginal in relation to the covenant. Some efforts have been made to overcome this perceived inequality with new ceremonies reflecting the understanding that women are fully a part of the people of Israel. These include a foot-washing ceremony, the 'Covenant of Washing' devised by Reform and Reconstructionist woman rabbis. However, it has proved difficult to construct a ritual which possesses the symbolic power of circumcision. To date, none of the innovations proposed has achieved widespread popularity.

Religious Majority

After circumcision, *bar mitzvah* is probably the most well-known Jewish rite of passage. Strictly speaking, it is not a rite but a status entered by a Jewish boy at the age of thirteen — if he does not mark the event, the boy is still *bar mitzvah*, a 'son of the commandment'. However, in popular terms, boys 'have' their *bar mitzvah*, meaning they participate in a ceremony which celebrates their new status, and from an anthropological perspective does in fact 'construct' it.

A community newspaper like the British *Jewish Chronicle* will typically carry several *bar mitzvah* announcements, some of them accompanied by photographs which show the *bar mitzvah* boy wearing special clothes that signify his new status – a *kippah* or skull-cap, and a *tallit* or prayer-shawl. The expressions on these photographs are diverse. Some are characterised by *gravitas*: a boy who is *bar mitzvah* has reached the age of religious majority or adulthood, and is regarded as now being responsible for his own observance of the *mitzvot* to a greater extent than previously. Others are joyous. *Bar mitzvah* can give some young boys a feeling of accomplishment; and it is marked for many by a party and presents. Finally, some boys look distinctively apprehensive. For many, *bar mitzvah* is something of a 'trial by ordeal'. It can take around a year of tuition for the boy to learn what is required for him to complete the synagogue ceremony, and he may also be expected to make a speech at any subsequent festivities.

As was mentioned above, *bar mitzvah* means 'son of the commandment' and its celebration constitutes a kind of religious coming-of-age ceremony. After it has been negotiated, the boy will be expected to keep the *mitzvot*. For example, he is expected to wear *tefillin* for weekday morning prayers. These are leather boxes containing Biblical passages on parchment (Exodus 13:1-10 and 11-16; Deuteronomy 6:4-9 and 11:13-21) and bound to the left arm and head with straps. He may also count towards a *minyan*, the quorum of adult males which Orthodoxy requires for communal prayer. As an *entrée* to full membership of the religious community, the day of a boy's *bar mitzvah* fittingly requires considerable preparation. The minimum expected of the boy is that he will be called up for an *aliyah*, to make a blessing over a section of the *sidra* or weekly *Torah* reading. However, many Orthodox families and congregations will also expect him to read part of the *Torah*, and some boys will tackle the *haftarah* (a reading from the Prophetic books) and a sermon or discourse on a point of *halakhah*, too. Although many children of religiously active parents will attend a *cheder* or weekend religion school for a few years, extra Hebrew studies are normally required, as are preparatory rehearsals of some kind.

At twelve, a Jewish girl becomes *bat mitzvah* or 'daughter of the commandment'. Whilst boys mark their attainment of religious majority with *Torah*-reading, and the 'laying' of *tefillin*, there has traditionally been little public ritual to mark the girl's new status, although even conservative authorities like Rabbi Ovadiah Yossef (former Sephardi chief rabbi of Israel, and present spiritual leader of the Shas party) advocate teaching her privately of her obligations.[25] This in part reflects the fact that, in Orthodox Judaism, women have played a lesser role in public religious expression. Women are not counted towards a *minyan*, and whilst there is no halakhic bar on their making an *aliyah*, *minhag* has excluded them from doing so. Similarly, women's *exemption* from positive ('do this') time-bound ('at this time') commandments has often been taken to imply their necessary *exclusion* from many forms of observance. Non-Orthodox Jews reject the belief that different gender roles assumed by halakhic sources are divinely ordained, and (with the exception of most Conservative congregations) permit the full participation of women in synagogue services and other rituals. Accordingly, some public celebration of *bat mitzvah* has also become the norm in many synagogues. In Reform Judaism, the *bat mitzvah* parallels the boys' service closely. At the same time, some Orthodox congregations (but not *Charedi* ones) have initiated maturity ceremonies for girls, but these do not include any activity that could be interpreted as leading worship. It is more usual for the celebrations to take the form of an annual service during which girls who have turned twelve during the previous year present readings of their choice in Hebrew or the vernacular. A girl who participates in this ceremony is known as *bat chayil*, 'daughter of worth', a name which recalls the 'woman of worth' (the JPS *Tanakh* translates the Hebrew as 'a capable wife') in Proverbs 31:10, traditionally recited to their wives by men on their return home from synagogue on Sabbath eve. In this way, Orthodoxy has sought to combat the attractiveness of Reform for some, and to provide a meaningful option for others who feel committed to tradition but also wish for a greater public valuing of their female religious lives.

Ostensibly, *bar* and *bat mitzvah* are individual rites, but like other rituals they also serve the collective needs of the community on several levels. Family and friends come together for preparation, service and secular festivities. All this serves to affirm group ties and social solidarity with the wider Jewish community. For small congregations particularly, there are also practical ways in which an individual boy's or girl's attainment of religious majority strengthens the synagogue. It increases the number of those who may count towards the *minyan* and can lead services. It may also give an economic boost to a community, in the shape of dues for membership or preparatory classes, or for the hire of a hall for the party afterwards.[26]

Cultural historians like Philippe Ariès have shown that childhood is not a fixed state but a social construct. In some cultures it extends well beyond puberty, or physical maturity. (For instance, in Britain today, the boundary between childhood and adulthood is normally thought to be crossed at around sixteen or eighteen years.) In others, quite young 'children' are regarded as 'adult' insofar as they are expected to dress and behave like their elders. Thus the rituals marking the boundaries between childhood and adulthood are also subject to change. Whilst *bar* and *bat mitzvah* are the ritual expressions of religious majority in Judaism today, this has not always been the case. Other rituals that have arisen to mark the assumption of religious responsibilities include the medieval school initiation ceremony, and Confirmation.

In his book *Rituals of Childhood*, Ivan Marcus recounts the elaborate rituals which marked a young boy's initiation into *Torah* studies in medieval Germany and France. Wrapped in a *tallit*, he would be carried to the teacher's house, where he would be shown a tablet with Hebrew characters on it. The teacher would read these, with the child repeating after him. The teacher then smeared honey over the letters on the tablet, and the child was expected to lick it off, and to consume various foods on which Hebrew words had been written. Further rituals completed the day: incantations to ward off forgetfulness, and a visit to a riverbank where the child would be told that his study of *Torah*, like the river, would never end.[27]

The existence of this school initiation ceremony indicates how some Jews in the past had different ideas from those widely held today about what constituted the major events of Jewish childhood. For these medieval Ashkenazim, the small boy's entry into Jewish education meant that he moved decisively from the informal-domestic to the formal-public context. But this notion and the associated rituals were gradually discontinued in the later Middle Ages. Its displacement in the fifteenth century by the *bar mitzvah* reflected changing ideas in Europe generally about the nature of childhood and the religious life. Amongst western Christians, a new emphasis was placed on the importance of consent and understanding on the part of those who participated in religious life. Child oblation to monasteries (the giving of children by their parents to the monastic life) was discouraged, with some orders demanding an age of reasoned consent, around twelve for girls and fourteen for boys. In short, religious adulthood was delayed, and more time created for childhood. This same process of new boundary formation took place in Judaism. Prior to the thirteenth century, young boys were permitted to wear *tefillin*, read *Torah* in synagogue, and participate in fasts. This usually began as soon as they could understand what was involved. But in a parallel to the deferral of oblation and other practices in Christianity, religious majority in Judaism was also postponed until thirteen, and boys who had not yet attained *bar mitzvah* were no longer encouraged or permitted to assume adult responsibilities. In both religious traditions, the changes reflect a view that maturity and reasoned consent are required for meaningful participation in religious duties, which Marcus associates with a medieval shift from 'acts' to 'reason'.[28]

Whilst medieval Ashkenazim believed that young boys entered the world of adult responsibility at an earlier age than that envisaged by the *Talmud*, the contemporary trend is to extend childhood beyond the twelve or thirteen years envisaged by classical rabbinic sources. This cultural development, coupled with other concerns about Judaism's survival in the post-emancipation environment, led to the creation of a Confirmation ceremony practised today in Reform, Conservative and Reconstructionist congregations. Many early reformers realised that whilst *bar/bat mitzvah* traditionally marks the beginning of one's full participation in Judaism, for many young people it is functionally the end-point of their religious education, and heralds a period of estrangement and non-attendance at synagogue. Beginning in Kassel, Germany, in 1810, there were attempts to counter this by replacing the *bar mitzvah* with a Confirmation ceremony at a later age (fifteen or sixteen). Christian practice certainly influenced the reformers, particularly their attempts to produce standard catechetical texts for use in instruction. Today, Confirmation is more likely to occur as a supplement to an earlier *bar* or *bat mitzvah*. Like *bat chayil*, it is a group experience. In addition to advanced Hebrew studies, emphasis may be placed on social action projects (visiting a nursing home; tutoring younger children) and group recreational activities. The aim is to raise levels of Jewish literacy and to give teenagers experiences of substance, which will make them more likely to lead adult lives characterised by commitment to Judaism.

Marriage

The traditional Jewish ideal is for men and women to marry early. The *Torah* emphasises that 'it is not good for man to be alone' and the story in Genesis 2:18-24 is held to imply that the uniting in marriage of a man and woman returns them to the state of completeness intended at Creation. For all observant Jews, marriage is a necessary vehicle for the fulfilment of the *mitzvot*. This is true not just with regard to procreation, the primary purpose of marriage (Genesis 1:28) but also because a loving couple will support each other practically and emotionally as they seek to raise 'a faithful house in Israel'. Marriage is, therefore, a sacred relationship. The Hebrew word for marriage, *kiddushin* (sanctification) expresses its special nature. In the *Kabbalah* this idea is taken even further. Marriage assumes a cosmic dimension, as the union between husband and wife mirrors the union of the *sefirot* of *tiferet* (the male principle, 'beauty') and *malkhut* (the female principle of 'sovereignty').

In the *shtetl* in times past (and today in *Charedi* communities) the sexes did not mix freely. Most marriages were arranged by a relative or professional matchmaker (*shadkhan*) and some couples did not meet before their wedding day. Nowadays a few meetings are usual before the couple decides in principle to marry, and a written or verbal agreement is made. For the majority of non-*Charedi* Jews, finding a suitable partner is a matter of personal responsibility, although some introduction agencies specialise in Jewish singles, and many synagogues organise events for the unattached, at which one may hope to meet a future spouse. Orthodox authorities advise against casual, 'just for fun' dating:

> Using as a paradigm the union effected between God and the Israelite community on Mount Sinai via the Torah, it is worthwhile to keep in mind that the first set of commandments, given amidst great pomp and fanfare, did not endure [Genesis 32]. The second set, transmitted in a more sober setting [Genesis 34], have remained with us to the present....Rather than falling in love and then marrying, it is probably better to marry and then rise in love....The end goal being an enduring, meaningful union, it is folly to let temporary infatuation obscure what is of ultimate significance. [29]

The marriage ceremony takes place under a *chuppah* or canopy, symbolic of the future marital home. This may be erected in any one of a number of locations. Most modern ceremonies take place in the synagogue, but hotels are also common venues, and some Ashkenazim hold their weddings out of doors. Like most rites of passage, the marriage ceremony is subject to variation, from one family to another as well as from region to region. Much variety stems from *minhag*, local custom which is sometimes (like the changing childhood rituals in medieval Europe) the product of acculturation. For example, in Oriental communities the bride's family may organise a henna party resembling those held by their Muslim neighbours. But the essentials described below would feature in most religious weddings.

Whilst marriage is sacred, in Jewish law it is also a contractual agreement, sealed by a marriage document known as a *ketubbah*. In ancient times in Jewish as in many other cultures, at marriage a woman passed from her father's authority to that of her husband. (The *Mishnah* speaks of a man 'acquiring' a wife, *m. kiddushin* 1:1.) So the *ketubbah* traditionally sets out the obligations that the husband will agree to take on in relation to his wife during the marriage, and his liabilities afterwards, should it end in divorce. These include the obligation to provide her with food and clothing, and sexual satisfaction. Before the couple stands under the *chupah* and the marriage ceremony begins, the *ketubbah* is signed by bride, groom and witnesses. Progressive communities have not abandoned the *ketubbah*, but modify its text to reflect their wish that marriage be a more egalitarian relationship between two equally responsible and active partners. The *ketubbah* is a fundamental element of the Jewish marriage (strictly speaking, a couple are not married without it) and is often a work of art, treasured for aesthetic as well as emotional reasons.

The couple is traditionally escorted to the *chupah* by their parents, who will stand next to them during the wedding. The ceremony that follows is a composite of two ancient rites – the betrothal and the wedding proper. (In some Oriental communities the bride was until modern times allowed a year between betrothal and marriage in order to prepare for the wedding day and assemble a trousseau, or dowry.) Firstly, the official (who is frequently a rabbi, but need not be) recites blessings over wine and for the betrothal. The couple drink the wine and the groom places a ring on the bride's right forefinger, saying, 'Behold you are sanctified to me with this ring, according to the Law of Moses and of Israel.' In progressive communities, the bride will make a similar declaration and place a ring on the groom's hand. After the ceremony, the ring (or rings) is frequently transferred to the finger usual in the country where the couple lives. The *ketubbah* is then read in Aramaic and the vernacular.

The reading of the *ketubbah* concludes the first stage of the ceremony. The second stage consists of a further seven blessings. Strikingly, the theme of these blessings (with the exception of the final one) is not love, but creation. God is praised as Creator of all things, of man, of man and woman, and of the Peace of the Garden of Eden. This emphasis highlights the interpretation of marriage as a naturally ordained state, and also suggests that by entering marriage the couple themselves are furthering the divine plan for creation.

After the blessings, bride and groom again sip wine. A glass is wrapped in paper or cloth and the bridegroom smashes it by stamping on it. The origins of this custom are unclear, but it is popularly interpreted as reminding those assembled of the destruction of the Jerusalem Temple.

Other mystical interpretations regard the glass as representing the couple. Just as the glass once shattered enters a new state from which it will never emerge, so it is hoped that the couple's married status will be permanent.

It is customary after the service for the couple to be left in a room alone for a period, known as *yichud*. In the past, this was the moment at which the marriage was consummated, but more commonly today it is a time to relax, to break the fast which most Orthodox couples have observed since the eve of the wedding, and generally recuperate before the festive meal and party.

Despite the high estimation of family life, and the idealised account of marriage in some Jewish texts, in the past the experience of traditional Jewish marriage was certainly a difficult one for many women. Until comparatively recently, repeated pregnancy and childbirth were dangerous experiences which shortened life expectancy. (Contraception and abortion are both generally forbidden by the *halakhah*.) Traditional folk-songs attest to the fatalism and apprehension with which some young women approached their wedding day:

> You will cry enough, sleep more tonight
> Tomorrow you are going
> Say good-bye to your sister-in-law
> And your three brothers
> And much as you cry, it won't help you
> You are going
> Why are you running to the mountains?
> The bridegroom's parents are taking you
> Don't hide yourself in the mountains, it won't help you....[30]

Interestingly, this song also attests to a significant community of sympathy between young women. The bride-to-be's relationship with her sister-in-law features prominently in the text as one which will be sadly missed.

Judaism regards as blessed the man who remains married to the bride of his youth. It also says that 'he that sends his wife away is hated' (*Gittin* 90b). But unlike Christianity and Hinduism, Judaism has always permitted divorce. The Biblical laws of divorce are not detailed (Deuteronomy 24:1-4) but later tradition evolved the *get*, the bill of divorce given by a man to his wife in order to release her from the marriage and permit her to marry another man should she wish to. Since this system allowed men to divorce their wives but not vice versa, halakhists added further conditions to minimise abuses. The *get* must be delivered and received freely, and clauses guaranteeing financial support to the divorced wife were inserted into the *ketubbah*, as mentioned above.

Despite these alterations, Jewish women who wish to live carefully observant lives remain vulnerable if their marriages breakdown. For example, in Britain, as in many other countries, an Orthodox Jewish woman can initiate and gain a civil divorce. But if she wishes to re-marry in the Orthodox synagogue, she must receive a *get* from her husband. Where this is not forthcoming (in cases of malice or desertion) the woman is an *agunah*, a 'chained wife' who is, halakhically speaking, anchored to her first husband and may not contract another marriage.

Several factors have combined to place the plight of *agunot* near the top of the contemporary Jewish agenda. Firstly, Israeli law confers responsibility for matters of personal status (marriage, divorce, conversion and so on) upon religious communities. There is no civil marriage; a woman must obtain a *get* in order to be regarded in any sense as divorced. Secondly, whilst *agunot* outside Israel may decide to place personal happiness above obedience to the *halakhah* and re-marry outside the synagogue, offspring from a second marriage will be regarded by Orthodoxy as *mamzerim*, illegitimate children. This status is passed on to subsequent generations, and has a number of practical implications as (for example) a *mamzer* cannot choose his or her own spouse freely, but must marry only another *mamzer*. Similar restrictions do not apply to the recalcitrant husband, however. Whilst polygyny was effectively banned amongst Ashkenazi Jews in the medieval period, it has remained halakhically permissible for Sephardi and Oriental Jews, and a *halakhic* carry-over from the days of plural wives means that a man may have legitimate children with a second woman without obtaining a divorce. Thirdly, the number of *agunot* is popularly thought to be increasing. Civil divorce is rising amongst Jews, and a growing proportion of Jewish men no longer regards it as a priority to fulfil their halakhic obligations towards their wives. Finally, awareness of the issues has been raised successfully by a number of Jewish women's groups, which lobby for remedies in particular cases and in more general terms.

Within Orthodoxy, efforts have been made to overcome this iniquitous position, whilst not undermining the status of the law. In Israel, the rabbinic courts in charge of personal status matters may arrange for the jailing of a husband who refuses his wife a *get*, but this does not always lead to a swift resolution. In 1993, *The Guardian* newspaper reported on an unusual but not unique case involving an Israeli couple of Yemeni origin:

> For the past thirty years, Yiha Avraham has been three words away from freedom. Ever since the 80-year-old Israeli was imprisoned in 1963, he has refused to say, "I am willing" – words which would free him, both from prison and from his 52-year marriage....
> Last week seven rabbis and religious judges made the latest attempt to persuade Mr. Avraham to do the decent thing.... But [he]... flatly turned down all inducements, including a place in an expensive old people's home.[31]

In the *Diaspora* the religious court or *bet din* may ask the civil authorities to help them effect the dissolution of a marriage – an unusual example of the halakhic system's need to co-operate with the extra-halakhic in order to counter an injustice which threatens to undermine the status and authority of Jewish law. In New York (since 1980), Canada (1990), and South Africa (1996), secular legislation has been enacted which allows a court to withhold a civil divorce where one party presents a barrier to the (religious) remarriage of the other spouse. The Canadian Divorce Act also allows a judge to penalise the recalcitrant spouse by awarding higher alimony and child support payments until the *get* has been delivered. In England and Wales, the Chief Rabbi initially proposed to address the *agunah* problem through the introduction of pre-nuptial agreements, but this met with difficulties, as English law does not at present recognise any contract that implicitly denies the concept of marriage as a life-long union.[32] Finally, in Spring 2002, Labour MP Andrew Dismore successfully introduced a bill empowering courts to delay civil divorce in the absence of a *get*. Having received Royal Assent, the Divorce (Religious Marriages) Act became law in July 2002.

Despite these efforts, there is to date no satisfactory resolution to problems faced by chained wives. In particular, whilst the new secular legislation may help prevent the creation of future *agunot*, it cannot help those women who already find themselves chained to vindictive husbands. Moreover, many of the *Diaspora* solutions are predicated on the assumption that the husband will at some point wish to re-marry, and so needs a civil divorce. But this is not necessarily the case. The various *get* laws are also of uncertain halakhic status. Whilst most were introduced with the support of Jewish women's rights groups and Orthodox rabbis, some authorities have come to the view that any *get* delivered under these terms is coerced, and therefore invalid. Significantly, the legal remedies proposed also offer little to women whose husbands are missing, including those whose husbands are thought to be – but cannot be proven to be – dead. For example, after the terrorist attacks in New York in September 2001, eight Jewish men were missing. As Jewish law cannot presume death, their wives became *agunot*. In an act of compassion, Orthodox rabbis ruled that DNA traces or dental remains could be regarded as 'conclusive signs of death', as could definitive evidence of a phone call or email made at the time of the attack on the World Trade Center. But, as the process of clearing the site continued, it remained unclear whether or not the women would be halakhically freed not just to re-marry, but even to mourn their husbands.

When attitudes and practices within the Jewish community as a whole are considered, consensus seems even more distant. Liberal Judaism, a British variation on the Reform theme founded in the early 1900s by Lily Montagu and Claude Montefiore, denies the existence of *agunot*, and accepts civil divorce as sufficient. Some Reform Jews adopt a similar position, but a growing reluctance to follow practices which appear to place the secular above the religious means that many Reform congregations will require a *get* to be issued before they will allow a second marriage within the synagogue. Finally, Reconstructionism argues that just as men and women share responsibilities equally in marriage, so they should share as equals the responsibility for ending that status. Divorce should be a joint inititiative, but a *get* is needed; giving the past 'a vote but not a veto' in this case means preserving the idea of *Jewish* divorce. It is clear that the range of solutions employed today reflects the current diversity of Jewish attitude towards *halakhah* and *minhag*. Whilst particular measures may end the suffering of individual women, the fact that they are predicated on different assumptions suggests that it is unlikely that Judaism will arrive at a universally acceptable solution to the *agunot* question in the near future.

Just as divorce has risen in the Jewish community, so has the number of marriages between Jews and non-Jews. This is not surprising because since emancipation, an increasing number of Jews participate in work and social activities with non-Jews. They also tend to assume non-Jewish values, which place personal freedom and romantic love above reliance on the services of the *shadkhan*.

The *halakhah* does not permit marriage between Jews and non-Jews, and in the minds of many non-Orthodox Jews too, inter-marriage and assimilation or loss of Jewish identity go hand in hand. In Britain, secular legislation (the 1949 Marriage Act) reflects the Orthodox position in restricting synagogue marriage to two persons both professing the Jewish religion. But in recent years, moves have been made within the Reform and Liberal communities to respond constructively to the realities of the situation. A British survey in 1993 found that fifty-three per cent of Jewish men between twenty and thirty-five had married or would consider marrying a non-Jew. In North America and outside the anglophone world, the figures are higher; approximately seventy-five per cent of Jews in Denmark marry non-Jews, and in Germany close to eighty per cent contract such marriages.[33] Unless efforts are made to maintain positive contacts with such Jews, they will be lost to the community.

In Britain, the RSGB and ULPS operate a joint outreach programme which, whilst not promoting inter-marriage, seeks to build up the couple's links with Judaism. Though many rabbis are not prepared to officiate at mixed-faith marriages, the medieval Orthodox practice of 'sitting *shivah*' (mourning) for a child who married a non-Jew, has been abandoned. Children born to Jewish fathers and non-Jewish mothers, are not, halakhically speaking, Jewish. But Liberal Judaism has overcome this by its recognition of patrilineal as well as matrilineal descent, and Reform Judaism permits the children of a Jewish father to attend *cheder* in the hope of fostering a commitment that may lead to future conversion. (Reform Judaism in America follows the British Liberal movement in accepting children from mixed marriages who self-identify as Jewish.[34]) Such measures are not acceptable to Orthodoxy, but it seems likely that present realities, and the demographic pressures exerted by an ageing Jewish population, will lead to the increased introduction of positive, but halakhic, responses to inter-marriage. These may include prolonged Jewish education for teenagers (the past decade has seen a remarkable growth in the number of Jewish day schools in Britain), since extended community involvement seems to increase the likelihood of one's finding a Jewish spouse, and a more proactive and positive approach to intending spouses who wish to convert to Judaism.

In the late twentieth century, progressive Judaisms have also been challenged to respond to gay and lesbian couples seeking to have their relationships recognized in a Jewish religious context. Halakhically speaking, sex between men is forbidden (Leviticus 18:22) and lesbian sex, whilst viewed more leniently in the *Talmud* (*Yevamot* 76a) is also forbidden as an 'Egyptian' practice (Leviticus 18:3). Despite this tradition of condemnation, since the early 1990s Reconstructionist rabbis have officiated at same-gender ceremonies and, in 2000, the Central Conference of American Rabbis (the American Reform rabbinic organization) also resolved that the relationship of a same-gender Jewish couple was worthy of affirmation through appropriate religious ritual. These moves are typically justified on the grounds that justice and civil rights are longstanding Jewish concerns. Acceptance of lesbian and gay couples is not universal within Reform and Reconstructionism, however. No rabbi is compelled to perform such ceremonies. Similarly, Jewish groups which at present do not approve rabbinical officiation at same-sex marriages are not necessarily homophobic. For example, the British Reform Assembly of rabbis includes openly gay and lesbian members, and whilst a ceremony under a *chupah* may not be acceptable, a special blessing or expansion of the ceremony of fixing a *mezuzah* (symbolizing the establishment of a Jewish home) may be carried out in recognition of the value of the relationship.[35] And in Israel, where Orthodox Judaism exercises authority in matters of personal status law, there is, for example, no legislation outlawing the participation of openly gay men in the armed forces.

Death and Mourning

Judaism cherishes life. Although bodily resurrection in the messianic age is presented as a normative doctrine in the *Mishnah* (*m. Avot* 4:17), Jews focus on the present life, rather than on the hereafter. The rationale for this is offered by many folk tales of pious figures from Jewish history, who weep on their deathbeds – because it is only in the present world that one may perform the *mitzvot*, and know the joy which such observance brings. In practical terms, this view of life as blessed means that it is forbidden to hasten the death of a *goses* or dangerously ill person.

Judaism defines death as the absence of a heartbeat and the cessation of respiration, traditionally tested by holding a feather or mirror close to the person's mouth and nose. Some authorities now recognise the concept of brain death. This permits organ donation for transplant surgery but acceptance of this definition is not universal (see chapter six). Immediately that death *has* been verified, arrangements are made for the interment of the body. It is forbidden to delay burial and, ideally, this takes place on the same day as death. The unburied state is seen as shameful, as is any unnecessary mutilation (for example, post-mortem examination) of the body. In many communities the special duties of respectfully washing the corpse and dressing it in a shroud (and *tallit*) are performed by a *chevra kadisha*, a 'holy fellowship' of volunteer men and women. The *Talmud* (*mo'ed katan* 27b) requires that both shroud and coffin be simple, 'out of deference for the poor' and perhaps also so that the bereaved do not abandon their dead for fear of financial ruin. Orthodoxy also requires burial in consecrated ground, and does not permit cremation, or the placing of the body on a shelf in a vault, on the grounds that this may constitute either a mutilation of the body, or a denial of the belief in bodily resurrection. Non-Orthodox Jews, however, may practise cremation because they believe in the immortality of the human spirit or soul, or because they reject, or are broadly speaking indifferent about, belief in any kind of post-mortem existence.

Jewish mourning is highly structured. Before the funeral, Orthodox Jews carry out the traditional rending of garments (*keri'ah*), a practice which recalls the actions of Jacob, Job and David in the Bible (Genesis 37:34, Job 1:20, 2 Samuel 1:11). Nowadays, rending often takes symbolic form, for example the discreet cutting of a tie or lapel. The desired swiftness of burial means that most rituals surrounding death occur after interment. During the period of seven days (*shivah*) after the funeral, family members are required to remain at home. They sit on low stools (or on pillows in some Oriental communities), and refrain from a range of physical and spiritual pleasures including bathing, sexual intercourse, and studying the classical Jewish texts. Because paid work is prohibited, the mourning family is effectively isolated from the everyday world, which inevitably leads to a concentration on the grieving process. There will also be visits from friends and fellow congregants who come to console and pray with the bereaved. Although one is a mourner by obligation for parents, siblings, children and spouse only, it is a *mitzvah* or good deed to comfort mourners – to help them begin to overcome feelings of loneliness and desolation.

After *shiva* is ended, less intense periods of thirty days and twelve months (in the case of one's parents only) begin. To a large extent normal life is resumed, but mourners do not attend most religious celebrations and parties. During the thirty days, they may also refrain from having their hair cut and in the case of men, from shaving. Bereaved sons traditionally say the mourner's *kaddish* in synagogues on weekday mornings for eleven months. At the end of one year, the death anniversary or, in Yiddish, *yahrzeit*, is marked by prayers and the lighting of a candle in the synagogue. This custom, which may be repeated on the *Shabbat* preceeding each anniversary of the death, is based on the Proverb, 'the lifebreath [soul] of man is the lamp of the Lord' (20:27). Like the *shiva* it is more widely observed than the restrictions relating to secondary mourning periods. It is also the custom in many communities for the dedication of a grave-marker or headstone to take place around this time.

Close family and friends of the deceased are clearly the prime beneficiaries of rites surrounding death and burial. The structured nature of Jewish mourning, with its programme for the gradual return of the mourner to normal life, eases the pain of loss and separation. But like *bar mitzvah*, these rituals may serve other latent functions. In a study of a modern Orthodox synagogue in urban Canada, Simcha Fishbane found that mourning rites were a means of re-socialisation for middle-aged men who had previously been estranged from the worship community. Saying *kaddish* regularly for parents provided a route to the maintenance or rebuilding of contacts with synagogue life. And, after the *yahrzeit*, a proportion would be reintegrated as active members of the community. The incorporation of the *kaddish*-sayers into the synagogue also attracted their immedate family, thus augmenting membership further.[36] Like all rites of passage, Jewish mourning rituals meet important communal needs as well as individual ones.

Food Laws

Over the centuries, the marking of life cycle events (and to a lesser extent, of the festival calendar) has increasingly taken place in public, communal space, notably the synagogue. But for most Jews the family home is, both practically and ideologically speaking, a significant site of religious expression. In chapter two it was suggested that after the destruction of the Jerusalem Temple in 70 CE, Judaism became increasingly democratic. In their devotion to *Torah* and *mitzvot*, all Jews could live lives of priestly divine service. In a similar way, in rabbinic thought the home replaces the Temple as a kind of sacred space, the place where one can fulfil God's laws. The sacredness of the domestic sphere is signalled in numerous ways. For example, many Jews will fix a *mezuzah* (an encased piece of parchment containing the words of Deuteronomy 6:4-9 and 11:13-21) to the outer door-post of the house. (Many Orthodox Jews place *mezuzot* on the right hand door-post of every room, except the bathroom.) But perhaps above all, the traditional Jewish home is characterized by the observance of *kashrut*, dietary laws which govern the preparation and consumption of food.

The dietary laws described below ensure that food preparation and consumption is a religious ritual for all observant Jews. However, as Susan Starr Sered has pointed out in her work on elderly Jewish women in Israel, because women have traditionally carried the burden of responsibility for making and cooking food, *kashrut* has been especially significant for their Jewish identity:

> *Kashrut* raises food preparation from a task that every woman in the world unthinkingly does in order to put food on her family's table to a religious ritual par excellence.... While the women of course cook in order to eat, they keep kosher and preserve tradition because this is what God wants them to do.... *kashrut* sacrilizes women's everyday life.[37]

Sered's remarks are based on her work with a group of women attending a Senior Citizens' Day Centre in Jerusalem in the 1980s. Of course, not all women experience Judaism in the way she describes. But her insights help to reinforce the importance of including a consideration of *kashrut* within any attempt to understand Judaism. An over-concentration on texts and public institutions will tend to result in an androcentric account of a tradition. To gain a more complete picture it is necessary (as has been attempted in this chapter) to look also at what Judaism is as a distinctive *culture*, and the patterning of this culture emerges nowhere more clearly than in the domestic sphere, the practices of everyday life.

The roots of the dietary laws are in the *Tanakh*. Leviticus 11 and Deuteronomy 14:3-21 identify certain foods as kosher ('right' or 'fit' to be eaten) and other ones as forbidden. These latter foods are commonly known as *terefah*, 'torn', since Exodus 22:30 specifically prohibits foods that have been 'torn' or attacked and killed by wild beasts. Only animals which have cloven hooves and chew the cud are permitted. These include cattle, sheep, goats and deer (see Deuteronomy 14:4-5). Fish must have scales and fins, whilst shellfish, eels and other sea creatures are all not kosher (Deuteronomy 14:9-10.) Regarding birds, the situation is less clear. The Bible (Deuteronomy 14:11-19) specifies certain species as prohibited, including the eagle, the stork, the heron and the ostrich. But the identity of many birds on the list is uncertain. Consequently, the practice is only to eat those birds known by tradition to be kosher, such as chickens, turkeys, ducks, and geese. Different communities maintain their own practices in this regard. Similar variation exists in relation to insects. The kosher locusts mentioned in Leviticus 11:21-2 are hard to identify, and so many rabbinic authorities, following the injunction to 'make a fence around the Law', forbid all insects. To avoid their accidental consumption, vegetables and fruit need to be washed and inspected before use. However, some observant Oriental Jews (from Yemen and Morocco) will eat those locusts which have a tradition of *kashrut*.

Kosher foods must be prepared appropriately before consumption. In addition to 'torn' meat, the meat of animals that have died from natural causes is forbidden (Deuteronomy 14:21). In rabbinic tradition, this law is understood to imply a requirement for animals to be ritually slaughtered in the manner known as *shechitah*. *Shechitah* involves the swift, horizontal cutting of the food- and wind-pipes of the animal or bird. Like the Islamic method of slaughter, it has been the subject of criticism from some animal welfare societies. Some Jews, especially in the Reform (and Liberal) communities, share these concerns and practise vegetarianism. From an Orthodox standpoint, however, the advocacy of vegetarianism is non-halakhic and goes against the grain of Jewish tradition (meat consumption is permitted in Genesis 9:3). *Shechitah* is also relatively humane, insofar as it renders an animal unconscious almost immediately, before pain can be registered.

Once slaughtered, the animal or bird is inspected to ensure that it is free from defects, and a rinsing and salting process known as 'kashering' or 'making-fit' is carried out to remove the remaining blood (in accordance with Leviticus 7:26-27; 17:10-14). This process lasts several hours, and used to be performed by women in the home. However, just as the negotiation of rites of passage is increasingly managed by religious professionals, so more often than not kashering is performed by the butcher today. The sciatic (thigh vein) nerve is also regarded as prohibited and therefore set aside, as this is the site of Jacob's wound when he wrestled the angel in Genesis 32 (see especially verses 26 and 33). Because the removal of the nerve is a very difficult process the custom in some countries is to discard the entire hindquarter of the animal. Historically, this has been the established practice in Britain, although in recent years a restaurant selling hindquarter meat has been opened in London. Finally, suet and similar edible fats are also *terefah* because of their association with Temple sacrifices (Leviticus 7:1-4; 22-25).

Like the selection and slaughtering of meat, the cooking process is circumscribed by numerous *halakhot*. Rabbinic interpretation extended a Biblical teaching against 'boiling a kid in its mother's milk' (Exodus 23:19; 34:26; Deuteronomy 14:21) to prohibit the cooking or eating together of any meat and any milk (and also the derivation of any benefit from such a mixture – for example, by selling it to a non-Jew). Because of these rules it is usual for Orthodox Jews to have separate sets of cooking utensils, crockery, and cutlery, one for meat (in Yiddish *fleischig*) and one for milk (*milchig*), and also to wait, after having a meat meal, before consuming a dairy one. In Oriental and *Charedi* circles the waiting period may be six hours, but most Ashkenazim are likely to wait for between one and three hours.

Why is the preparation and consumption of food so heavily ritualised in Judaism? The tradition itself is ambivalent. The Bible links *kashrut* with the holiness or separation of the Jewish people:

> I am the LORD your God who has set you apart from other peoples. So you shall set apart the clean beast from the unclean, the unclean bird from the clean. You shall not draw abomination upon yourselves through beast or bird or anything with which the ground is alive, which I have set apart for you to treat as unclean. You shall be holy to Me, for I the LORD am holy, and I have set you apart from other peoples to be Mine (Leviticus 20:24-6).

Some medieval philosophers attempted to find additional rationale for the detailed laws, perhaps out of a desire to encourage *reasoned* observance, or to counter anti-Jewish polemics. Maimonides (*Guide of the Perplexed*, 3.48) argued that the *kosher* diet was a healthy one: it enabled Jews to avoid the consumption of what he felt to be dirty, unwholesome animals like the pig. It also prohibited rich, indigestible dishes combining meat and dairy produce. In contrast, Nachmanides linked holiness with spiritual self-restraint. For him, prohibited animals and birds were predators, whose violent characteristics could be passed on to those who ate them, whilst permitted species were calmer, and promoted human refinement. However, mainstream Judaism regards such explanations of *kashrut* as auxiliary. The *halakhah* commands allegiance because of its divine nature, not because of any justification provided by an extra-halakhic authority.

With the advent of modernity, Jews have adopted a wide range of approaches to *kashrut*. The *Charedim* and Orthodox communities value careful observance of the dietary laws. In the western world some aspects of *kashrut* have become less taxing. Orthodox Jews can buy pre-prepared products that have been certified *kosher* by a *Bet Din* or rabbinic board. These can be readily identified by the presence of a registration mark on the packaging. (Kosher butchers, restaurants and so on are similarly licensed.) Alternatively, where such marks are not available, the wider trend towards detailed ingredients listing on labels and wrappings means that observant Jews can check the product's contents and avoid that which is *terefa*. In contrast, the women in Sered's earlier cited study came from traditional Middle Eastern communities (e.g. Kurdish, Yemeni, Iraqi) and tended to expend considerable effort in preparing their families' food. Highly complex and sometimes physically demanding processes were involved, but the women were proud of knowing what was the right procedure: they never needed to ask a rabbi questions involving *kashrut*.[38]

Conservative Judaism tends towards observance of *kashrut*, as much on account of the laws' function in creating and maintaining a distinctive Jewish identity, as because of their perceived divine nature. For similar reasons, while in the late nineteenth century Hebrew Union College served a *terefah* banquet (including shellfish) to its first rabbinic graduates, and the Pittsburgh Platform described the dietary laws as 'apt rather to obstruct than to further modern spiritual elevation', some Reform Jews today choose to keep some of the food laws (particularly those found directly in the Bible, such as the lists of forbidden and permitted animals).

Non-Orthodox attitudes towards the dietary laws (including here those of the nominal or residual Orthodox described in chapter three) reveal the extent to which, despite the rabbinic theory ('careful observance of all applicable *mitzvot* at all times') ritual practice or performance is not a matter of absolutes – yes or no; kosher or *terefa* – but of *occasional distinctions*, of observances which for many Jews today are subject to ongoing re-negotiation. Some, for example, will keep a kosher kitchen at home but are willing to eat non-kosher foods in restaurants or in non-Jewish homes.

This eases the practicalities of relations with non-Jews. It could also be regarded as signalling the distinctiveness of the Jewish home in relation to the wider non-Jewish world. But observant Orthodoxy is unwilling to sanction what it regards as a weakening violation of *kashrut*.

Also significant, but arguably far removed from traditional *kashrut* observance is the popular consumption of kosher-style foods by contemporary American Jews in particular. In a 1990 article anthropologist Jack Kugelmass describes what he calls 'ethnic theme park restaurants', restaurants in New York's Lower East Side which promise diners food-like-mama-used-to-make but deliver (more satisfying) extravagant portions of non-supervised but stereotypically Jew-*ish* food such as bagels, fried fish and chicken soup. Kugelmass interprets the suburban Jews who visit them as seeking nostalgic – but temporary – connection with an idealized past: 'The chicken fat, the music, and the curios on the wall are Jewish vehicles for an exercise of generalized ethnic nostalgia that is permitted and, indeed, mandated by American culture in our day.'[39] Whilst both the ritual performance (the nature of the food itself, and the context in which it is consumed) and the rationale for the activity (nostalgia or comfort-seeking rather than divine service) undeniably differ sharply from those recognized by traditional Judaism, what is clear is that food continues to play a significant role in the construction of Jewish identity and experience today. The selection, preparation and consumption of Jewish food will no doubt continue to change, as will the range of plausibility structures, justifications or explanations on which it is grounded. However, what does seems certain is that understanding Jewish food will remain an important task within the enterprise of understanding Judaism.

Synagogue and Prayer

Much of this chapter has concentrated on the concept of sacred time expressed in the religious calendar and the life cycle of the individual Jew. Sacred places, or more accurately, sacred *spaces*, are also recognised by Judaism. Israel has been regarded as a Holy Land since ancient times. (This is discussed in more depth in chapter six.) The keeping of *kashrut*, *Shabbat* meals, and the *seder* in the home means that it becomes a sacred space – a place where one can fulfil God's laws. The synagogue is also an important sacred place in Judaism. Because the synagogue's sacredness is not intrinsic – the space is 'made sacred' by the rituals performed within it – what follows will describe not just the typical structure of the synagogue building, but also the key features of Jewish worship.

The origins and early development of the synagogue are the subject of controversy. Tradition traces the institution back to the time of the Babylonian exile that followed the destruction of the first Temple in 586CE. Jews living distant from Jerusalem were unable to offer the sacrifices prescribed in Leviticus and so met to pray, sing Psalms and study. Texts like Ezekiel 11:16 and Psalm 74:8 are thought to allude to their meeting-places which, it is argued, continued to exist alongside the sacrificial cult once the Temple had been restored. However, there is no explicit reference to synagogues at this early period, which casts doubt on the traditional account. What does seem more certain is that the synagogue had become an established institution by the early centuries of the Common Era. The Christian New Testament describes Jesus and his early followers speaking in synagogues in Israel and *Diaspora* (Matthew 4:23; Acts 13:5, 14:1) and the *Mishnah* takes its existence for granted. Whatever the historicity of these accounts, it is clear that their authors expected ancient readers to be familiar with the term. Today, most sizeable Jewish communities have a synagogue building, managed by a council or committee and perhaps employing a professional cantor or *chazan* to lead services.

The word 'synagogue' comes from a Greek word meaning 'assembly' and as this implies, the present day synagogue is a building in which Jews meet for worship and other activities. The range of Hebrew and other names given to the building over the centuries indicates the diversity of functions which it has served. These include *Bet ha-Keneset* (house of meeting), *Bet Ha-Midrash* (house of study), *Shtibl* ('room') and *Shul or Shool* (Yiddish for 'school'). Outside Britain, some Reform communities also use the name 'Temple', signalling a conviction that the synagogue does not merely substitute for the Jerusalem Temple, but has superseded it.

A central feature of any synagogue is the ark (*aron kodesh*) or sanctuary (*heikhal*). This reflects the significance of the *Torah* in Judaism: it is indicative of its status that in 66CE, when a synagogue was attacked in Caesarea, the Jews there did not try to protect the building, but instead carried their *Torah* scroll to safety (Josephus, *Jewish War* 2.285-291). At its simplest, the ark is a cupboard or curtained recess housing the scroll or scrolls of the *Torah* (*sefer torah*). Because it is generally the focal point of the synagogue, the ark is often highly ornate, as are the mantles and silver finials which protect and adorn the scrolls themselves. Portions from the *Torah* are read from these hand-written scrolls on *Shabbat* morning, on festivals, and in some Orthodox synagogues on Mondays and Thursdays as well.

The other common prominent features include the *bimah* – a raised platform or desk from which the *Torah* is read, the *ner tamid* or eternal light which burns above the ark to symbolise the divine presence, and seating for the congregation. In Orthodox synagogues men and women will sit separately. Depending on the nature of the building, women may occupy a ladies' gallery or an area behind a *mechitzah* or partition. In *Charedi* synagogues and in some older buildings (such as the Gothic Old-New synagogue in Prague) women occupy an entirely different room from which they can (with some difficulty) observe what is happening in the main body of the synagogue, through a small window or grill in the wall.

Many synagogues will be decorated in some way. The commandment in Exodus 20:4-5 prohibits the making of representational art for the purposes of worship, but not art *per se*. Much synagogue decoration therefore consists of geometrical design or decorative calligraphy: figurative art is rare and avoids human faces. Highly decorative ritual objects may also be present, for example a *menorah* (seven-branched candlestick) or *chanukiah*. Although rebuilt and renovated several times during the past four centuries, the Rhodes synagogue pictured in chapter one still reflects the influence of Ladino-speaking Jews who fled to the island during the Spanish Inquisition. It is decorated with huge chandeliers, a black and white mosaic tiled floor, and attractive wall paintings of flowers, geometric designs and calligraphy.

It was suggested earlier that there is a relation between the definition of sacred space and the rituals that it houses. This is apparent when the use and structuring of sacred space in Orthodox and Progressive synagogues are compared. In the typical Orthodox synagogue (as in Rhodes), the *bimah* occupies a central position, which reflects the importance the community ascribes to *Torah* reading and study. The location of the *bimah* also means that both those who are called to read the *Torah* and the leader of the service (any suitably skilled adult males) are placed amongst and not distinguished from the congregation. In contrast, many Progressive communities site the *bimah* on a (virtual or actual) stage in front of the congregation, whose seats are arranged auditorium-style, as in a theatre. The leader, who is often the rabbi, faces the congregation, guiding their

Two East End Synagogues

Fieldgate Street Great Synagogue: In the early twentieth century, London's East End was home to a hundred thousand Jews, many of them immigrant families who fled persecution and hardship in Poland, Romania and Russia. Wartime bombing and upward social mobility encouraged dispersal to the suburbs; today only four thousand mostly elderly Jews remain in the district.

The Fieldgate Street Great Synagogue opened in 1899, at the height of Jewish immigration. Whilst not a large building it was 'great' in comparison with the average *shtibl* or prayer-room used by traditional Jews in Eastern Europe.

The photograph shows one boarded window. In autumn 2000, during a period of violence in the Middle East, stones were thrown at the synagogue and racist graffiti painted on the door. Attempts to attack Israel by threatening Jews elsewhere in the world are not infrequent.

Synagogue of the Congregation of Jacob: Many synagogues reflect the architectural idiom of the surrounding culture. This may be due to a desire to make use of current styles, or simply because the building was previously used for other purposes. The Synagogue of the Congregation of Jacob opened in 1921 in a converted chapel.

The synagogue's interior walls show traces of wall paintings. These decorations, and the hand-painted *pinkasim*, community record books, are typical of chasidic congregations in Eastern Europe. Today neither the Congregation of Jacob nor Fieldgate Street are *Charedi*. Both are affiliated to the Federation of Synagogues, a body formed in the 1880s to meet the needs of Eastern European Jews, who were generally more traditional in orientation than the existing, more Anglicized Jewish community in England.

worship. In short, as anthropologist Seth Kunin notes, whilst there is a clear democratization of sacred space in Orthodox synagogues, in many Reform and Liberal ones there is clear differentiation between the space occupied by the congregants and the rabbi:

> These examples suggest that in spite of the democratic principles which are central to Progressive ideologies, general access to sacred space is minimised in comparison to Orthodox synagogues, the only significant exception to this being the position of women.[40]

As this analysis implies, the present-day synagogue functions chiefly as a place of public prayer and worship, although prayers do not have to take place in a synagogue. A *minyan* or quorum of ten may meet in any suitable room for communal worship. Private and spontaneous prayers are also valued. In fact, the majority of prayers mentioned in the Bible are those of individuals who approach God for assistance. Examples include Hezekiah's simple appeal for recovery in 2 Kings 20:1-3 and Hannah's prayer (1 Samuel 1:10-16) which has often been regarded as a model of correct behaviour in approaching God.

In ancient times, worship centred around the Jerusalem Temple, where the priests or *kohanim* made sacrificial offerings each day, accompanied by the psalm-chanting Levites. Following the Temple's fall, fixed prayer times referred to by the early rabbis as *avodah she-ba-lev* or 'service of the heart' were introduced which recalled the rhythm of the Temple day. Morning and afternoon prayers (*shacharit* and *minchah*) corresponded to the twice daily sacrifices. Evening prayer (*maariv*) corresponded with the daily burning of fats and limbs, and additional services on *Shabbat* and festivals imitated those added to the basic rituals at those times. This schedule has persisted to the present day. Both men and women are commanded to pray daily, although with the exception of some Progressive communities, women are not expected to wear the *tallit* or the *tefillin* donned by men for morning prayers.

Key to the order of service is the *Shema*, the most well known of Jewish prayers, which consists of three Biblical passages, Deuteronomy 6:4-9, Deuteronomy 11:13-21 and Numbers 15:37-41. The *Shema* expresses the injunction to meditate on the *mitzvot*, to teach them to one's children, and to keep the laws regarding *tefillin* and the *mezuzah*. Its opening declaration is sometimes described as a Jewish 'creed', since it declares belief in the unity of God, and it is traditionally the last prayer recited by or on behalf of a dying person.

Following this, a central series of *berakhot* or benedictions known as the *amidah* is recited. *Amidah* means 'standing' because the prayer is recited standing, facing Jerusalem. The blessings are:

'Fathers', praising God for choosing and remembering the patriarchs
Acknowledgement of God's power to sustain life and revive the dead
Acknowledgement of God's holiness
Prayer for wisdom and knowledge
Prayer for *teshuvah*, or repentance
Request for pardon from sin
Prayer for release from trouble
Prayer for healing
Prayer for 'blessing of the years' (sustenance)
Prayer for the ingathering of exiles
Prayer for true justice administered by good leaders
Prayer against the *minim* (sectarians)
Prayer for the righteous and pious
Prayer for the rebuilding of Jerusalem
Prayer for the coming of the Messiah, a descendant of David
Prayer for God to accept prayers
Prayer for the return of the divine presence to Zion
Thanksgiving
Prayer for peace for the people of Israel

Such is the status of the *amidah* that it is known in many traditional sources as *ha Tefillah, the* prayer. However, its origins are uncertain, and in particular, the target of the exclusionary *birkhat ha-minim* has attracted considerable debate. Some scholars have suggested that is was introduced to flush out heretics who would be unwilling to recite a benediction calling for their own downfall. Moreover, it has been suggested that the heretics or *minim* referred to were early Jewish Christians. An early version of the prayer recovered from the Cairo Genizah (a depository for worn-out copies of sacred Jewish writings) refers to 'the Nazoraeans who are the *minim* (i.e. heretics of our day)'.[41] However, there is no widespread evidence to support the idea that Jews cursed all Christians during prayers, and sources from the patristic era seem to indicate that, for several centuries,

COMMON GROUND

Christians were welcome in many synagogues (see chapter five).

The *amidah* is modified on *Shabbat* and followed on festive days by *hallel* (Psalms 113-118). Reform and other Progressive prayer books also regularly omit or alter some *berakhot* (for example, to excise references to a personal Messiah), while preserving the basic pattern of the prayer.

Like the *amidah*, public reading of the *Torah* (on *Shabbat*, on Monday and Thursday in Orthodox communities, and on other prescribed festivals, e.g. at *Purim*) has been a hallmark of Jewish worship for centuries. In the first century CE, Josephus claimed that all Jews could repeat the law 'more readily than their own names', because each week men assembled to listen to and study it (*Against Apion*, 2.175-177). This is an apologetic exagger-ation, but the antiquity of public proclamation of the law seems secure. Following a practice outlined in the *Bavli*, the *Torah* (Pentateuch) is divided into fifty-four sections or portions. On each *Shabbat* morning, one portion or *sidra* of the *Torah* is read in Orthodox synagogues. (Many Progressive communities shorten the passage, cutting some genealogical passages, to arrive at a lectionary which approximates the Jerusalem *Talmud* in reading the *Torah* over three years.) The number of men (in Progressive synagogues, women too) called up to read the *Torah*, or to recite the accompanying blessing, if an expert member of the congregation is to do all the reading, varies. On *Shabbat* morning the number in Orthodox synagogues is seven. In the afternoon, and on Monday and Thursday, when the first section of the forthcoming *sidra* is read, the number is three. After reading the *Torah*, a section from the Prophetic books (*haftarah*) is also read, and, particularly in modern and non-Orthodox synagogues, a sermon may be preached.

Following the readings, or on weekdays, after the *amidah*, a series of prayers concludes the service. On weekday evenings when services are short, these consist of the *alenu*, proclaiming the divine and universal kingship of Israel's God, and another prayer which looks forward to the coming of God's kingdom on earth. The service finishes with *kaddish*. Many Jews who are not otherwise especially observant, attend services in order to say *kaddish* for a dead parent. Such a rite cannot be performed at home since, like other liturgical elements which involve public proclamation of God's holiness (e.g. the *amidah*), only it can be recited where a *minyan* is present.

This service structure would be recognised by most religious Jews, although, since Enlightenment and emancipation, liturgical innovations have proliferated. As outlined in chapter three, liturgical changes made for aesthetic reasons were the harbingers of later, more wide-ranging reform. Most of these early modifications involved the removal or shortening of the *piyyutim*, early medieval poems which embellished the main prayers but added significantly to the length of the service and expressed ideas in language that the nineteenth century reformers found superstitious and outdated. There was also a move to translate the liturgy from Hebrew into the vernacular, and to adapt prayers to remove references to doctrines that *modernes* no longer found plausible. These included belief in bodily resurrection, and in the future coming of a Messiah. (Progressive Judaism prefers to speak of the immortality of the human spirit, and the goal of the Messianic Age, an age of justice and the triumph of God's will, for which all Jews must work.) Whilst there has been a return to Hebrew in recent years, innovations continue. In particular, there are new liturgies for the *chavurot* which are so central to Reconstructionism, and to commemorate new feast days, such as Holocaust Memorial Day, Israel Independence Day, and Jerusalem Reunification Day. The synagogue and worship will continue to be of central importance for Judaism – and because of that, change too will be unending.

Notes

[1] Ahad Ha-Am, 'one of the people', was the pen-name of Asher Ginsberg (1856-1927).

[2] *Shabbat* 25b, *Shulchan Arukh*, Orach Haim 263:3, *Mishnah Berurah* 263:12. The *Mishnah Berurah* of Israel Meir Ha-Kohen (1838-1933) is a commentary on the *Shulchan Arukh*.

[3] L. Jacobs, 'Electricity', in *The Jewish Religion; A Companion*, Oxford: Oxford University Press, 1995, p. 143.

[4] *Service of the Heart: Weekday Sabbath and Festival Services and Prayer for Home and Synagogue*, Union of Liberal and Progressive Synagogues, 1967, pp. 61-62.

[5] S. C. Heilman, *Synagogue Life: a Study in Symbolic Interaction*, New Brunswick: Transaction Publishers, 1998, pp. 31, 51-52.

[6] Alpert and Staub, *Exploring Judaism*, p. 86.

[7] A. Agus, 'This Month is For You: Observing Rosh Chodesh as a Woman's Holiday', in E. Koltun (ed.), *The Jewish Woman: New Perspectives*, New York: Schocken, 1976, pp. 84-93.

[8] Dobrinsky, *A Treasury of Sefardic Laws and Customs*, p. 260.

[9] A. J. Koltach (ed.), *The Concise Family Seder*, New York: Jonathan David, 1987, p. 16.

[10] Discussed in Eisen, *Rethinking Modern Judaism*, pp. 249-250.

[11] Ibid., p. 247.

[12] Koltach, *Seder*, p. 8.

[13] S. Gaon (ed.), *Book of Prayer of the Spanish and Portuguese Jews' Congregation, London*, Vol. Two: New Year Service, Oxford: Oxford University Press, 1971, p. 106.

[14] P. Goodman (ed.), *The Yom Kippur Anthology*, Philadelphia: Jewish Publication Society, 1971, pp. 54-55.

[15] S. Pepys, *Pepys Diary*, Vol. One, Folio Society, 1996, p. 313.

[16] M. Hilton, *The Christian Effect on Jewish Life*, SCM Press, 1994, p. 52.

[17] Eisen, *Rethinking Modern Judaism*, p. 116.

[18] Kaplan, *Judaism as a Civilisation*, pp. 448-451.

[19] Esther 4:16 describes a fast undertaken by Esther before she

petitioned the king. In the medieval period it became common to fast on the day before *Purim*.

[20] Hilton, *Christian Effect*, pp. 24-9; B. Morris, *Anthropological Studies of Religion: An Introductory Text*, Cambridge: Cambridge University Press, 1987, pp. 248-252.

[21] A. van Gennep, M. B. Vizedom and G. L. Caffee (trans.), *The Rites of Passage*, Chicago: University of Chicago Press, 1969, p. 20.

[22] R. M. Geffen (ed.), *Celebration and Renewal: Rites of Passage in Judaism*, Philadelphia: Jewish Publication Society, 1993.

[23] L. Davidman and J. Stocks, 'Varieties of Fundamentalist experience: Lubavitch Hasidic and Fundamentalist Christian Approaches to Contemporary Family Life', in J. S. Belcove-Shalin (ed.), *New World Hasidim: Ethnographic Studies of Hasidic Jews in America*, New York: State University of New York Press, 1995, p. 120.

[24] M. Wiener (ed.); E. J. Schlochauer (trans.), *Abraham Geiger and Liberal Judaism: The Challenge of the Nineteenth Century*, Cincinnati: Hebrew Union College Press, 1981, p. 113.

[25] Dobrinsky, *A Treasury of Sephardic Laws and Customs*, p. 33.

[26] S. Fishbane, 'Contemporary *Bar Mitzvah* Rituals in Modern Orthodoxy', in J. N. Lightstone and F. B. Bird (eds), *Ritual and Ethnic Identity: A Comparative Study of the Social Meaning of Liturgical Ritual In Synagogues*, Waterloo, Ont.: Wilfred Laurier University Press, 1995, p. 166.

[27] I. G. Marcus, *Rituals of Childhood: Jewish Acculturation in Medieval Europe*, New Haven: Yale University Press, 1996, p. 1.

[28] Ibid., pp. 117-127.

[29] R. P. Bulka, *Jewish Marriage: A Halakhic Ethic*, New York: Ktav, 1986, pp. 6-7.

[30] D. Shai, 'Family Conflict and Cooperation in Folksongs of Kurdish Jews', in S. Deshen and W. Zenner (eds), *Jewish Societies in the Middle East*, Washington: University Press of America, 1982, p. 279. J. R. Cohen reports that some women formed societies to sing for weddings, 'Women's Roles in Judeo-Spanish Sephardic Song', in S. Silberstein Swartz and M. Wolfe (eds), *From Memory to Transformation: Jewish Women's Voices*, Toronto: Second Story Press, 1998, p. 54.

[31] D. Brown, 'Refusal to say a Short Sentence Lands Israeli Husband a Long One', *The Guardian*, 22 February 1993, p. 1.

[32] H. Jacobus, 'Getting Together', *Jewish Chronicle*, 11 August 2000, p. 22.

[33] J. A. Romain, *Till Faith Do Us Part: Couples Who Fall in Love Across the Religious Divide*, Fount, 1996, pp. 12-14.

[34] J. A. Romain, *Faith and Practice: A Guide to Reform Judaism Today*, RSGB, 1991, pp. 167-170.

[35] Ibid., pp. 229-230.

[36] S. Fishbane, 'Jewish Mourning Rites: A Process of Resocialisation', in Lightstone and Bird (eds), *Ritual and Ethnic Identity*, pp. 169-184.

[37] Susan Starr Sered, *Women as Ritual Experts: The Religious Life of Elderly Jewish Women in Jerusalem*, New York: Oxford University Press, 1992, pp. 88-89.

[38] Sered, *Women as Ritual Experts*, p. 89.

[39] Eisen, *Rethinking Modern Judaism*, p. 261 and J. Kugelmass, 'Green Bagels: An Essay on Food, Nostalgia and the Carnivalesque', *YIVO Annual* (1990), 57-80.

[40] S. Kunin, *God's Place in the World: Sacred Space and Sacred Place in Judaism*, Cassell, 1998, p. 105.

[41] R. Kimelman, 'Birkhat ha-minim and the Lack of Evidence for an Anti-Christian Jewish Prayer In Late Antiquity', in E. P. Sanders (ed.), *Jewish and Christian Self-Definition. Vol. 2. Aspects of Judaism in the Graeco-Roman Period*, SCM Press, 1981, pp. 226-244.

5

Jewish/Non-Jewish Relations

No religion is an island (A.J. Heschel)

Early Encounters

As discussed in chapter one, Judaism is in no small way the product of encounter and dialogue with the non-Jewish world. Jews have always existed amidst and alongside other ethnic and religious communities, and this has inevitably impacted on their theologies, ritual practices and other forms of cultural expression. This chapter will outline some of the contours of the history of Jewish/non-Jewish relations, looking not just at the events themselves but also at their consequences and significance for Jewish and non-Jewish (or Gentile) perceptions of themselves and each other.

Since the origins of Israel and Jewish self-understanding lie in the *Tanakh*, it is there that this study must begin. Crucial to the Biblical account of Israel's formation is a series of covenants or contracts between God and humanity. The first of these is made with the family of Noah, a man whom God allowed to survive a great flood sent to destroy the corrupt world. God promises Noah that the world will never again be ravaged by a flood; the rainbow symbolises this promise. In exchange, Noah is subject to certain injunctions which the *Talmud* later clarified as the requirement to refrain from blasphemy, idolatry, sexual immorality, murder, theft, and the eating of live flesh, and to establish courts of justice (*Sanhedrin* 56a; *Avodah Zarah* 2b). Interestingly, this covenant (*berit*) is made not just with Noah and his descendants (who themselves, according to Genesis 10, represent some seventy different nations) but also 'with every living thing that is with you – birds, cattle, and every wild beast as well – all that have come out of the ark' (Genesis 9:10). All sentient creatures are subject to the dominion and protection of God.

As Genesis continues, non-Jews are not excluded from the account, but the view emerges that the people Israel (the name comes from that given to Jacob in Genesis 35) serves a special function in the divine plan for the world. In Genesis 12:3 and 18:18 Abraham and his descendants are portrayed as participants in a second covenant through which humanity as a whole will benefit. Finally, Exodus 19:4-6 develops this idea further, qualifying the nature of Israel's special mission. This third covenant – one not with the whole world, nor with a single family, but with the whole people Israel – enjoins them to observe commandments in exchange for their adoption as the treasured possession of God:

> You have seen what I did to the Egyptians, how I bore you on eagles' wings and brought you to Me. Now then, if you will obey Me faithfully and keep My covenant, you shall be My treasured possession among all the peoples. Indeed all the earth is Mine, but you shall be to Me a kingdom of priests and a holy nation.

The differences in these covenants are indicative of the ambiguities in the Biblical text concerning the relation of Jews and non-Jews or Gentiles (like this English word, the Hebrew *goyim* has its origins in a word meaning, 'peoples' or 'nations'). For the early Biblical writers and their audiences, the challenge was to reconcile the realities of a universe in which peoples who worshipped other deities and spirits often seemed to prosper, with belief in the God of Israel, who created and governed the whole world. In some texts pagan deities are dismissed as inferior or as non-entities: 'All the gods of the peoples are mere idols,' says 1 Chronicles 16:26. Elsewhere, there are warnings of what will happen to Israel should the people turn to other cults. Hosea 3:1 likens Israel's lack of faith to the behaviour of an adulterous woman; Deuteronomy 28:36 links deities of wood and stone to exile and dispossession. Perhaps the most famous narrative account of the clash between Israel's God and those of other nations is in 1 Kings 18, where Elijah confronts the prophets of Baal. Yet, at the same time, the Biblical model of a powerful (if not omnipotent) God means that the persistence of other religions demands explanation, or integration into this world-view. Deuteronomy 4:19 suggests that Israel's God permits the nations to worship other deities, whilst Isaiah 2:3 looks forward to an age in which all peoples will come to recognise God. Finally, Malachi 1:11, a text which is admittedly difficult to interpret, may even suggest that in sincerely performing their sacrifices, pagans are unknowingly worshipping God. *If* it does so, then the text represents a bold attempt to make some kind of theological space for other cults and religions within the world-view of Biblical Judaism. However, the verse is capable of other (perhaps more compelling) readings. Its reference to the honouring of God's name 'among the nations' could speak of the faithfulness of *Diaspora* Jewry, or simply of God's universal power, as is the case in some Psalms:

> Praise the LORD, all you nations
> Extol Him, all you peoples!
> For great is His steadfast love towards us;
> the faithfulness of the LORD endures forever.
> Hallelujah (Psalm 117)

The writing and redaction of the Biblical text took place during times when Israel (people and land) was subject to the authority of a succession of different Middle Eastern powers (Assyrians, Babylonians and Persians). Hosea is generally dated to the eighth century BCE, the time of the first Assyrian invasions of Israel; the major part of Deuteronomy more likely belongs to the late seventh century BCE, a period in which Assyrian power waned and the Babylonians were ascendant. In contrast, Malachi was compiled during Persian rule. Beginning with Cyrus the Great, whom Isaiah 44:28 describes as God's shepherd, due to his decision to allow Judaeans exiled by the previous Babylonian regime to return home, the Persians allowed considerable freedom to local forms of cultural and religious expression, as a means of promoting loyalty within the empire and fostering cohesion. Previously destroyed shrines like the Temple in Jerusalem could be rebuilt (the Second Temple was completed in 515 BCE).[1] Such an environment could explain the relative optimism of the later text.

In the fourth century, the Persians were succeeded by the Macedonian king Alexander III (sometimes styled 'the Great'). Alexander's reign was brief (336-323 BCE) but the consequences for Judaism of his conquest of the Middle East were immense. He and his successors (the Ptolemies in Egypt and the Seleucids in Syria-Babylonia) founded such cities as Alexandria and Antioch, and established administrative and other structures that planted pockets of Hellenistic culture across the region. Greeks were encouraged to immigrate to the new territories and the Greek language was the medium in which much important business was contracted. Jews (and their non-Jewish neighbours) began to use Greek, not just in dealings with others, but also when formulating and articulating their own identities. Inevitably, this led to deeper exchange between Jewish and Greek ideas and concepts. When the *Torah* was translated into Greek in the mid-third century BCE, the result was a work which, whilst close to the Hebrew text, inevitably also embraced Greek concepts. This book, known as the *Septuagint* (often abbreviated to LXX[2]) was later rejected by the rabbis. Nevertheless, their work also betrays the influence of Greek concepts and legends, and their Hebrew includes a number of Greek 'loan words'. The rabbis understood *Torah* as a living organism, and thought that dialectical discussion of it could bring the learned closer to the divine world. In much the same way, some Greek philosophers spoke of the *logos*, the 'word' or pervading principle that ordered the universe.[3]

The interaction between Hellenism and Judaism was not uniform in nature and scholarly opinions are divided on the issue of how the textual, epigraphical, and other archaeological evidence from the period should be interpreted. A general consensus holds that chronologically, the first communities to be in some sense Hellenized were in the Diaspora, particularly Egypt (where the *Septuagint* was produced). In Judaea where the Jewish population was more dense and the land perhaps less attractive to Greek settlers, the process was slower and less significant. Yet there are dangers in drawing such simplistic distinctions in the account of Hellenism's influence. Contemporary debates about Jewish identity inevitably impact on the writing of history. Portrayals that contrast a strong, resistant Judaea with a weak, apostasising Egyptian Jewry may in part be reflections of present day conceptions of Israel and *Diaspora* as centre and periphery in Jewish life. In Judaea, too, there were those who consciously wished to embrace the philosophy of the new power, or who absorbed it in subtle ways. Drawing on evidence relating to Greek administration, trade, and education as it impacted upon the region, Martin Hengel has argued that from as early as 'the middle of the third century BCE *all Judaism* must really be designated *"Hellenistic Judaism"* in the strict sense' – essentially, that one cannot separate Palestinian or Israeli Judaism from its Hellenistic,

Diaspora counterparts. Whilst this view has received considerable criticism – Hengel does not find a great deal of evidence to support his views about the pervasive use of Greek at such an early date – there was a strong Hellenizing party in Jerusalem by the second century BCE, as 1 and 2 Maccabees attest.[4] These extra-canonical books describe how Ptolemaic suppression of Judaism, coupled with the corruption of the Hellenizing party who controlled the High Priesthood in Jerusalem, led Judas Maccabeus to launch a successful revolt re-establishing a degree of Judaean independence in 164 BCE. (Celebration of the Maccabees' re-dedication of the desecrated Temple is the origin of *Chanukah*, discussed in chapter four.) Yet whilst Maccabean success seemed to represent a victory for the re-assertion of Jewish culture, Judas' descendants, the Hasmoneans, quickly adopted many of the trappings of the Hellenistic dynasties, including the use of Greek mercenaries.

Intermittent military conflict with the Seleucids, and continued disagreement about the appropriate relation between Jewish culture and Hellenism, helped to create the conditions for inter-Jewish conflict. The final years of the Hasmonean dynasty were marred by civil war. When Queen Salome Alexandra died in 67 BCE, a struggle for the throne broke out between her sons, Aristobulus II and Hyrcanus II. The dispute provided the Roman general Pompey with a pretext for the invasion of Judaea and in 63 BCE Jerusalem was conquered, reducing the briefly independent nation to a client state.

The reign of the Herodians and then direct Roman rule by a procurator (instituted by Augustus in 6 CE) did not represent the end of Hellenism but accelerated and concentrated its impact upon the Jews of *eretz Israel*. Predictably, then, it was also during the Roman era that the most famous and ultimately most devasting (pre-Christian) violent conflict occurred between an occupying force and her Jewish subjects.

Until relatively recently the Roman Empire was commonly portrayed in much western popular culture as a largely peaceful, tolerant age. (Ridley Scott's epic film, *Gladiator*, has done much to dispel such images.) School textbooks teaching Classical civilisation or the Latin language presented images of toga-wearing citizens who populated a world consisting largely of gracious villas, luxurious bath-houses, and orderly, prosperous market-places. There were many reasons for this emphasis. As late as the mid-twentieth century, history in general focused on elite characters and concerns – the rise to power and career of leaders and prominent others, and the domestic and foreign policies they pursued. Social history and 'history from below' – the history of those groups including women, the poor, and others traditionally marginalised within society - have only come to the fore since the early 1960s. Political expediency also contributed to the benign account of earlier Empires. European cultures used it to justify their own 'civilizing' conquest of the peoples of Africa and Asia.

Such a positive interpretation of Roman life and thought finds some support in the words of the Romans themselves. A first century BCE inscription from Halicarnassus, Asia Minor, celebrates Augustus (the first Emperor) as the originator of an era in which,

> Land and sea have peace, the cities flourish under a good legal system, in harmony and with an abundance of food, there is an abundance of all good things, people are filled with happy hopes for the future and with delight at the present.[5]

However, this epigraphical evidence is a distortion of the experience of the vast majority of Rome's subjects and citizens. In the book *Pax Romana and the Peace of Jesus Christ*, Klaus Wengst stressed that the peace of the Roman age was secured by violence in the form of military conquest by the legions and harsh justice meted out by Roman officials like the procurator of Judaea, Pontius Pilate (26–36 CE) who executed Jesus of Nazareth. Those who lived in conquered lands were subject to physical and economic oppression, required to pay taxes, tolls and tribute to support the conquerors' war machine. Wengst perhaps presses his case too far in suggesting that the experience of the masses during this period differed from that under other regimes. The ancient world was marked by deep social and economic division. A small minority enjoyed considerable wealth whilst the labouring masses (the free and enslaved poor) who constituted around ninety-five per cent of the population enjoyed a precarious existence, living at (or below) subsistence level.[6] However, he is correct in highlighting the strictures that the imperial cult imposed on the religious expression of the empire's subjects.

From the time of Julius Caesar (100-44 BCE), cultic honours were paid both to and on behalf of the emperor, although the imperial cult was instituted formally in Rome only after Augustus' death. The cult was the only form of pagan belief and practice in the Roman Empire to be (more or less) systematically organised across provinces. Some classical scholars have deemed its impact sufficient to merit the assessment that 'Rome's main export to the empire was the cult of the emperors'.[7] Its practice included sacrifices presented by a special priesthood and offered to dead emperors whose statues were housed in temples like those of other deities. At the same time, offerings were also made to other deities on behalf of the emperor, reflecting a belief that the ruler enjoyed a kind of special relationship with them – that he was *divine* if not truly a *deity*. The *Res Gestae*, admittedly not a neutral source, refers to 'continued sacrifices for my [Augustus'] health at all the couches of the gods'; Pliny the Younger speaks of similar worship offered for the welfare of Trajan (98-117 CE); this identification of divinity and imperial power was also reflected in imperial iconography or image-making and the language of the poets. In Horace's *Odes* a parallelism of function is established between Jupiter [Jove] and Augustus:

> We believe that Jove is king in heaven because we hear his thunders peal; Augustus shall be deemed God on earth for adding to our empire the Britons and the dread Parthians (3:5:1-4).

In Europe today, the notion that a ruler like the Roman emperor be regarded as somehow possessed of divinity may appear strange. However, the ancient world was familiar with cults that celebrated kings or other figures of power. For Greek and Roman polytheists alike, omnipotence was not expected of divinity – a human of exceptional power might plausibly be a deity too. Rome's subjects who (like those Jews who maintained that worship was due only to the God of Israel) did not participate in the imperial cult ran the risk of being labelled as anti-social and separatist. Whilst according to Roman writer Suetonius, Julius Caesar granted Jews certain rights to observe *mitzvot* and meet for worship (Suetonius, *Iul.* 42.3), freedom to observe Judaism was at best uncertain, at worst precarious, and on occasion denied. In 139 BCE Jews had been temporarily expelled from Rome for the offence of introducing their rites to Romans (Modestinus, *Digest*, 48.8.11). In another of his *Lives of the Twelve Caesars*, Suetonius also describes restrictions under Tiberius (46-48 CE):

> [Tiberius] abolished foreign cults, especially the Egyptian and the Jewish rites, compelling all who were addicted to such *superstitions* to burn their

religious vestments and all their paraphernalia. Those of the Jews who were of a military age he assigned to the provinces of less healthy climate, ostensibly to serve in the army; the others of the same race or of similar beliefs he banished from the city, on pain of slavery for life if they did not obey (*Tiberius* 36)

It is important to note that in this passage Suetonius mentions both Egyptian and Jewish rites – the Romans were not exclusively or uniquely concerned with Jewish religious practice. Moreover, included among those expelled from the city are people holding 'similar beliefs,' most likely proselytes to Judaism. Finally, Suetonius' emphasis on *superstition* is a common theme in pagan assessment of Judaism. In particular, observance of circumcision, of dietary laws, and of sacred time in the form of *Shabbat*, was seen as puzzling by the classical writers.

Probably the most extensive Roman account of Jewish history and religion is that of the late first century CE historian Tacitus. His *Histories* provides a synthesis of negative assessments of Judaism in the ancient world. For example, in a counter-reading of the Exodus story, he describes the Jews as having been driven out of Egypt because they were a source of disease – an anti-Jewish tradition with long roots stretching back to Egyptian writers like Apion and Manetho, whom Josephus (introduced in chapter three) criticised in his two-volume *Against Apion*. Tacitus writes:

> Most authors agree that once during a plague in Egypt....King Bocchoris approached the oracle of Amman and asked for a remedy, whereupon he was told to purge his kingdom and to transport this race [the Hebrews] into other lands, since it was hateful to the gods. (*Hist.* V. 3:1-4)

Like Suetonius, Tacitus is also representative of elite Roman perspectives (he held several public offices) on Jews when he describes them as impious and insular:

> The Jews regard all as profane that we hold sacred; on the other hand, they permit all that we abhor (*Hist.* V. 4:1)

> The Jews are extremely loyal toward one another, and always ready to show compassion, but toward every other people they feel only hate and enmity. They sit apart at meals and they sleep apart.... (*Hist.* V. 5:5)

But how did Jews view their non-Jewish rulers and neighbours? For some, the prefect's rule brought welcome respite from internal strife and the threat of Greek attacks. 'Pray for the welfare of the empire, because but for the fear of it we would swallow one another alive', says *m.Avot* 3.2, whilst Philo described the early years of emperor Gaius' reign (37-41 CE) in glowing terms:

> Indeed, the life under Saturn, pictured by the poets, no longer appeared to be a fabled story, so great was the prosperity and well being, the freedom from grief and fear, the joy which pervaded households and people, night and day (*Embassy to Gaius* 13).

At the same time, for other Jews the hardships of Roman rule prompted discontent. (Philo himself led an unsuccessful embassy to Gaius to re-assert Jewish rights following organised persecutions in Alexandria.) For some, belief in a forthcoming messiah, an 'anointed one' who would restore the House of David and gather scattered Jewry to the land of Israel, inspired militant anti-Roman action. From 6 CE onwards there were sporadic incidents of violence; in 66 CE the militant tendency prevailed and the Jews revolted against Rome.

Just why the Jews warred against Rome remains an open question. The motives of the revolutionaries were not uniform. Despite his anti-Jewish sentiments, there is probably a degree of truth in the words of Tacitus, who in describing the siege of Jerusalem in 70 CE, spoke of the Jews there possessing 'three generals, three armies' (*Hist.* V. 12-3). There were in fact several wars being conducted during this period: Jewish civil war (prompted by dissatisfaction with hypocrisy and corruption amongst the Judaean elites), Jewish-Roman conflict, and further conflicts between Jewish and non-Jewish subjects of the empire. For Josephus, the cessation of Temple sacrifices on behalf of the Roman state and the *princeps* (*Jewish War* 2.409) precipitated the conflagration, but he also mentions other contributory incidents. For example, in Caesaraea in 66 CE hostilities surrounding the construction of Greek-owned workshops on a site adjacent to the city's synagogue erupted into violence (*Jewish War* 2.284-91).

During the early part of the revolt the Jews met with some successes. *Sicarii* insurgents infiltrated Jerusalem in Autumn 66 CE, managing to kill representatives of the Jerusalem priesthood and the Roman garrison based in the city. When Cestius was sent to pacify them, the rebels were able to mobilise a large number of fighters from among the festival pilgrims and to resist the Roman advance. Eventually, Cestius broke off his attempted siege and retreated to Caesaraea, during which time (Josephus tells us) he was harried by other Jews. However, news of Cestius' defeat prompted Nero to appoint Vespasian (accompanied by his son Titus) to quell the revolt. From this point Jewish defeat was only a matter of time. With areas of sparse and mixed population quickly retaken, Jerusalem was isolated and surrounded by the imperial forces. Moreover, Jewish infighting continued. As late as Spring 70 CE John of Gischala and his group of Zealots managed to steal their way into the inner court of the Temple during *Pesach* and attack a rival faction led by Eleazar ben Simon. All this happened despite the fact that the siege of Jerusalem by Titus was already under way.

Josephus offers a long description of the siege of Jerusalem. His account is problematic, given his status as a favourite of Emperor Vespasian, but in its essentials is probably reliable. Certainly, the picture painted of the violence and famine experienced by troops and civilians alike is plausible. According to Josephus and to Roman historians, Titus did not want to destroy the Temple and attempted to negotiate a surrender. Arguably, these accounts are idealised and Titus wished to smash a building that served as an ideological impetus to resistance. Whether entirely by intention or not, the Temple complex was burned in August 70 CE, the city as a whole being taken a month later.

Although a few fortresses elsewhere remained in Jewish hands as late as 74 CE (notably Masada, which has assumed iconic status in contemporary Israeli culture), the fall of Jerusalem effectively signalled the end of the Jewish revolt against Rome. Jewish leaders and the *menorah*, the seven-branched candlestick from the Temple, were taken to Rome for a victory procession. The Arch of Titus, which recorded their sufferings in the Roman Forum, survives to this day.

With the destruction of Jerusalem and the Temple, Judaism had lost its ideological centre. The shattering nature of the defeat led to increasing pessimism on the part of Jewish writers, a trend only exacerbated in the aftermath of the unsuccessful revolt led by failed messiah Simon bar Kokhba in 132-135CE. In the early rabbinic literature, the image of Rome is predominantly negative, and Roman rule referred to in hostile terms. Continued subjection to Rome was never interpreted, however, as an indication of a failure on the part of Judaism's God. Like the prophetic writers mentioned at the beginning of this chapter, Rome's Jewish subjects also assimilated their non-Jewish opponents into the traditional Jewish world-view. In this extract from *Genesis Rabbah* 63:9, Rome is likened to Esau, the type of the Gentile, as opposed to Jacob (Israel), the archetypal Jew:

> A prefect once asked a member of the family of Sallu:
> 'Who will enjoy sovereignty after us?'
> He took the pen and paper and wrote:
> And after that his brother emerged, his hand clasping Esau's heel; and his name was called Jacob.
> Of this it was said:
> 'See how ancient words become new in the mouth of a Sage!'[8]

Jews and Christianity

Christianity grew out of Judaism and was in its early years essentially one of the parties within it. Some of Jesus' own teachings were close to those of the Pharisees. Like them he was willing within certain boundaries to modify *Torah* legislation for the sake of individual well being. And both stressed a new sense of intimacy between God and every human, expressed in the unusual but not unique reference to God as 'Father'.[9] After Jesus' death, Peter and other early Christians continued to participate in the Temple cult at Jerusalem (Acts 3:46). In later years, Christian liturgy reflected these origins, giving prominent place to the Psalms. Theological writings similarly deployed images and categories already found in the Hebrew Bible, which despite – or perhaps because of – Marcion was regarded by the early church as forming part of the canon of holy scripture.[10] However, as Christianity broadened to embrace non-Jewish members its relationship with Judaism was problematised. Was Christianity a new way of being a Jew, or was it something else? If something else, was Judaism still a valid means of achieving meaningful relationship with God? Within Christian theological discourse these questions are particularly associated with Paul, a Jew who played a prominent role in the Jesus movement's energetic mission to the Gentiles around 36–60 CE. Paul's writings are preserved in the New Testament (Romans, Corinthians I and II, Galatians, Philippians, Thessalonians I and Philemon.)[11] They suggest that he soon recognised that the inclusion of non-Judaizing Gentiles within the church (Acts 15:5 notes the contrary position held by some members of the Jerusalem community) had implications for the church's relation to Israel. Most famously, Paul's letter to the early Christian community in Rome presents his attempts to wrestle with the issues. On the one hand, Paul considers Israel's priority and position in the divine plan. 'What advantage has the Jew? Of what is the value of circumcision?' he asks, continuing, 'Much in every way. To begin with, the Jews are entrusted with oracles of God...' (Romans 3:1-2). Elsewhere, he writes:

> They are Israelites, and to them belong the sonship, the glory, the covenants, the giving of the law, the worship, and the promises; to them belong the patriarchs, and of their race, according to the flesh, is the Christ, who is God over all, blessed for ever. (Romans 9:4-5)

> I myself am an Israelite, a descendant of Abraham, a member of the tribe of Benjamin. God has not rejected his people whom he foreknew. (Romans 11:1-2)

In chapter 11, non-Jewish or gentile Christians are reminded that they are 'branches' grafted into the essential, supportive Jewish root (11:17-24) and towards the end of the epistle, Paul describes a collection made amongst the gentile churches to raise money for poor Jewish Christians in Jerusalem, arguing that such activity is justified because 'the gentiles have come to share in their [Jews'] spiritual blessings' (Romans 15:27).

At the same time, Paul's letter also attempts to make sense of the continued rejection of Jesus' teaching and the early church's mission by the majority of Jews. Despite the denial in 11:2 that God has rejected the Jewish people, Paul does regard Israel as having 'stumbled'. The passage 9:30–10:21 appropriates Hebrew Bible terminology to describe their failure to comprehend God's message through Jesus. Other texts like 2:28-29 can be interpreted to belittle Jewish *praxis*, whilst 3:20 says 'no human being will be justified in his sight by works of the law, since through the law comes knowledge of sin'.

As 2 Peter 3:16 notes, Paul is not easy to interpret. For some Christian leaders like Martin Luther, passages such as Romans 3 have formed the basis of a Christianity which asserts the necessity of 'justification by faith' alone and has as its correlate a stereotype of Judaism as mechanistic and devoid of spiritual value. More recently, Christian attempts at rapprochement with Judaism have taken their start from the parable of the olive tree in Romans 11.[12] Any attempts to analyse Paul, be they in the service of anti-Judaism or of positive relations between Jews and Christians, face considerable difficulties. Paul was not a systematic theologian. His letters are situation-specific, sometimes rushed and imperfectly thought out, and were not intended to serve as timeless guides for the institutional church that developed long after his death. A reading of Romans which can, however, make some sense of it as a textual whole, is offered by Walters in *Ethnic Issues in Paul's Letters to the Romans*. Walters locates the epistle in the period 55-58 CE. Just a few years earlier (*circa* 49 CE) the emperor Claudius issued an edict expelling Jews from Rome. Those who had to leave included Jewish Christians (see Acts 18:2) with the result that the Christian community in Rome henceforth was Gentile in character and developed independently of the synagogue. When Claudius died in 54 CE Jews and Jewish Christians returned to the city in considerable numbers, but the different ethnic and religious groupings found it difficult to accommodate themselves to the changes that had occurred in the intervening period. The Gentile church had developed a non-Jewish identity and regarded itself as superior to Judaism, having adopted the edict's rhetoric about Jews as troublemakers. Similarly, Jewish self-understanding had also crystallised around notions of ethnic identity and was less able to include Christianity.

In this context, Paul's letter to the Romans can be seen to focus not (as Luther would have it) on the question of 'how one is to be saved' but on the inter-relation of Jews and Gentiles, all of whom participate in and are subject to the divine plan. The criticisms of the hypocrisy and unfaithfulness of some Jews are made by Paul in order to pre-empt and curtail Gentile boasting against Israel. Israel's failure (in the eyes of the early church) can be faced because, like the errors decried by the prophets of the Hebrew Bible, it does not imply that the election and covenant are at an end.[13]

Despite Paul's emphasis on the faithfulness and impartiality of God, the church increasingly came to picture Israel as in error, and derived from this the notion that Jews and Judaism were dispossessed, rejected and even cursed by God. Competition between early Christianity and early Judaism provided the basis for the tragic history of Christian persecution of Jews and Judaism. As Christianity tried to justify its existence and its separate identity, it did so in opposition to Jewish religion. As Rosemary Radford Ruether phrases it in her controversial work *Faith and*

Fratricide:

> For Christianity, anti-Judaism was not merely a defense against attack, but an intrinsic need of Christian self-affirmation....The *adversus Judaeos* literature was ...[created] to affirm the identity of the church, which could only be done by invalidating the identity of the Jews. [14]

After Paul, the fall of the second Temple in CE 70 and the failure of the later Bar Kokhba revolt in 132-135 CE were both taken as proofs that Jews were in error in their refusal to accept Jesus as Messiah. Texts by the Church Fathers show a more decided hostility to Judaism than is found in the New Testament, where criticisms are directed at particular individuals or parties and the controversies (Mark 2:23–3:6, for example) read more like the in-fighting of factions belonging to the same extended family than polemic between different religions. Gregory of Nyssa described Jews as:

> murderers of the Lord, killers of the prophets, enemies and slanderers of God; violators of the law, adversaries of grace, aliens to the faith of their fathers, advocates of the devil, progeny of poison snakes, ...whose minds are held in darkness, filled with the anger of the Pharisees, a sanhedrin of satans.

Also writing the fourth century, Augustine, the most influential of the Church Fathers, constructed Jews as 'Witness People' – a people doomed to lead lives of suffering as a sign for their culpability in the death of Jesus:

> To the end of the seven days of time, the continued preservation of the Jews will be a proof to believing Christians of the subjection merited by those who, in the pride of their kingdom, put the Lord to death....

> The Jews have been scattered throughout all the nations as witnesses to their own sin and our truth. They themselves hold the writings that have prophesied Christ....[15]

A close reading of the Patristic material raises further questions, however. Most of these early texts were written for internal Christian consumption. That the Church Fathers felt a need to remind their fellow-believers of the damned and damnable status of Jews suggests, then, that this position was not shared by all. Did some form of positive relation exist between at least some Jews and Christians? Was this what elicited the Fathers' condemnation?

While those who were competing with the nascent rabbinic movement for power and authority became increasingly visceral in their approach to Judaism and to Jews, this was not the full picture of Jewish-Christian relations in the first centuries of the Common Era. Among the ranks of ordinary Christians, many seem to have experienced no difficulty in combining allegiance to Jesus with a respect for Judaism that sometimes took the form of direct participation in synagogue life.[16] To the Church Fathers, this Judaizing behaviour represented a powerful threat. Although later Christian polemic operated in a context in which Jews were a marginalised minority, in antiquity Judaism was not in retreat. For example, the second century bishop Melito of Sardis has the dubious honour of being credited with having introduced the charge of 'deicide' into Christian rhetoric on Jews:

> Him whom the nations worshipped and whom the uncircumcised admired and the gentiles glorified, for whom even Pilate washed his hands, Him have you slain in the great feast….You have slain your Lord in the midst of Jerusalem. (*Peri Pascha*, lines 672-76).

Though not mitigating the violence of either Melito's language or its mutations in later theology, archaeological evidence poses new questions about the context in which these words, from *Peri Pascha* (an Easter sermon), were first spoken. Well into the Common Era, Sardis was the location of a flourishing Jewish community, as is evidenced by the discovery in 1962 of a large, imposing synagogue located in the city centre. This building formed part of a gymnasium complex and was decorated expensively with marble and mosaics. In contrast, the Christian church was much smaller and in a poorer, less desirable location. Perhaps Melito was not, then, so much a powerful oppressor of Jews as he was a desperate leader attempting to persuade his community that Judaism had been superseded *despite appearances to the contrary?*

It is dangerous, however, to use archaeology to re-construct the context of a textual source such as the *Peri Pascha*. The dating of the Sardis synagogue is not clear; the remains visible today may date from as late as the fourth century, rather than from Melito's day. Nevertheless, such evidence is a reminder of the confidence of some ancient Jewish communities, and as Cohick notes, because most second and third century Christian groups held little power socially, *any* political influence of the Jewish community in Sardis is likely to have been greater than that of Melito's

The Sardis Synagogue: The Sardis synagogue dates from the second to fourth centuries CE. It reflects a large, prosperous, urban Jewish community, and could have accommodated up to a thousand people, although it was probably not purpose-built.

The picture shows a large table, perhaps used as a *bimah* (reading desk). It is supported by eagles, and flanked by lions – a reminder that the Biblical injunction against graven images has been diversely interpreted. These carvings date from an earlier period and were apparently re-used in the synagogue, a common practice in the ancient Near East.

congregation.[17]

Christianity's rise to power as the official religion of the Roman Empire from the fourth century onwards signalled a troubling period for Jews in the 'Christian world'. Christendom made it possible for doctrinal anti-Judaism to become social and economic in its expression. Constantine (called the Great) who first proclaimed Christianity as the official religion of the Empire, issued the following law (*Concerning Jews, Heaven-Worshippers and Samaritans*) in 315 CE:

> We wish to make it known to the Jews and their elders and their patriarchs that if...any one of them dares to attack...another who has fled their dangerous sect and attached himself to the worship of God [Christianity], he must speedily be given to the flames and burnt together with all his accomplices.
>
> Moreover, if any one of the population should join their abominable sect and attend their meetings, he will bear with them the deserved penalties.

Although generally speaking Judaism was not outlawed, Jews were subject to degradation, restriction and frequently, violence. The view that Jews should persist as a 'sign' of the folly of those who reject God's plans for human salvation helped justify the abuses. *Adversus Judaeos* literature in late antiquity and the early Middle Ages perpetuated the early Patristic emphasis on finding Biblical proofs of the Jews' folly. It also continued to adopt a *presentist* approach to Jews, believing that individuals living a millennium or more after the time of Jesus were somehow just as guilty of Jesus' death as were the parties described as petitioning Pilate in Matthew 27. The great creativity in medieval Judaism – the writing of the Talmuds and great commentaries – was largely ignored. Augustine's earlier judgement that Jews 'have remained stationary in useless antiquity' could plausibly be attributed to some ninth and tenth century Christian writers (*Tractatus Adversus Judaeos*, PL.42: 51-67).

Although early medieval Christian attitudes towards Jews and Judaism were in continuity with those of the Church Fathers, the 1090s are generally held to be a turning point in Jewish-Christian relations. Shortly after the year 1000, a new emphasis on sacred place emerged within medieval Christianity. Muslim presence in Israel and (particularly) Jerusalem was considered an affront to Christendom. Eventually in 1095 Pope Urban II preached the first Crusade, a campaign to send Christian armies to re-take the 'Holy Land', rebuild sites associated with the life of Jesus, and assure the safe passage of pilgrims. While Muslims were Urban's primary concern, Jews living in Christian lands represented an easier target for some of the armies as they made their way to Jerusalem. Despite the attempts of some bishops and nobles to protect Jews living under their jurisdiction, there were bloody massacres and forced conversions, particularly in the Rhineland region. In the short term, the killing of perhaps five thousand people had a significant impact on the region's Jewish community.[18] In the longer term, it signalled the beginning of an era that would culminate in the expulsion of Jews from many Western European countries. England has the dubious distinction of being the first country to expel its Jewish subjects in 1290. But France (1380), Spain (1492) and Portugal (1497) all followed suit, as did major continental cities like Prague (1542) and Vienna (1670). The result was that many Jews moved eastwards, particularly to modern day Poland and Russia, or, in the case of significant numbers of Sephardim, to Greece and Turkey. For almost five hundred years, eastern Europe (dominated religiously by Catholicism and the Orthodox family of churches) would be the centre of Jewish life and scholarship – until that, too, would be destroyed by violence.

The inability of church and nobles to control the outpouring of popular anti-Jewish sentiments during the first Crusades was symptomatic of a general shift towards a widespread and fervent anti-Judaism within much of European society. This antipathy found expression in the mythology and popular culture of medieval Christendom. In 1144 a young boy of twelve was murdered in Norwich at Easter, and rumours circulated that the local Jewish community had committed the crime, seizing him and enacting a facsimile crucifixion in order to mock Christ's Passion. The story was recounted by a monk, Thomas of Monmouth, in 'The Life and Passion of the Martyr St. William of Norwich'. Thomas argued that such a murder was committed annually by Jews in a town selected by the drawing of lots, and that, as such constant enemies of Christianity, Jews ought to be destroyed. Within a century the ritual murder charge, thought to be supported by the cry of guilt in Matthew 27:25, had spread throughout England and to continental cities, especially in German-speaking parts of Europe. Wherever the accusation emerged, it had practical consequences for the local Jewish population. Lincoln's Jewish leaders were massacred, and others imprisoned in the Tower of London, following their alleged murder of 'Little St. Hugh', whom according to legend they had previously fattened on bread and milk. The 'blood libel' as it is often known, fixed Jews in many Christian minds as at once both super- and sub-human. Described as capable of organising internationally to plan and commit the murder, Jews were also thought to *require* Christian blood in order to ensure their survival. In the *Prioress's Tale*, Geoffrey Chaucer stepped aside from his usually derisory style to recount the murder of a child by Jews, alluding to the story of Hugh and thereby placing an image of demonic, murderous Jews at the heart of English literary and cultural tradition:

> The serpent Satan, our first enemy,
> ...has his wasps' nest in the hearts of Jews.[19]

The late medieval cycle of massacre, expulsion, and re-admission, also fed the legend of the Wandering Jew. In essence the story describes a Jewish cobbler who refused Jesus rest against the wall of his house along the road to the crucifixion. Because of his meanness, the cobbler was cursed to wander eternally until Jesus' Second Coming. First published in Germany in 1602, it had previously circulated orally and eventually fed into antisemitic concepts that the Nazis employed in their propaganda.

Although the massacres and blood libels were popular in origin, anti-Jewish attacks were not confined to the poorer sections of society. In 1215 the Fourth Lateran Council issued a series of edicts against Jews. The ideological motivation behind the measures is clearly illustrated by this extract from the first paragraph of Title Sixty-Eight:

> Whereas in some provinces of the Church a difference in clothing distinguishes Jews and Saracens, in certain other lands such disorder has developed that no differences are discernible. Thus it sometimes happens that Christians mistakenly have intercourse with Jewish or Saracen women, and Jews or Saracens with Christian women. Therefore, lest these people...seek to excuse the sin of intercourse, we decree that these people of both sexes, in all Christian provinces and at all times, shall be readily distinguishable from everyone else by their type of clothing.[20]

This represents a clear example of the role that the *social construction of difference* played in medieval relations between Jews and Christians. The Church sought to ensure the visible presence within, and therefore the more effective marginalisation of, the non-Christian Other in its midst. Like the penalties attached to dhimmitude (see later) in the Muslim world, the Council's decisions were not implemented uniformly. Where they were enforced, the wearing of a distinctive badge was generally required. In thirteenth and fourteenth century France, this took the form of a yellow circle of cloth, whilst in England stripes of fabric were sown across the chest, sometimes in the shape of Tablets of Law. In the German Empire, legislation of 1270 required male Jews to wear a distinctive cap, which can be seen in many medieval and early modern pictures.

In the thirteenth century the *Talmud* also became a target of Christian polemic. For Christians, the *Talmud* was a heretical departure from the Bible. Some Jews attempted to argue that the text was in fact a kind of commentary or *midrash* on the Hebrew Bible, and as such was similar in character to the New Testament, but they did not meet with success. In 1239 Pope Gregory IX ordered that copies of the *Talmud* be handed over to Christian clergy, pending clarification of the accusation made by Nicholas Donin of La Rochelle (a Jewish convert to Christianity) that it contained blasphemies against Jesus. Following the resulting disputation-trial, Louis IX ordered that all copies of the *Talmud* be confiscated and burned. Twenty-four cartloads of books were lost, jeopardising *Talmud* study and the rabbinic academy in Paris. This tragic event, recalled in the traditional Ashkenazi liturgy for the 9th *Av* (see chapter four) was repeated across Europe. Notable burnings took place in Italy under the instructions of the Inquisition, and later in Poland in 1757, following a disputation with the Frankists, a Christianising offshoot of the Shabbataean movement.[21]

How did Judaism survive in this environment? How does one maintain a distinctive religious culture when one lives as a minority in a generally hostile world? Medieval Jewish life and thought was structured primarily by *halakhah*. The Vatican required Jews to assume particular forms of dress and occupation in order to maintain Jewish visibility and distinctiveness and thereby preserve the integrity of Christian society. At the same time, *responsa* and codes were (in a sense) Jewish means to promote loyalty, co-operation, and therefore survival amidst difficult conditions. Within the strictures of the framework enforced by the wider state, the Jewish community was largely self-regulating. In particular the *Cherem* (ban of excommunication) and other sanctions discouraged nonconformity in the form of deviance from halakhic norms or other anti-social behaviour.

Medieval Jews were not always passive victims. They tried to defend themselves not simply by acting to strengthen the Jewish community but also on occasion by fighting Christian crusaders and through polemical or apologetic literature.[22] Some of the written responses to Christianity were very sophisticated. For example, Rashi carefully refuted christological interpretations of Biblical prophecies, especially of Isaiah, a book so beloved of Christian writers and artists that it has sometimes been called the fifth gospel. Others were far more crude. The invocation to God to 'Pour out Your fury on the nations that do not know You' (from Psalm 79:6) was inserted into the *haggadah* at this time. The medieval Jewish world also had its own legends and folk tales deriding Jesus and the Christian religion. Most famous amongst these was the *Toledot Yeshu*, a grouping of folk tales about Jesus and his followers, compiled around the tenth century. (Other texts include the *Nizzachon*, a guide to strategies for countering Christians in, for example, public disputations.) In these accounts of Jesus' life, he is said to have been the illegitimate son of Mary, fathered by a Roman centurion Panthera (a story found also in the work of second century pagan writer Celsus) or perhaps to have been the result of Mary's rape by a neighbour. In an inversion of Christian values, Peter and Paul are commended for having taken a misguided belief-set out from the realm of the Jewish world and into Gentile society. In short, *Toledot Yeshu* is an acerbic attack directed at Christian belief. It is perhaps unsurprising that, long after its popularity amongst Jews waned, it was reprinted and used by Christian antisemites. Despite their claims, however, it was never the official, rabbinic assessment of Christianity.

Co-existent with the conflicts, there were positive contacts between Jews and Christians, and not all Jews were without resources or power. Like the polemics of the Church Fathers, the Lateran Council's legislation to prevent social contacts between Jews and Christians implies that these were taking place. Jewish thinkers like Maimonides influenced Christian theologians of the stature of Thomas Aquinas. Not insignificant minorities of European Jews also enjoyed positions of considerable economic and political influence, as Court Jews (employed by nobles to raise taxes, provision armies, or oversee the growth of new industries) or bankers during periods when Church law prohibited Christians from lending money at interest. Particularly on the frontiers of Christian Europe, such as in early medieval Hungary, Sicily and Spain, Christian-Jewish interaction took place within a larger framework of heterogeneity, and Jews tended to suffer fewer restrictions than in the west. The popes struggled to enforce canon law separating Christians from non-Christians (including Jews). For example, in the thirteenth century, papal legates repeatedly failed to persuade the Hungarian kings to enforce the Lateran Council's ruling on distinguishing clothing, and to exclude Jews from public office.[23] However, particularly in the late medieval period, the position of even the wealthy few was precarious and unpredictable. In the twelfth century, York was the home of one of England's most prosperous Jewish communities. Yet in 1190, in the wake of the Third Crusade, the city's Clifford's Tower was the site of a siege at the end of which one hundred and fifty Jews died – many at their own hands as an alternative to forced conversion. And in relatively tolerant Hungary, 1290 saw anti-Jewish violence predicated on accusations of Jewish host-desecration in Pozsony (a town with a sizeable German community).[24]

In Western and Central Europe, as late as the twentieth century, mainstream Christianity continued to hold that Jews were responsible for Jesus' death and that their religion was not a valid means of relation with God. This was true in the Roman Catholic Church and also in Protestant churches. Moreover, both Catholicism and Protestantism generally agreed that there should be some convergence of civil and religious power and authority. As Christianity moved from the medieval era to that of the Reformation, Jewish experience in much of Europe was not, then, greatly improved.

In *That Christ Was Born a Jew* (1523), Martin Luther originally tried to persuade Jews that the Hebrew Bible pointed to Christ. He regarded anti-Jewish hostility and violence as a hindrance to the winning of converts, writing, 'If the apostles, who also were Jews, had dealt with us Gentiles as we Gentiles deal with the Jews, there would never have been a Christian among the Gentiles'. However when his missionary project was not realised, Luther's attitude changed. In 1543 he wrote *Against the Jews and their Lies*, a lengthy pamphlet which displays the arrogance he had earlier so decried:

> I shall give you my sincere advice:
>
> First, to set fire to their synagogues or schools....This is to be done in honour of our Lord and of Christendom, so that God might see that we are Christians....Second, I advise that their houses also be razed and

destroyed.....Third, I advise that all their prayer books and Talmudic writings, in which such idolatry, lies, cursing and blasphemy are taught, be taken from them.....[25]

In addition to these measures, Luther advocated that rabbis be prohibited from teaching on pain of death, that Jews be forbidden from travelling, that usury be outlawed and that efforts be made generally to rid Christian Europe of 'this insufferable devilish burden'.

John Calvin did not share Luther's position, describing Jews as the children of Abraham and arguing that Judaism and the Hebrew Bible were important components of salvation history. However, he did believe that conversion to Christianity was desirable, since only in Christ was the promise first made to Jews fulfilled.

Not all Catholics and Protestants adopted their leaders' positions, and of course not all leaders were anti-Jewish, although very few were prepared to countenance recognition of Judaism. However, some Christians associated with the Radical Reformation articulated views of Jews and Judaism that came close to doing so. For some Radical Reformers (early Anabaptists), the emphasis was on 'inner Word' as opposed to the externals of religion; there was also to be no coercion in matters of faith. Thomas Müntzer (1489-1525), considered a leader of the first generation of radicals, regarded suffering as a sign of divine election. In this respect, persecuted Christians and Jews shared a common bond. Some of Müntzer's successors, like Hans Denck, rejected the Lutheran law-gospel dichotomy and developed a Christian universalism that regarded 'true believers' of every nation as the Friends of God. However, the sentiments of these Christians were not accepted by other groups or by all members of their own churches. Like many Jews in this period, thousands of early Anabaptists were slaughtered at the hands of Protestant and Catholic authorities.[26] A similar fate met sixteenth century Lithuanian unitarian Jacob Palaeologus, who was executed in Rome in 1585. He argued that Jews, Christians and Muslims formed a kind of 'interfaith Church' and would all be able to accept the Messiah in due course (events to be determined by God, rather than by human endeavor). In the meantime, as people of God they should develop contacts and attitudes of mutual respect, and aid one another in times of crisis.[27]

Müntzer, Denck, and Palaeologus did not represent majority trends within Christianity. Their visions of a society more tolerant of religious difference were not realised, either during or after the Reformation. And, as was discussed in chapter three, while increasingly freed from legal restrictions and the constraints of the ghetto (*judería* in some Spanish towns), post-Enlightenment Jews were still frequently regarded as outsiders or as alien to European society. This was true across many areas of life. For example, Abraham Geiger (the pioneer reformer discussed in chapter three) was greatly interested in the comparative study of religions. He even wrote on Jesus, whom he regarded as a Pharisee-type figure, similar to some Galilean wonder-workers mentioned in the early rabbinic texts (both of these ideas have been subsequently developed by twentieth century Jewish scholars, David Flusser and Geza Vermes). But, as a Jew, a career in academic theology was not open to him.[28] If, by the eighteenth-century Christendom was at an end, one of its defining characteristics, anti-Judaism, had endured. Whilst critical of traditional Christianity, many Enlightenment personalities kept alive Christian anti-Judaism by infusing it with contemporary scientific – or pseudo-scientific – notions. In fact it was only in response to the Holocaust or *Shoah* that a major re-configuration in relations between Jews and Christians began to occur. Those events will be considered later in this chapter, but first the discussion will turn to the Jewish-Muslim encounter.

Jewish-Muslim Relations

Like Jews and Christians, Jews and Muslims have a difficult and complex history of inter-relation. Islam was born in the Middle East. Like Christianity, it claims a close relation with Judaism because Muslims trace their ancestry to Abraham and to his son, Ishmael, born to the slave Hagar. In the Hebrew Bible, the story is recounted in Genesis 16:15ff; the Quran, 37:99-110, recounts Ishmael's story and identifies him with the nearly sacrificed son of Genesis 22.[29]

For Muslims, the Quran is the revealed word of God, received and transmitted without corruption by Muhammad. It is 'the Clear Sign' (Q 98:1), the eternal and final revelation given to the last prophet. As such it cannot be translated or imitated. Many non-Muslim scholars would disagree and see both Jewish and Christian influences in the Quran and *hadith* (authoritative traditions which describe a deed or saying of Muhammad's). Amongst the most radical of current views is that advocated by Patricia Crone and Michael Cook. In *Hagarism*, they argue that in Islam's early period there was a striking intimacy between Jews and Arabs (based on common opposition to Persian dominance) and that Muhammad's message was originally one which sought to justify this (on the grounds of Abrahamic descent) and thereby legitimise joint Arab-Jewish conquest of the Holy Land. However, at the same time, Muhammad's message was also messianic in character, suggesting that the Ishmaelites in general, and more particularly, he, would play a vital role in redemption history. In this dual message was the germ of an Arab religious identity distinct from that of the future Muslims' Jewish mentors.[30]

This account of early Muslims as Arab judaizers is highly controversial. Some of the non-Islamic sources used by Crone and Cook (including the seventh century *Doctrina Iacobi*, a Greek anti-Jewish tract; an eighth century Jewish apocalypse, *Secrets of Rabbi Simon ben Yochai*, and an Armenian chronicle ascribed to Bishop Sebeos) are themselves doubtful in origin and of questionable value as historical sources. The reconstruction is therefore inevitably almost as speculative as it is bold in its attempt to offer a new articulation of Islam's origins. Less problematic is the general conclusion that Jewish influence shapes some of the traditions found in the Quran. Muhammad, whose prophetic ministry began around 610 CE and ended with his death in 632, lived in the Arabian Peninsula, where Jews had lived for some centuries. Fourth century texts refer to the 'community of Israel' found in the region, and whilst Makkah (Muhammad's birthplace and the home of his first followers) was not necessarily the thriving town portrayed in the Quran, it is not impossible that Muhammad had either direct or indirect contact with Jewish and Christian tradition (Q 106:2).

Several Quranic passages evoke the Hebrew Bible narrative (and the New Testament) including Q 4:156-9, 162-6, and 19:30-40, and early Islamic practice suggests Jewish influence. As seventh century Jews would have done, Muhammad's followers refrained from eating pork, blood, and any animals that died of natural causes or as the result of being gored by other beasts (Q 5:1-4). Until the revelation at Q 2.142f. Jerusalem, not Makkah, served as the *qiblah* or direction of prayer for Muslims. Perhaps most significantly, Islam shares with Judaism its emphasis on the unitary nature of God, the importance of sacred text, and the prophetic office as the means whereby the text was made known to the world. The first of Islam's five pillars, the *Shahadah*, emphasises these elements in a way that resonates with the *Shema*, the central affirmation of Jewish belief:

> *Shahadah*: 'There is no God but God: Muhammad is the messenger of God.'

> *Shema*: 'Hear O Israel, the LORD our God, the LORD is One'.

Perhaps, then, Muhammad's mission did begin by assuming some continuity with Judaism (and to a lesser extent, with Christianity). After a few years, however, it passed into sharp distinction from it:

> O Believers! Take not take the Jews and the Christians as friends; they are friends of each other. Whosoever of you makes them his friends is one of them. God does not guide the people of the evildoers (Q 5:56).

> Thou [Muhammad] wilt surely find the most hostile of men to the believers are the Jews and the idolators, and thou wilt surely find the nearest of them in love to the believers are those who say 'We are Christians' (Q 5:85).

These extracts from the Quran attest to early Islam's *milieu* as being one in which different world-views vied for adherents, and different factions related in ambiguous ways. Muhammad hoped that the Madinah Jews in particular would accept his claims; when they and the Christians did not, he condemned them.

Despite this opposition, Islam did not consider Jews as unfavourably as it did polytheists. Whilst according to the Quran, 'religion, with God, is Islam', and for its adherents Islam uniquely embodies both the essence and the expression of what religion should be, Jews are regarded as possessing elements of the ultimate religion, and accordingly their continuing existence has been tolerated. Specifically, Jews (together with Christians, Sabaeans and Zoroastrians) have been regarded as *ahl al-kitab*, people of the book. In his introductory book on Muhammad, Martin Forward summarises well what was entailed in this designation:

> Quranic references to *ahl al-kitab* are partly hostile, because Jews and Christians have misread and disobeyed their scripture; and partly friendly, exhorting them to restore the pristine purity of their faith and to join battle with Muslims against infidelity and irreligion.[31]

As Muhammad enjoyed increasing political successes, eventually ruling the Hijaz (the western part of the Arabian Peninsula), ambivalence of attitude found formal embodiment in dhimmitude. When the Jewish inhabitants of Khaybar (north-west of Makkah) surrendered to their Muslim conquerors in the 620s, they signed a treaty or *dhimma* under which they were permitted to continue practising Judaism and cultivating the land in exchange for an annual payment. This practice was soon extended to other Jews and Christians living under Muslim rule. They were not required to adopt Islam, but had to pay a range of taxes to ensure their freedom. These included the *jizya*, a poll tax levied on males above puberty. The receipt for the *jizya* was originally a piece of parchment worn around the neck, or a seal worn on the wrist or chest. It was needed if the *dhimmi* wished to travel freely. In addition to financial penalties, there were restrictions on the public expression of Jewish religion. The building of new synagogues was prohibited (although older ones could be restored) as was the sounding of the *shofar*. Viewed negatively, over time the *dhimma* contract ceased to be an agreement between two parties and assumed more of the character of a legalised persecution. In the late thirteenth century, kabbalist Isaac ben Samuel of Acre (now Akko in Israel) fled his home and sought refuge in Christian Spain, claiming that 'in the eyes of the Muslims, the children of Israel are as open to abuse as an unprotected field'. Similarly, nineteenth-century European travellers in the Middle East reported that both churches and synagogues in Jerusalem were in severe states of decay.[32] Yet, for much of the medieval period Jews fared better in Muslim lands than in Christian ones. Under Islam, there was some persecution but Jews were not killed nor forcibly converted *en masse*, as during the Crusades. (The Quran teaches that there must be no compulsion in religion, Q 2:256.)

The degree of protection afforded to Jews by the *dhimma*, and the sometimes relaxed attitude to the enforcement of its penalties, facilitated the growth and flourishing of medieval Jewish communities in Muslim lands. As Babylon declined as the hub of Jewish scholarship, Spain assumed this mantle, with Córdoba becoming an important centre. The *halakhah* of this period often betrays Islamic influence. For example, whilst polygyny was banned for Ashkenazi Jews, Jews living in the East continued to accept the practice. Indeed, when Yemeni Jews emigrated to Israel in the 1940s, some of the arrivals were party to polygynous marriages. Outside the religious sphere, Jews and Muslims were able to mix with relative ease socially, intellectually, and professionally in trade and administration. (Even where intercourse was less free, the practicalities of *dhimmi* life could promote Jewish and *Christian* interaction as the two communities experienced similar penalties and restrictions.) In such a context, some Jewish individuals rose to positions of considerable prestige and power. Hasadai ibn Shaprut was doctor and advisor to the Sultan of Córdoba and Samuel ibn Nagdela, vizier of the ruler of Granada. Most famously, in the late twelfth century the Córdoba-born philosopher and halakhist Moses Maimonides (who fled Spain when it was conquered by the less tolerant Almohads) became both spiritual head of the Cairo Jewish community and physician to its Muslim ruler, the Kurd Saladin.

After the early seventh century, Jews collectively were rarely in a position to exercise political power over either Muslims or Christians, although in the eighth century the Khazars, a people in southern Russia, embraced Judaism, and Khazaria remained under Jewish rule for two centuries. Nevertheless, several Jewish thinkers endeavoured to address the issue of whether it was possible to make theological space for Islam and Muslims within Judaism. Maimonides' *Thirteen Principles of Faith*, for Orthodox Jews today still a classic articulation of belief, are shaped by their author's experiences in the Muslim world. Some of them bear the scars of polemical encounters with Islam. They assert the truthfulness of the Biblical prophets and Moses' identity as 'the chief of the prophets, both of those that preceded and of those that followed him'. Accordingly, the commandments should be obeyed and will never be superseded. These statements represent a direct rebuttal of the Muslim view that Muhammad was the greatest prophet of God, and that the Quranic account of history should be favoured over the corrupted version given in the *Tanakh*. Yet Maimonides also regarded Islamic monotheism as positive (he preferred it to Christian trinitarianism) and worthy of Jewish recognition. The principles which stress the unity and incorporeality of God and that 'to him alone it is right to pray' seem to owe much to a dialogue with Muslim philosophy and align Jewish thought with Islam, and against Christianity and its belief in a God who exists in three persons: Father, Son and Holy Spirit.[33]

Spanish poet and philosopher Judah ha-Levi (1075-1141) also explored the relations between Judaism, Christianity, and Islam. His *Kuzari* is written in the form of an imagined dialogue between the King of the Khazars and a rabbi. The king wishes to know what the teachings of Judaism are before he allows himself and his people to be converted and the rabbi explains and defends these teachings, particularly in relation to the challenges posed by Islam, Christianity, and Platonic philosophy. In this dialogue (which contrasts notably with the Enlightenment writings of Mendelssohn, discussed in chapter three) ha-Levi did not seek to reconcile reason and Judaism; instead, he argued that Judaism was based on revelation – a source of higher, surer truth than could be arrived at through rational enquiry – as delivered to her prophets. For ha-Levi, prophecy was both the origin (Moses' receipt of *Torah* at Sinai) and the basis of Israel's divinely mandated mission to the world. Israel functioned as a kind of intermediary between God and humanity; Judaism was the seed from which the tree of Christianity and Islam grew:

> God has a secret and wise design concerning us, which should be compared to the wisdom hidden in the seed which falls into the ground....The original seed produced the tree bearing fruit resembling that from which it had been produced.

Contained within this model was an assertion of the superiority of the Jewish seed. In the Messianic Age, those peoples who had an imperfect form of the truth would be converted or assimilated to Judaism's higher substance. The religions of the Gentiles merely serve to introduce and pave the way of the expected Messiah. If they acknowledge Him when He comes, they will become one tree.[34]

For many contemporary Jewish writers, ha-Levi's particularism and his view of Jews as a spiritually superior race, is problematic. However, ha-Levi lived in the same turbulent times inhabited by Maimonides; his views must be assessed in the light of this context. Spanish Jewry found itself caught up in conflict between zealous Muslims (the Almoravids and Almohads) and equally determined Christian forces embarking on the *Reconquista*, or reconquest of Spain. In such a dangerous environment the *Kuzari*'s recurrent emphasis on the historic mission of Judaism, and its commitment to belief in the coming of the Messiah, function as a much-needed call to Jewish faith and self-assuredness.

In more recent times, complex politics have again problematised the Jewish-Muslim relationship. Judaism has always had a geo-political dimension. According to the *Mishnah*, the land of Israel is holier than any other land (*m. Kelim*, 1:6). Since Biblical times the land of Israel has been the object of Jewish prayers, often linked with messianic expectations. The rise of Zionism amongst Jews in the late nineteenth century was in part a secular development, influenced by nationalist aspirations in Europe; it was also the product of religious hopes, as traditional Judaism held that God's law could be only imperfectly observed in *galut*. Similarly, Islam has a strong political dimension, which fed into the Arab nationalism of the early twentieth century onwards. At the heart of Islam is the fundamental concept of *tawhid* – unity, balance, or making one. It follows then that the desire to expand Muslim territorial rule is a reflection of the religious desire to see the world reflect and respond faithfully to the underlying unity or oneness of God. Moreover, within the Islamic world-view, Jerusalem enjoys a status surpassed only by that of Makkah and Madinah. Muslims call Jerusalem *al-Quds* ('the Holy') and believe that it was mystically visited by Muhammad (a tradition that both attests Islam's recognition of earlier sacred traditions and asserts Muslim superiority over it).

In short, both Islam and Judaism regard Israel, and especially Jerusalem, as sacred. Hence the political conflicts between Jews and Palestinian Arabs (a minority of whom are Christian); Israel and her neighbours, have tended to impact negatively on wider Jewish-Muslim relations. When David Ben Gurion declared the creation of the State of Israel on 14 May 1948, combined Arab armies immediately launched attacks on the new country, and many Jews living in the aggressor nations found their lives there were no longer tenable. Subject to various forms of hostility, they emigrated *en masse* to Israel and North America. Just as these Jews found themselves the victims of anti-Israeli feeling extended to Jews and Judaism more generally, so the Palestinian conflict has clouded Jewish attitudes towards Muslims and Islam. Jews are not untouched by the phobias that can blight western media coverage of Islam.

On a more positive note, the foundations of Jewish-Muslim dialogue, leading to more peaceable relations between the two traditions, do exist. Progressive rabbi Ignaz Maybaum coined the term 'trialogue' to refer to dialogue between Jews, Christians, and Muslims. Despite the devastating political turmoil through which he had lived (he was born on the European mainland and fled the Nazi regime in the 1930s), Maybaum was optimistic about the future:

I hold the view that all three monotheistic forms of expressing holiness

have equal capacity to contribute to the one world relgion, which has its
birthplace in the Middle East. Today the Middle East is becoming…the
birthplace of the revival of monotheism, uniting Jew, Christian and Muslim
in their search for terrestrial holiness, spiritual holiness, and that holiness
which is human and universal. This unity can be the very aim to which Jew,
Christian and Muslim aspire. The whole era looks to the Middle East. I
speak of a new era in the Middle East.

Maybaum's conception of the 'trialogue' and its participants is not
without problems. In particular, he contrasts the prophetic nature of
Progressive Judaism with Orthodoxy's emphasis on *halakhah*, describing
Orthodox Judaism as 'Islamised' and a 'Judaism without prophecy'. In
his attempts to teach with clarity, Maybaum sometimes comes close to
stereotyping the various participants. On the one hand, there is the lively,
self-critical Progressive Jewish (and Christian) stance, and on the other,
that of the rigid, mechanistic Orthodox Jew and the Muslim. However,
Maybaum's sincerity and thoughtfulness in seeking to wrestle with the
issues cannot be doubted. Moreover, his critique grows out of his belief
that Judaism, Christianity, and Islam are profoundly close in nature. This
is illustrated by his re-reading of ha-Levi's tree parable as one that does
not need to imply any spiritual superiority on the part of Jews and Judaism:

> Judah ha-Levi and Maimonides see Judaism as the seed which brings forth
> the tree with the two branches: Christianity and Islam….But…there is
> Christianity and Islam within Judaism…Christianity and Islam are already
> there within the 'seed' itself and not merely later in the tree with the two
> branches.

> With this understanding the dialogue ceases to be an intellectual enterprise
> and becomes a meeting similar to a meeting of kinsmen. Brothers meet
> brothers.[35]

More recently, in 1995, the International Council of Christians and
Jews, which had been promoting dialogue between Jews and Christians
since the 1940s, decided to establish the Abrahamic Forum for trilateral
dialogue between Muslims, Christians and Jews. The intention was to
create a council functioning at institutional, academic and grassroots levels
to break down barriers of mistrust between the three traditions. Perhaps
predictably, the Forum's first conference, held in Germany in October

1999, focused on monotheism. A subsequent meeting, *Convivencia*, in Seville (July 2000) resulted in the creation of 'Guidelines for Future, Steps in Promoting Jewish-Christian-Muslim Relations'. More accurately, these 'guidelines' are a series of questions for future exploration in the areas of theology, ethics, and religion and society. Many questions grouped under 'religion and society' attest to the extent to which the development of positive relations among the three traditions, and between Judaism and Islam particularly, is circumscribed by ongoing political disputes and differences over the interrelation between 'religion' and 'the state':

> Is religious nationalism a desirable, legitimate or even feasible concept? Does nationalism itself serve as substitute for religion? What are the consequences of viewing national identity in religious terms?….We need to address the whole relationship between secular democracy and religion; whether they are compatible, contradictory, and/or reconcilable….Is it only a secular, pluralistic democracy that enables and guarantees true '*Convivencia*' of the three monotheistic traditions…or do we lose more than we gain from such a context?[36]

Modern Antisemitism and the Shoah[37]

During the Holocaust or *Shoah*, the persecution and murder of upwards of six million Jews (among them one and a half million children) was pursued as a matter of political policy, by a regime that ultimately intended also to destroy Christianity. At the same time, the Nazis borrowed much of the grammar of persecution from the medieval church, and what historian Lucy Davidowicz famously called 'the war against the Jews' could not have been waged without the support and participation of many individual Christians and church bodies.[38]

By the time Hitler was appointed to the Chancellorship of Germany in 1933, Jews had gained legal equality in most European lands. (Emancipation was not universal. For example, in Romania most Jews were barred from voting, and access to education beyond the most basic level was severely restricted. In Russia, educational establishments imposed quotas and Jews were largely confined to the Pale of Settlement.) No longer compelled to stay in the ghetto, they could (at least in theory) live, study and earn a living wherever and in whatever manner they chose. Yet anti-Judaism was still embedded in European culture. The post-Enlightenment world remained saturated with Christian concepts and rhetoric. In *Oliver Twist*, Dickens portrayed a Jewish fence, Fagin, in animal-like and demonic terms. Other nineteenth- and early twentieth-century novelists shared, or made powerful connection with, anti-Jewish sentiments. Du Maurier's sensational *fin-de-siècle* novel *Trilby* featured the villainous Svengali, whilst in *Ulysses* (often described as *the* great twentieth-century novel) James Joyce recounts the singing of the 'Ballad of Sir Hugh or the Jew's Daughter' by one character to another. The popularity of these works, which have their equivalents outside the anglophone world, suggests that what occurred during the Nazi era was in many ways not an 'interruption' but grew organically out of the culture of Europe.[39]

Although continuity between Nazi policy and the teachings of the early church undeniably exists, this is not to say that National Socialism was in no way distinctive in its hatred of Jews. Like their medieval predecessors, the Nazis abhorred Jews and regarded their social acceptance as dangerous to the well-being of the German nation. However, their hatred was infused with new racist pseudo-science. German racists claimed that the Germans were the descendants of ancient Aryans, a people purer than, and superior to, all other races. Their blond hair, blue eyes, and fair skin all evidenced inner qualities lacking in other peoples. Jews were regarded as a con-taminating presence within the German state, an anti-race or *Gegenrasse*. In *Mein Kampf*, Hitler argued that the Germans had of necessity to dom-inate the 'racially inferior', as 'all great cultures of the past perished only because the originally creative race died out from blood poisoning'.[40] Hence, whilst the Church traditionally sought to convert Jews to Christianity, and advocates of Enlightenment hoped to normalise Jews by promoting assimilation, for the Nazis there was ultimately but one final solution to the 'Jewish problem' – extermination.

Although *Mein Kampf* had established Hitler's murderous intent towards Jews as early as 1925, once in power the Nazis proceeded towards their final solution of the 'Jewish problem' in a series of measured stages. It may be that they feared protest from the establishment, or it may be that policy evolved or emerged over time in response to changing political, social, and military conditions. Between 1933 and 1935 Jews were dismissed from the civil service and their access to a variety of professions was curbed, whilst *shechitah* was outlawed (ostensibly on animal welfare grounds). In September 1935, the Nuremberg Laws were promulgated, depriving Jews of their citizenship and prohibiting marriages or sexual relations between those of 'German or related blood' and Jews, who had recently been defined racially, to include those who had at least one Jewish grandparent. Through this programme of legislation, and by means of more sporadic boycotts of Jewish businesses and violence, the Nazis attempted to 'Aryanise' the German economy. The *de facto* as opposed to *de jure* removal of Jews from the German state (and later, from German occupied territories such as Austria) was also promoted by Adolf Eichmann's policies of voluntary and forced emigration.

In 1941 (when Germany occupied or exercised a decisive influence over large tracts of Europe including Austria, the Channel Islands, Czechoslovakia, Poland and parts of the Soviet Union), the Nazis moved to implement the systematic destruction of Jewry. From the Nazi standpoint the size of the Jewish populations in Poland and Russia rendered the earlier policies of boycott, control, and emigration unfeasible: nearly a tenth of the population of occupied Poland was Jewish. The prior abuse of Jews, and their subsequent relegation to the status of 'non-persons' in the eyes of many non-Jewish Europeans, had prepared the ground for the murderous programme of the early 1940s. Initially by small, mobile army units known as *Einsatzgruppen*, and later in an extensive network of concentration- and death-camps located primarily in Poland, eastern Germany, Estonia and Yugoslavia, Jews were abused and killed. They died by gassing and starvation, and also by shooting and physical attacks including beating, medical experimentation, sexual assault and torture. Towards the end of the war, when the concentration-camps in the east were dismantled, many thousands lost their lives on the so-called 'death marches' as they were forced to walk from Poland to camps in those western regions that remained within the diminishing Reich.

Like their medieval ancestors, those Jews who were murdered and abused by the Nazis were not always passive victims. Many avoided or sought to avoid deportation to the camps engaged in resistance, most famously in Warsaw, where several thousand Jews armed with makeshift weapons managed to delay the dissolution of the ghetto by some four weeks. Even in the concentration-camps rebellion was not unknown. In late 1944, Greek Jews working in the crematoria at Auschwitz blew up one of the ovens; other revolts occurred in Chelmno, Ponary, Sobibor and Treblinka. However, lack of resources and effective organisation meant that the resistors could not significantly threaten the Nazi regime. Moreover, ghetto and camp inhabitants were aware that violent protest by a few could result in an immediate massacre of the entire population.

Despite stereotypes concerning Nazi 'efficiency', it is impossible to estimate accurately the number of Jews killed during the *Shoah*. Pre-war statistics did not always record the Jewish population in a given region, and during the Cold War many of the archives held in the Soviet bloc were hard to access. As suggested earlier, probably somewhere between six and a half and seven million Jews died: nearly two-thirds of European Jews and one-third of the Jews in the world.

During this time of devastation for Jewry, how did the victims' non-Jewish neighbours respond? In particular, how did the members of the various Christian churches behave? Of course, some Christians were themselves subject to persecution. Consistent opponents of the Third Reich, Jehovah's Witnesses were deported to concentration-camps. Dietrich Bonhoeffer, a leader of the Confessing Church (which denied the possibility of an accommodation between Nazism and Christianity) was hanged for his part in a plot to kill Hitler, and some small groups like the Hutterian Brethren were expelled *en masse* during the 1930s.[41] However, the majority of Christians in Nazi-occupied territories suffered little impediment on account of their faith.

Despite (or perhaps because of) this position of relative security, few of the Jews' Christian neighbours did much to counter the Nazis' antisemitic policies. The war-time Pope, Pius XII, has recently been the subject of tremendous controversy: how much did he know of the likely fate of Italy's Jews, and why did he seemingly do little of significance to assist them? Academic and popular opinion is sharply divided. Arguably, Pius' behaviour was characterised by indecision. Although he privately sheltered some Jews and made general statements against injustices, calls for more outspoken public help were resisted on the grounds that the Holy See wished to remain neutral, and that condemning atrocities against Jews could lead to reprisals against Catholics in German-controlled lands. Given the circumstances, such prevarication was hardly neutral: it reflected a value scheme which placed the Catholic Church over the lives of individual Jews. In this respect, institutional Christian responses (both Catholic and Protestant) to the Nazi persecution of Jews were largely uniform. Most groups made the preservation of the church community the priority. Without doubt, centuries of Christian denigration of Jews and Judaism made possible a reluctance to include the Jewish people within the sphere of Church concern. Christian anti-Judaism was a necessary, although not a sufficient, cause of the *Shoah*.

Aside from the resistance and partisan activity referred to earlier, how did Jews respond to the Holocaust or *Shoah*? For many living in the pre-modern Jewish communities of Eastern Europe, the primary mode of response was halakhic, as illustrated at the end of chapter two. Observance during this time was in effect a form of resistance, a refusal to capitulate to the Nazi world-view. It created a sense of order and meaning in an environment that must often have seemed anomic. This benediction was composed by inmates in Bergen-Belsen, Spring 1944. It refers to the fact that scholars in the camp ruled that leavened bread could be eaten at *Pesach* since *Torah* is the wellspring of life:

> Our Father in heaven, behold it is evident and known to Thee that it is our desire to do Thy will and to celebrate the festival of Passover by eating matzah and by observing the prohibition of leavened food. But our heart is pained that the enslavement prevents us and we are in danger of our lives. Behold, we are prepared and ready to fulfil Thy commandment, "And ye shall live by them and not die by them".
>
> We pray to Thee that Thou mayest keep us alive and preserve us and redeem us speedily so that we may observe Thy statutes and do Thy will and serve thee with a perfect heart. Amen. [42]

Many literary and artistic responses also emerged during the *Shoah* and subsequently. These take the form of memoirs and diaries (most famously that of the Dutch girl Anne Frank), poetry, paintings, films and novels. Their creators frequently express both a sense of compulsion to write – in order to discharge their 'duty' to tell others what happened – and the feeling that it is almost impossible to capture adequately in words or images the true horror of events.

In the postwar period, Jews continue to try to make sense of the *Shoah*. Some of these responses have taken the form of theodicies – attempts to justify the traditional belief in an omniscient, omnipotent, benevolent deity in the face of tremendous evil (see chapter six). As the events of the *Shoah* become increasingly distant in time, however, the impulse to theodicy has seemingly waned. In part this may be because the need to make religious sense of events is less acute for the generation that did not directly experience the *Shoah*, or it may be a tacit acknowledgement of the failure of each theodicy that has been proposed. Whatever the reasons, attention has increasingly focused on the issues of remembrance and memory (also touched on in the next chapter) and, to a lesser extent, on the development of relations between Jews and non-Jews. Such a move arises from the conviction that the way forward is for Jews and non-Jews to talk and to do things together, if a recapitulation of the dark days of the war is to be prevented.

Jewish-Christian Relations in the Aftermath of the Shoah

Heschel's dictum reproduced at the beginning of this chapter is taken from a talk given in 1965, the time when Jews and Christians were first beginning to talk and write publicly about the religious implications of the Shoah. For Heschel,

> The misery and fear of alienation from God make Jew and Christian cry together....
> Our era marks the end of complacency, the end of evasion, the end of self-reliance. Jews and Christians share the perils and the fears; we stand on the brink of the abyss together.[43]

One needed courage to participate in interfaith dialogue, but in the postwar world, parochialism was simply not an option.

A significant number of contemporary Jews and Christians share Heschel's view and have attempted to promote relations of mutual respect and tolerance. On the institutional front, much work has been done by the Council of Christians and Jews (CCJ) in Britain and elsewhere by the other member councils of its International 'parent', the ICCJ. CCJ was founded in 1942 and since then has established over sixty local branches across Britain and the north of Ireland. At branch level, typical activities include speaker meetings, joint Bible and other textual study, and social events such as musical evenings or parties at festival times.

These contacts and a growing awareness of both the long history of Christian anti-Judaism and the churches' inaction during the *Shoah* have prompted many churches and denominations to issue statements on Judaism and Jewish-Christian relations. Of these, the best known are those produced by the World Council of Churches (WCC) Consultation on the Churches and the Jewish People, and a series of Catholic documents which have initiated non-supersessionist readings of the Christian story, including *Nostra Aetate* (a document of the Second Vatican Council, 1965) and more recently, *We Remember: Reflections on the Shoah*, published in 1998. *We Remember* stresses the evils of antisemitism, concluding that,

> we wish to turn awareness of past sins into a firm resolve to build a new future in which there will be no more anti-Judaism among Christians or anti-Christian sentiment among Jews but rather a shared mutual respect.

However, its failure to confront directly the problematic role of Pope Pius XII proved disappointing for many Jews and for some Christians, too. Moreover, the stress on the need to explore 'whether the Nazi persecution of the Jews was not made easier by the anti-Jewish prejudices embedded in some Christian minds and hearts', and the reference to Holocaust perpetrators and bystanders as 'erring sons and daughters of the Church', though pertinent, places the emphasis on individual Christians and not (as some wished it to do) on the institution of the Church itself.

The everyday effectiveness or impact of official church statements is hard to judge. Amongst some participants in Jewish-Christian dialogue there tends to be a mildly pessimistic assessment of the extent to which the Churches have consistently followed up on their theological developments and made serious efforts to reach the 'grass roots' with their new teachings. In 2000, for example, many interfaith activists were disappointed by the publication of *Dominus Iesus*, which seemingly contradicted *We Remember* by re-asserting the traditional Catholic denial of the possibility of salvation for those outside the church. However, the recent shift in many denominations towards an increased emphasis on lay education suggests that positive official statements on Jews and Judaism will indeed have a profound influence on the thinking and actions of many Christians in the future. In order to survive, many churches will expand the educational opportunities offered to ordinary members, including education on Judaism and interfaith relations.

Despite positive developments in the Jewish-Christian relationship, then, participants in the dialogue would argue that much remains to be done if the past history of misunderstanding and violence is to be transcended. Within Europe, the Americas and the Middle East, there remains a concern about the extent to which official changes in policy and theology are 'owned' by the average adherent of, say, Christianity.

The empowerment of Asian and African Christians will also impact on Jewish-Christian relations. For a new generation of church members and leaders, relations with Islam or with African traditional religions are of more pressing concern. In Jewish communities, similar issues remain, although these are sometimes regarded (by both Jewish and Christian participants) as being of lower priority, in part because Judaism does not need to understand its relation with Christianity in order to understand itself. *but see 170*

As noted earlier in this chapter, Judaism has a long tradition of making some kind of theological space for other forms of religious expression; this activity can be traced back to the Noahide laws. In the last twenty or so years those radical-conservatives, the Lubavich Chasidim, have made some efforts to encourage worldwide observance of these laws by Gentiles. This project's potential for success at effecting widespread inter-religious co-operation is, however, limited. It is most likely to appeal to Christians wishing to judaize their faith. There is also a loosely organised movement known as the *Bene Noach*, 'Sons of Noah', which draws its membership from non-Jews who believe in the Jewish God, reject Christianity, follow the Noahide laws and yet retain a Gentile identity. Many *Bene Noach* rely on the Lubavich (and other relatively open *Charedim*) to teach them how the *Talmud* and later rabbinic tradition has enhanced the laws in Genesis 9.

On a different, and arguably more radical front, some Jews have tried to offer a rationale for religious dialogue with non-Jews, and for relations with the Other which move beyond practical expediences and take the beliefs and convictions of that Other as seriously as One demands to be taken Oneself. These efforts result from a concern (found particularly in Progressive circles) that, whereas many Christian churches have done much to revise their supersessionist theologies and acknowledge the role of Christianity in persecuting Jews, there has been a reluctance by some Jewish dialogue participants to take Christianity seriously and to acknowledge that it, too, may be, 'a great faith tradition in the service of God and humanity'.[44] In September 2000, a group of Jewish scholars and rabbis published a statement on Christians and Christianity, titled *Dabru Emet*, 'speak the truth' (Zechariah 8:16). The statement, endorsed by members of a range of different Jewish denominations, appeared in *The New York Times* and other publications across the United States and Europe. It contains eight proposals aimed at encouraging Jews to understand

Christianity within the framework of Judaism. According to the authors, Jews need a Jewish way of understanding the basic beliefs of their Christian neighbours, with whom they are already in frequent social and cultural contact. Additionally, learning more about the other will enrich their understanding of Judaism. The eight statements on Jewish-Christian relations are:

1.   Jews and Christians worship the same God....as Jewish theologians we rejoice that, through Christianity, hundreds of millions of people have entered into relationship with the God of Israel.

2.   Jews and Christians seek authority from the same book – the Bible....

3.   Christians can respect the claim of the Jewish people upon the land of Israel....Many Christians support the State of Israel....As Jews, we applaud this support. We also recognise that Jewish tradition mandates justice for all non-Jews who reside in a Jewish state....

4.   Jews and Christians accept the moral principles of *Torah*...this...can be the basis of an improved relationship between our two communities. It can also be the basis of a powerful witness to all humanity for improving the lives of our fellow human beings....

5.   Nazism was not a Christian phenomenon....Too many Christians participated in, or were sympathetic to, Nazi atrocities against Jews....We recognise...those Christians who risked or sacrificed their lives to save Jews during the Nazi regime....We applaud those Christians who reject the teaching of contempt, and we do not blame them for the sins committed by their ancestors.

6.   The humanly irreconcilable difference between Jews and Christians will not be settled until God redeems the entire world as promised in Scripture....

7.   A new relationship between Jews and Christians will not weaken Jewish practice. An improved relationship will not accelerate the cultural and religious assimilation that Jews rightly fear....

8.   Jews and Christians must work together for justice and peace....Separately and together we must work to bring justice and peace to our world. In this enterprise, we are guided by the vision of the prophets

of Israel....[45]

The long-term consequences of this statement remain to be seen. Point five has proven to be particularly controversial in its assertion that Nazism represented more of a rupture from, than a continuation of, Christian culture. This view implicitly critiques those commentators who argued (for example) that *We Remember* did not go far enough in acknowledging Christian responsibility for the Holocaust. The suggestion in Point two, that Jews and Christians share a common Bible, is a commonplace in dialogue circles but is also open to dispute, given that (for example) Christianity both orders the books of the Hebrew Bible differently than Judaism, and believes that there are two testaments, an older and a 'New' one. From its Christian readers, *Dabru Emet* has aroused a mixed response, on account of the lack of reference to a Trinitarian God, and the brevity of the reference to the need for justice for non-Jews living in Israel. As Jim Aitken suggests, however, 'this should not obscure the genuine sentiments of filiality behind *Dabru Emet*'.[46] There are also many religious Jews (typically from Judaism's Orthodox wing, following Soloveitchik, who was introduced in chapter three), for whom dialogue with Christians or other believers should be confined to a social policy-type agenda, rather than a theological one.

Jewish 'reluctance' to enter into dialogue on theological matters has many causes. In general terms, as mentioned earlier, whereas the founding story of Christianity itself leads many Christians to feel a desire to work out a relationship with Judaism, Jews do not 'need' to understand Christianity in order to make sense of their own tradition. There are also more specifically religious objections to dialogue with Christianity. For example, thinkers like Eliezer Berkovits challenge the kind of sentiments voiced in *Dabru Emet*. In his *Faith After Auschwitz*, he argued that Nazism was an outgrowth of Christian anti-Judaism: 'what was started at the Council of Nicaea was duly completed in the concentration-camps.'[47] Moreover, for the religious Jew,

> the idea of interreligious understanding is ethically objectionable because it makes respect for the other man [sic] dependent on whether I am able to appreciate his religion or his theology.... I am duty bound to respect the dignity of every human being no matter what I may think of his religion.[48]

Also from an Orthodox perspective, the outspoken Zionist thinker Yeshayahu Leibowitz has argued that whilst dialogue on non-religious issues is possible between Jews and Christians, dialogue between Judaism and Christianity as world-views is neither desirable nor possible:

> The Christian symbol is that of the deity who sacrifices his only son for man [sic]. This is the great contrast between the theocentric religion, in which man strives to serve God, and anthropocentric religion, in which God fulfills man's need for salvation. The actual manifestation of Jewish faith in daily living was, historically, the system of *Mitzvot*, the *Halakhah*, the organization of man's life as a programme of service to God in day to day existence.[49]

For these Orthodox writers (but not for all Orthodox Jews[50]), whilst effective communication and co-existence with non-Jews is possible, there is no such thing as a 'Judaeo-Christian tradition'. Religious Jews are, therefore, as varied in their attitudes to relations with other traditions as they are in their approaches to other matters.

Judaism and Other Religions

This chapter has focussed on relations between Jews, pagans, Christians and Muslims. Earlier in this book, Jews' and Judaism's encounter with the secularised world of modernity was explored in some depth. These *foci* are, perhaps, predictable. Jewish life and thought developed alongside pagan culture at first and then in contexts shaped by other monotheistic traditions with whom it shares a family relationship as well as one of geographical proximity and co-existence. However, such an account does not provide a full picture of either popular or scholarly encounters between Jews and non-Jews. For example, in the medieval period small Jewish communities existed in India, the most famous of these being the Cochin Jews of southern India and the *Bene Israel* ('Sons of Israel') whose main centres were Bombay, Calcutta, Old Delhi, and Ahmadabad. Increased international trade and western European colonial activity ensured that contacts between Jews and adherents of Indian religions were renewed in the nineteenth- and early twentieth-centuries. To date, relatively little work exists on the inter-relation of Jews and Hindus, although certain Cochin customs (synagogues are entered barefoot; many marriages are arranged, and women often wear bindis[51]) suggest that the negative Biblical passages on polytheism and worship involving images have not prevented all of Judaism's Indian adherents from being influenced by the wider religious *milieu*.

Work on the encounter between Judaism and Hinduism has been undertaken by Gandhian specialist Margaret Chatterjee. In *Gandhi and his Jewish Friends*, she explores the common ground between Gandhi and his Jewish associates in South Africa and Europe, all of whom were committed to discovering and pursuing a universalistic ethic, the inner core of religion minus its accrescence.[52] A later work draws comparisons between Hindu and Jewish experiences of modernity and between Israeli and Indian experiments with statehood in the late twentieth- and early twenty-first centuries. Since 1947, contemporary Indians and Jews alike have found that what was a longed-for, spiritually momentous state – the attainment of national independence – is less than divine once achieved, and that diversity within and between different religious communities is not easily managed. Despite the cultural prejudices of some early Zionists (Herzl argued that a Jewish state in Palestine would form a European 'wall against Asia'), these undeniable similarities of experience could, Chatterjee argues, make for future amity between the nations and their peoples.[53]

In recent years a community of sympathy has also been established between some Jews and Tibetan Buddhist freedom-strugglers. In the late 1990s a '*Seders* for Tibet' campaign was mounted in America, encouraging Jews to invite Tibetan guests to their family celebrations, or to insert into the *Haggadah* material from Tibetan history. Whilst the primary intention was to raise awareness of the Tibetan cause in the Jewish community, the use of Buddhist material in a Jewish liturgical context implicitly suggests that Jewish values of freedom and liberation have universal significance, and in some profound sense draw on a Source that transcends, and is greater than, that which is boundaried by conventional Jewish religious understanding.

At the same time, a substantial minority of western converts to Buddhism are Jewish, and still others seek to incorporate Buddhist techniques such as meditation and chanting into more traditional forms of Judaism. From an Orthodox perspective, this is a dangerous syncretistic move. But for practitioners their lifestyle, sometimes described as 'Jew-Bu', or 'Ju-Bu', builds upon and exposes an underlying unity between the otherwise differing traditions.

On a slightly less 'positive' note, recent studies have also drawn attention to a Japanese fascination with Jews and Judaism. As Goodman and Miyazawa note, as news of the *Shoah* emerged at the end of the war, many defeated Japanese identified with Jews, seeing themselves similarly as victims of the conflict. Anne Frank's diary has been widely read in Japan and *Fiddler on the Roof* is the country's longest-running musical: audiences empathise with Tevye the milkman and his struggle to hold on to tradition in a rapidly changing world. At the same time, crude antisemitic stereotypes persist even in educated, respectable circles. Surveys indicate that Jews are regarded as less trustworthy than Christians and Buddhists. In politics, the Global Restoration Party (GRP) aims to 'smite the traitors who are selling out Holy Japan to the diabolical Jewish cult' and suggests that Japan was defeated in World War II not by the USA and her allies, but by World Jewry. More commonly, economic recession and growing immigration are not infrequently blamed on secretly plotting 'Jewish corporations' and the Freemasons. [54] What fascinates scholars about these complex images of Jews is that, in Japan, they persist and develop in a context that is largely devoid of a visible Jewish presence. (There are around one thousand Jews in the country today.) Moreover, unlike Christianity or Islam, the religious traditions with which most Japanese associate (Buddhism, Shinto, or one of many New Religious Movements) do not discuss Judaism in any depth, if at all. For Goodman and Miyawaza, antisemitism in Japan indicates the extent to which 'the Jew' as scapegoat has been planted deeply in the Japanese psyche. Independent of any historical realities, Japanese images of Jews fulfil certain psychological and ideological needs – they explain the anomie felt by many Japanese today, and offer a means for the continued expression of wartime chauvinism and xenophobia. Viewed in a wider context, the Japanese case acts as a reminder that, despite the important repudiation of supersessionism by many churches, anti-Jewish *theology* is not the only factor behind poor Jewish/non-Jewish relations. Once established in the collective psyche, the negative image of 'the Jew' persists, independent of actualities but always (as the recent appearance of the GRP attests) capable of translation into negative policies or actions. The promotion of good Jewish/non-Jewish relations must therefore be the task not just of religious professionals but of societies and cultures as a whole.

Notes

[1] See J. M. Cook, 'Persia', in B. M. Metzger and M. D. Coogan (eds), *The Oxford Companion to the Bible*, Oxford: Oxford University Press, 1993, pp. 582–583 or R. J. Coggins, *Haggai, Zechariah, Malachi*, Sheffield: JSOT Press, 1987, p. 9.

[2] The name Septuagint comes from the number of translators referred to in the second century BCE *Letter of Aristeas*. (L. L. Grabbe, *Judaism from Cyrus to Hadrian, Vol. I: The Persian and Greek Periods*, Minneapolis, Fortress Press, 1992, pp. 179–180; 200–201.

[3] See M. Hengel; J. Bowden (trans.), *Judaism and Hellenism*, SCM Press, 1981, p. 174.

[4] Hengel, *Judaism and Hellenism*, p. 104. Hengel's critics include Louis Feldman. His points are expressed, however, in a manner that betrays the influence of contemporary concerns. For example Hellenization is equated with intermarriage. See Grabbe, *Judaism Vol. One*, pp. 148–153.

[5] Augustus, *Res Gestae* 12, quoted in K. Wengst, *Pax Romana and the Peace of Jesus Christ*, SCM Press, 1987 p. 9.

[6] See J. J. Meggitt, *Paul, Poverty and Survival*, Edinburgh: T & T Clark, 1998.

[7] P. Garnsey and R. Saller, *The Roman Empire: Economy, Society and Culture*, Duckworth, 1987, p. 164.

[8] See N. de Lange, 'Jewish Attitudes to the Roman Empire', in P. Garnsey and C.R. Whittaker (eds), *Imperialism in the Ancient World*, Cambridge: Cambridge University Press, 1978, pp. 255-281.

[9] D. P. Gray, 'Jesus was a Jew', in M. Perry and M. Schweitzer (eds), *Jewish-Christian Encounters Over the Centuries: Symbiosis, Prejudice, Holocaust, Dialogue*, New York: Peter Lang, 1994, pp. 1-25; J. T. Pawlikowski, 'Jesus – A Pharisee and the Christ', in M. Shermis and A. E. Zannoni (eds), *Introduction to Jewish-Christian Relations*, New York: Paulist Press, 1991, pp. 174-201.

[10] According to Marcion (d. 160) the Christian message rejected the claims of law. Marcion believed that Paul alone appreciated this distinction;

the evangelists were blinded to it by their Jewish heritage. Hence, the only normative scriptures were Pauline letters and a version of Luke. Marcion's claims prompted the church to assert the authority of both gospels and 'Old' Testament. The New Testament canon was accepted by almost all Christians by the early fifth century.

[11] I and II Timothy, Titus, Ephesians, Colossians and II Thessalonians are of doubtful authenticity.

[12] K. Stendahl, *Paul Among Jews and Gentiles*, Philadelphia: Fortress Press, 1976.

[13] J. C. Walters, *Ethnic Issues in Paul's Letter to the Romans: Changing Self-Definitions in Earliest Roman Christianity*, Valley Forge: Trinity Press International, 1993. There is little evidence concerning the enforcement of the edict. However, even partial expulsion would create the kind of impulses to re-definition that Walters envisages. See Grabbe, *Judaism. Vol. 2*, pp. 397 – 399.

[14] R. R. Ruether, *Faith and Fratricide*, New York: Seabury Press, 1974, p. 181.

[15] See R. Michael, 'Antisemitism and the Church Fathers', in Perry and Schweitzer (eds), *Jewish-Christian Encounters*, pp. 101–130.

[16] J. G. Gager, 'The Parting of the Ways: A View from the Perspective of Early Christianity: "A Christian Perspective"', in E. J. Fisher (ed.), *Interwoven Destinies: Jews and Christians Through the Ages*, New York: Paulist Press, 1993, p. 72.

[17] L. H. Cohick, 'Melito's *Peri Pascha*. Its Relationship to Judaism and Sardis in Recent Scholarly Discussion', in H. C. Kee and L. H. Cohick (eds), *The Evolution of the Synagogue: Problems and Progress*, Harrisburg, PA: Trinity Press International, 1999, pp. 123-140.

[18] M. Saperstein, *Moments of Crisis in Jewish-Christian Relations*, SCM Press, 1989, pp. 17–19.

[19] G. Chaucer, *The Canterbury Tales*, Oxford: Oxford University Press, 1998, p. 162.

[20] L. B. Glick, *Abraham's Heirs: Jews and Christians in Medieval Europe*, Syracuse: Syracuse University Press, 1999, pp. 187-188.

[21] S. Krauss; W. Horbury (rev. and ed.), *The Jewish-Christian Controversy from the Earliest Times until 1789. Vol. I. History*, Tübingen: J.C.B. Mohr, 1995, pp. 153-161; 184-185.

[22] See J. Cohen, 'Medieval Jews on Christianity: Polemical Strategies and Theological Defense', in Fisher, *Interwoven Destinies*, pp. 77-89 and

Krauss, *The Jewish-Christian Controversy*.

[23] N. Berend, *At the Gate of Christendom: Jews, Muslims and 'Pagans' in Medieval Hungary, c. 1000 – c. 1300*, Cambridge: Cambridge University Press, 2001, pp. 161-162.

[24] Ibid., pp. 199-200.

[25] F. Sherwin (ed.), *Luther's Works*, Vol. 47, Philadelphia: Fortress Press, 1971, pp. 268-269; compare W. I. Brandt (ed.), *Luther's Works*, Vol. 45, Philadelphia: Fortress Press, 1971, pp. 199-229.

[26] G. H. Williams, *The Radical Reformation*, third edition, Kirksville: Sixteenth Century Journal Publishers, 1992, pp. 120-36, 1267, 1269.

[27] Williams, *The Radical Reformation*, pp. 1123-1125; 1264-1266.

[28] S. Heschel, *Abraham Geiger and the Jewish Jesus*, Chicago: University of Chicago Press, 1998; D. Flusser, *Jesus*, Jerusalem: Magnes Press, 1968; G. Vermes, *Jesus the Jew: A Historian's Reading of the Gospels*, London: SCM. Press, 1973.

[29] Quranic references are from *The Koran*, trans. A. J. Arberry, Oxford: Oxford University Press, 1983.

[30] P. Crone and M. Cook, *Hagarism: The Making of the Islamic World*, Cambridge: Cambridge University Press, 1977.

[31] M. Forward, *Muhammad: A Short Biography*, Oxford: Oneworld, 1997, p. 55.

[32] Bat Ye'or, *The Dhimmi: Jews and Christians under Islam*, Associated University Presses, 1985, pp. 48; 352.

[33] The Principles are reproduced in *The Authorised Daily Prayer Book of the United Hebrew Congragations of the British Commonwealth of Nations*, trans. S. Singer, Eyre & Spottiswoode, 1962.

[34] J. ha-Levi, *The Kuzari: An Argument for the Faith of Israel*, New York: Schocken Books, 1964, pp. 226-227.

[35] I. Maybaum, *Happiness Outside the State: Judaism, Christianity, Islam: Three Ways to God*, Oriel Press, 1980, pp. x, 56-57; *Trialogue Between Jew, Christian and Muslim*, Routledge and Kegan Paul, 1972.

[36] R. Weyl, 'Convivencia – Enhancing Identity Through Encounter Between Jews, Christians and Muslims: The ICCJ 2000 Annual Conference in Seville, Spain', *ICCJ News*, 25 (Autumn 2000), p. 3. See also *From the Martin Buber House* 28 (Autumn 2000), issue on 'The Concept of Monotheism in the Abrahamic Traditions'.

[37] The Nazi persecution has been named 'Holocaust', 'genocide', '*Shoah*' or '*Churban*' (this latter term, implying a devasting destruction which paves

the way for something new, is particularly associated with the work of Ignaz Maybaum). 'Holocaust' is the word used by the LXX to describe offerings sacrificed in the Temple. Its theological overtones are problematic for some. '*Shoah*' means 'catastrophe'. It is commonly used in Israel, France, and increasingly in the anglophone world.

[38] L. Dawidowicz, *The War Against the Jews ,1933-1945*, Harmondsworth: Penguin, 1977.

[39] C. Dickens, *Oliver Twist*, Harmondsworth: Penguin, 1985 (first published 1837-1839); G. Du Maurier, *Trilby*, Harmondsworth: Penguin, 1994 (first published 1894); J. Joyce, *Ulysses*, Harmondsworth: Penguin, 1992 (first published 1936).

[40] A. Hitler; R. Mannheim trans., *Mein Kampf*, Boston: Houghton Miffin, 1962, p. 289.

[41] M. J. Wright, 'The Nature and Significance of Relations between the Historic Peace Churches and Jews during and after the *Shoah*', in S. E. Porter and B. W. R. Pearson (eds), *Christian Jewish Relations Through the Centuries*, Sheffield: Sheffield Academic Press, 2000, pp. 400-425.

[42] N. N. Glatzer (ed.), *Language of Faith: A Selection of the Most Expressive Jewish Prayers*, New York: Schocken, 1975, p. 216.

[43] Heschel, pp. 310–11.

[44] Tony Bayfield, in M. Braybrooke, *Christian-Jewish Dialogue: The Next Steps*, SCM Press, 2000, p. 118.

[45] T. Frymer-Kensky *et al.*, *Christianity in Jewish Terms*, Boulder, Col.: Westview Press, 2000, pp. xvii-xx.

[46] J. Aitken, 'Jews and Christians Take Counsel', *Church Times*, 20 October 2000, p. 17.

[47] E. Berkovits, *Faith After the Holocaust*, New York: Ktav, 1973, p. 41.

[48] Ibid., p. 47.

[49] Y. Leibowitz; E. Goldman (ed.), *Judaism, Human Values and the Jewish State*, Cambridge, Mass: Harvard University Press, 1995, p. 259.

[50] See for example, D. Novak, *Jewish-Christian Dialogue: A Jewish Justification*, Oxford: Oxford University Press, 1989.

[51] A 'spot' or 'drop', which takes the form of a red mark on a woman's forehead, and plays an important role in traditional Hindu marriage ceremonies.

[52] M. Chatterjee, *Gandhi and his Jewish Friends*, Macmillan, 1992.

[53] M. Chatterjee, *Studies in Modern Jewish and Hindu Thought*, Macmillan, 1997, especially pp. 152–3. See also H. Ucko (ed.), *People of God, Peoples of*

God: A Jewish-Christian Conversation in Asia, Geneva: WCC, 1996, in which a shared history of subordination to the West is seen as a basis for dialogue between European Jews and Asian Christians.

[54] D. G. Goodman and M. Miyazawa, *Jews in the Japanese Mind: The History and Uses of a Cultural Stereotype*, Free Press, 1995, pp. 6, 254-256.

6

Judaism and Jewish Continuity: Into the Twenty-First Century

All is foreseen, but freedom of choice is given (m. Avot 3:16)

In an age which champions pluralism and voluntaryism, how does one ensure the transmission of a distinctive identity to a new generation? This challenge is not unique to Judaism: in the early twenty-first century, many groups are confronted by similar questions. But in Jewish communities the discussion is particularly lively. Demographically speaking, the world Jewish population has not recovered from the *Shoah*. Moreover, Jewry is steadily ageing. Outside *Charedi* circles, Jews typically marry late and birthrates are low. Increasing rates of exogamy also mean that many children who have one or more Jewish parents do not self-identify as Jews or feel drawn towards the Jewish religion. Given these changes, it is hard to predict the future of Judaism.

In the last decade, much energy has been devoted to the exploration and promotion of 'Jewish continuity'. The term 'continuity' is an interesting one. It assumes firstly that practices and values can be passed on from one generation to another; and, secondly, that these practices and values are worthy of transmission: that is, that they will be appropriate and useful in the future. Yet the fact that so much effort is expended on continuity-oriented conferences, publications, and projects also suggests a lack of confidence that these two propositions hold true. Book titles like *Will We Have Jewish Grandchildren?* evoke the sincere concerns of some Jews.[1] Most Jews today live in societies where change is rapid and regarded as desirable. This does not always fit easily with Judaism's sense of tradition. At the same time, the events of the *Shoah* and the founding of the State of Israel compound the sense of inter-generational distance within Jewish communities. Many young Jews have parents or grandparents who live in contexts markedly different from those of their youth. (For example, Jews from the former Soviet Union are the largest country-of-origin group in contemporary Israel; most arrived during the late twentieth century.) These experiences of rupture and dislocation mean that some adults feel ill-equipped to socialise the new generation, that is, to transmit a meaningful sense of identity and belonging. But if some observers are pessimistic or anxious, others are determined to respond positively to the challenges on the horizon.

Responses to the Shoah

The *Shoah* or Holocaust is the most obvious example of a modern threat to Judaism's continuity. The suffering and destruction of millions caused some to question or abandon belief in a benevolent, omnipotent and just God: perhaps Judaism is philosophically or theologically untenable in a post-Auschwitz world? Despite the unprecedented and shocking nature of the experience (its brutality; its deployment of technical apparatus, juridical procedure, and violence; its occurrence within a culture in which many Jews felt 'at home'), atheism has not been the majority response. In one of the most radical responses, Richard Rubenstein has rejected traditional Jewish theology after the Holocaust, because (he believes) it leads to problematic and offensive conclusions:

> Traditional Jewish theology maintains that God is the ultimate, omnipotent actor in historical drama....I fail to see how this position can be maintained without seeing Hitler and the SS as instruments of God's will.[2]

Yet what Rubenstein is calling for is not atheism, but rather an exploration of new ways of theorizing Jewish life.

Chapter two described how some carefully observant Jews approached their rabbis for guidance on a host of halakhic questions raised by life under National Socialism. Whilst *responsa* were sought on specific and concrete issues that may sometimes appear trivial to non-Jewish observers (or to non-halakhically oriented Jews) they convey profound meanings. As Yaffa Eliach writes,

> The Jew superimposed his [sic] own system of values on a society that

World Jewish Population, 2000

The world Jewish population was estimated at 13.2 million at the beginning of 2000. This figure is provisional – many estimates count as Jewish all those who, when asked, identify as such. An individual's subjective definition does not necessarily coincide with the halakhic one, nor does it measure communal affiliation, belief or behaviour.

Countries with largest Jewish populations

Country	Jewish Population	% of Total World Jewish Population
USA	5,700,000	43.2
Israel	4,882,000	37.0
France	521,000	3.9
Canada	362,000	2.7
Russia	290,000	2.2
UK	276,000	2.1
Argentina	200,000	1.5
Ukraine	100,000	0.8
Brazil	98,000	0.7
Australia	97,000	0.7

(source: *American Jewish Year Book*, Vol. 100, New York: The American Jewish Committee, 2000.)

Jews are concentrated in a few predominantly urbanised countries (nearly 95% of Jews live in the ten states listed). They are also widely dispersed: over ninety countries have recorded populations of at least one hundred. Religious Jews in these small communities face significant challenges. It may be difficult to sustain religious institutions such as a synagogue, *bet din*, or a cemetery. Of course new technologies provide people living in countries like Cuba, Nigeria, Philippines, and Slovenia with unprecedented access to Jewish education, but they also promote a new degree of homogenisation, hastening the demise of some unique religious and cultural traditions.

viewed him as a non-person, a commodity earmarked for death. Within a lawless frame of reference, he continued to attempt to observe law, as if to proclaim: "I observe my tradition, therefore I am a human being".[3]

Responsa from this era imply a belief that the events of the Holocaust are not unique and that they can be contained or managed within a traditional Jewish framework. As was also highlighted in chapter two, the *responsa* do not question the essentials of Jewish theology, the reality of God and the covenant. Rather, they emphasise the need to question and explore the nature of human response to God amidst changing conditions.

In addition to the implicit theology found in the *responsa* of *Charedi* communities, there have been many notable attempts at constructing more explicit Jewish theologies of the *Shoah* and in particular at formulating theodicies, although none has gained widespread acceptance. Orthodox theologian Eliezer Berkovitz applied a variant of what philosophers of religion term the 'Free Will Defence', arguing that the *Shoah* was possible because God shuns intervention in earthly affairs. This divine restraint is necessary in order to grant humans the freedom to act for good or evil, and hence the ability to enter willingly into a relationship with God.

Berkovitz' theodicy has a Biblical precedent in the Psalmists' notion of the mysterious 'hiding of the [divine] face':

> Rouse Yourself, why do You sleep, O Lord?
> Awaken, do not reject us forever!
> Why do You hide Your face,
> ignoring our affliction and distress?
> We lie prostrate in the dust;
> our body clings to the ground.
> Arise and help us,
> redeem us, as befits Your faithfulness (Psalm 44:23-26)

Also drawing on Biblical concepts, others have suggested that God somehow willed or actively permitted the *Shoah*, as punishment for modern Jewry's rejection of *Torah* and increased assimilation to non-Jewish ways. Satmar rebbe Joel Teitelbaum famously outlined a similar position in his 1961 book, *Va-Yoel Moshe*, which interpreted the *Shoah* as a divine punishment for the sin of secular Zionism.[4] Many Jews and non-Jews find these interpretations of the *Shoah* deeply problematic. But it is important to appreciate how deeply many *Charedim* in particular were (and are) disturbed by the gulf between the life advocated by traditional Judaism, and the realities of modern, largely secular, civilization. Whilst most Jews welcomed emancipation, the increased accessibility of non-Jewish society and culture was regarded with sorrow by those who believed that assimilation would gradually destroy Judaism. For Teitelbaum, secular Zionism's campaign for a nation-state in Palestine was symptomatic of a dangerous desire to normalize the Jewish people. It entailed a rejection of both the Jews' historic identity as God's chosen people, and the traditional teaching that mass return to the land would only take place in an age of divine redemption. In short, as Norman Solomon notes, 'not unnaturally they feared, and believed they witnessed, the prophesied chastisement of Israel, with but a small and faithful remnant escaping'.[5]

Writing from a quite different perspective, Ignaz Maybaum, whose work was introduced in the previous chapter, also sought to explain the Holocaust whilst retaining the Biblical concepts of covenant and election. For him, the events were terrible but ultimately presented Jews with creative opportunities. The destruction of eastern European Jewish communities brought to an end what Maybaum saw as the negative 'medievalism' which still characterized much Jewish existence in the early twentieth century. Post-war, Jews could move fully into the modern era and into better relations with other groups, especially Christians. In this sense, the *Shoah* was part of God's plan for Israel, and Adolf Hitler a modern version of Nebuchadnezzar, whom God describes in Isaiah 52:13 as 'my servant'. (It is interesting to note here that Rubenstein wrote after Maybaum, but not consciously in response to him.)

Like most theodicies, Maybaum's interpretation of the *Shoah* is profoundly troubling. In religious terms, his suggestion that God somehow used Hitler to purge the Jewish people is a difficult one. And from a more dispassionate perspective, Maybaum's distinction between 'modernity' and 'Orthodoxy' is rather simplistic. However, Maybaum himself was not unscathed by the *Shoah*; he does not write from a position of easy distance from its horrors. Maybaum fled Germany in 1939, and lost family, friends and colleagues in the catastrophe: his writings are never glib. They attest to an often deeply moving determination to make sense of the Holocaust in a way that follows through and does not abandon traditional belief in a God who acts in history and has chosen the Jewish people.[6]

In addition to posing philosophical challenges to Judaism, the *Shoah* has had significant *practical* implications. Those who died included many who might have been expected to play a major role in ensuring Judaism's continued vitality. A large number of the Nazis' victims came from traditional communities that valued *Torah* study and the carefully observant life. Reform Judaism, of which Germany had for more than a century been the intellectual power-house, also suffered greatly. Amongst those who perished was Regina Jonas, the first ever woman rabbi, who was ordained in Germany on behalf of the Union of Liberal Rabbis in 1935. Before her own final deportation to Auschwitz, Jonas played an important role in helping new arrivals at the Theresienstadt camp to cope with their feelings of shock and disorientation.

In the aftermath of the *Shoah*, survival was the prime concern. Living in displaced persons' camps in the immediate postwar era, many former prisoners married and started new families. This drive to ensure physical continuity was reinforced when the newly proclaimed State of Israel was attacked by five Arab nations in Spring 1948, and again during the Six Day War in 1967. To many, the practical necessity of defence seemed to be infused with an almost sacred character. Philosopher Emil Fackenheim seemed to capture this mood when he suggested that, 'the authentic Jew of today is forbidden to hand Hitler yet another, posthumous victory....we are, first, commanded to survive as Jews, lest the Jewish people perish.' Although Fackenheim intended his statement to be a religious one (he believed that Jews were obligated to remember the *Shoah's* victims, and to keep faith with the world and with Judaism's God) it often came to be seen as legitimising a collective, secular Jewish struggle for survival.[7]

In relation to Judaism as a *religious* tradition, the post-*Shoah* emphasis on survival has mixed implications. On the one hand, without a viable Jewish population, Judaism is seemingly doomed. But at the same time, survival of the Jewish people does not necessarily depend on or imply the persistence of a particular set of beliefs or practices. From a religious viewpoint, survivalism carries with it the danger that the existence of a Jewish people or state becomes an end in itself, and the traditional Jewish religious *foci* of God, *Torah*, and Israel (conceived in broad terms) recede in importance. For example, in his 1957 work on American Judaism, Nathan Glazer described what he regarded as a problematic 'stubborn insistence on remaining a Jew, enhanced by no particularly ennobling idea of what that means'.[8]

In a 1982 book, British Reform Rabbi Dow Marmur expressed similar concerns to Glazer's, and argued that it was time for Jews to look *Beyond*

Survival.[9] New generations of Jews needed to know why they should survive, if meaningful Jewish religious life was to continue. In the last ten years Marmur's position has assumed normative status within Judaism. The concern is for continuity with Jewry's past rather than purely physical survival. As Marmur puts it, the motivation for religious parents today must be, 'Not just "Don't give Hitler a posthumous victory!", but the *veshinantam levanecha* of the *Shema*, "you shall teach [Torah] diligently to your children".[10] An affirmative emphasis on the content of Jewish religious tradition is regarded as vital. For 'right-wing' Orthodoxy, the focus must be on study and observance as traditionally conceived. For others, the reinvigoration of Jewish life takes place in relation to the new State of Israel (religious Zionism), or is manifest in responses to pressing moral and ethical issues. This return to ethics is not an anti-halakhic stance akin to that of some of the early reformers (discussed in chapter three). For Robert Gordis, the Biblical and rabbinic legislators' concern for the concrete and the relevant means that Judaism's classical sources are replete with insights and rulings which help those grappling with the pressing issues of today, including ecology, democratic freedom, and the threat of nuclear annihilation.[11]

So, religious Jews seek to divert survivalist impulses into ones that work for Jewish continuity. But increasingly, as long-term security for Israel seems (at least periodically) within reach and new generations feel more distant from the events of the Nazi era, the drive for physical survival has given way to an increasing desire to memorialise the *Shoah*. The *Shoah* is remembered in many ways: in the minds of those who experienced the events (or who have family and friends who did); in the memoirs and biographies written by or about survivors; in theological and religious works; in art, film, literature, and educational resources; and increasingly in public monuments, museums, and joint acts of remembrance like *Yom Ha-Shoah* or Holocaust Memorial Day. Remembrance and commemoration are certainly important, but there is disquiet in some circles about the impact that these activities have on other efforts to transmit a positive religious identity to new generations of Jews.

It is not an exaggeration to say that for some Jews, the Israel-founded *Yom Ha-Shoah* has assumed a significance to rival that of *Yom Kippur* and *Pesach*. Conceived as a 'Day of Holocaust and Heroism', it was established by the new State's Parliament in 1951 and is observed during the same month as *Pesach*, on 27th *Nisan*, which is the anniversary of the Warsaw

Ghetto uprising. Both the name and the timing reflect the early desire to overturn the perception that those who died were passive victims, and to place emphasis on acts of armed resistance, which seemed more in keeping with the determination required of Israel's first citizens. Although fundamentally secular in origin, it is now marked annually not just in Israel but also in *Diaspora* communities. However, this practice raises several issues for Judaism. *Yom Ha-Shoah* originated in a context that regarded the modern State of Israel as the sole guarantor of Jewish existence. Israeli political speeches made on the day still focus on this principle, and portray the state as a 'never again!' response to the Holocaust. As such, as Jacob Neusner has noted, its observance is intended to serve a specific secular purpose in promoting a sense of shared goals and identity:

> The place of the Holocaust in the civil religion of Israel is easy to understand: it forms a critical element in the public explanation of why there must be a State of Israel, why it must be of its present character and not some other, and why every citizen must be prepared to support the State in peacetime and fight for it in war.[12]

What are the implications for Jewish religious tradition of the incorporation of *Yom Ha-Shoah* into the liturgical calendar? On the one hand, it reflects the idea that all Jews can understand themselves as one people, defined by a shared heritage and history. And as noted in chapter one, Judaism cannot be adequately understood without reference to the Jewish people. But observance of *Yom Ha-Shoah* can also be interpreted as problematic. Does its religious commemoration implicitly equate Judaism with Jewish history? Does it confuse religion with ethnicity? These profound question are just some of the reasons why, in *Diaspora*, acceptance of this Israel-born day of remembrance is far from universal.

Many religious Jews live in contexts that offer them a calendar of several possible Holocaust memorial days. *Tisha Be-Av* (9th *Av*) a fast day commemorating the destruction of the First and Second Temples, is the preferred day for Holocaust remembrance amongst Orthodox groups. But some also have national days, like Britain's Holocaust Memorial Day (27th January, the anniversary of the liberation of Auschwitz, first marked in 2001) and the springtime Days of Remembrance of Victims of the Holocaust proclaimed by the United States Congress in 1980 (the date in 2004 is April 18th). In addition to local custom, a range of interpretative factors may affect one's preference for one date over another. For example, observing a national memorial day (one marked by the population as a whole, rather than by the Jewish community alone) may reflect a desire to locate Jewish experience within the context of wider human activity and reflection. In contrast, opting for the ninth of *Av* may signal a view of the *Shoah* which denies that it poses unique challenges for Judaism, and places it firmly within traditional Jewish frames of reference. (The Holocaust is in some sense 'like' the destruction of the Temples.) Just decades after the end of World War II, it is still too early to predict which (if any) memorial day will eventually assume normative status. But whichever date prevails in the future, the choice will reflect and construct the ways in which Holocaust memory has been shaped by, and shapes, Jewish religion in the future.

In addition to days of remembrance (memorials in time) a growing number of monuments has been erected, and museums opened, with the aim of ensuring that the memory of the *Shoah* does not fade. The desire to document and teach about the Nazi war against Jews stems from a variety of impulses. The wish to avert future tragedy is certainly one; the present generation also faces the challenge of trying to find ways of remembering events and honouring victims without the guiding presence of survivors, many of whom are now aged or dead. Recently founded examples of museums and memorials include the United States Holocaust Memorial Museum (America's national institution for the documentation, study, and interpretation of Holocaust history); the Beth Shalom Holocaust Memorial Centre in Nottinghamshire, England; and a permanent exhibition housed in London's Imperial War Museum.

Aside from the former camps like Auschwitz, the major Holocaust shrine remains, however, *Yad Vashem*. This educational-memorial complex, situated on Memorial Hill in Jerusalem, is maintained as a religious site (for example, visitors are asked to cover their heads) and its name is derived from Isaiah 56:5, which promises 'a monument and a name', i.e. remembrance, to those who hold fast to the covenant with God. Foreign dignitaries visiting Israel tour *Yad Vashem* as a matter of course, to acknowledge Israel's identification with the victims of the *Shoah*.

The early emphasis of *Yad Vashem* was on resistance, especially the Warsaw ghetto uprising. It also projected a zionist understanding of Israel as the only true *locus* of Jewish continuity. Recently, growing attention has been paid to the life of European Jewry before the war, and to the cultural and human loss which resulted from the Nazi persecution. For example, in 1987 a Children's Memorial was opened. Its dark and cavernous space, lit only by reflected memorial candles, creates a sombre atmosphere in tribute to the one and a half million children who died during the *Shoah*. And in 1992, the Valley of the Communities – a kind of rock maze, with the names of annihilated settlements carved into the walls – was dedicated. It is the largest single monument at *Yad Vashem* and houses an important centre for the study of prewar Jewish life.

Just as some kind of memorial day has attained significance in the lives of many Jews, so pilgrimages to sites commemorating, or associated with, the *Shoah* have become something of a rite of passage for many North American, British and Israeli teenagers. These visits to former camps, or the sites of lost or dwindling Jewish communities, offer young adults a model of what it means to be Jewish which is quite different from that associated with *bar* or *bat mitzvah*, or confirmation – but one which in many respects confers no less a burden of responsibility on them than that conveyed by the traditional rituals. Survivor-guilt, a new-found awareness of Jewish identity, and the desire to prevent future genocides, are just some of the issues which Jewish teenagers are prompted to work through.

What are the implications for Judaism of the increasing prominence given to memory and pilgrimage? On one hand, remembrance of past events can be a spur to positive reconciliation between Jews and non-Jews. Many young Germans, for example, have little or no contact with Jews and scant knowledge of Judaism. Summer programmes (bringing together Jewish and non-Jewish students from Europe, Israel and America) allow the grandchildren of the wartime generation to confront the past together, and – perhaps - to attempt to move forward positively.

But there are also fears that the emphasis on *Shoah* may be damaging to the Jewish future. There are legitimate questions to ask about the morality of the growing commercialisation of the Holocaust. Auschwitz draws many casual tourists as well as reverential travellers to southern Poland; trans-global entertainments corporations make profits from films, books, and computer games that exploit the events of the *Shoah* for at least partly financial ends. To what extent does this trivialize the suffering of National Socialism's victims? At the same time, radical Jewish thinkers like Marc Ellis have critiqued what they regard as the political abuse of the Holocaust as a tool to 'organize and police the Jewish community' in

Israel and the United States. For Ellis, the Holocaust has been de-historicised in much popular discourse. By this he means that there is comparatively little in-depth discussion of the actual events. Instead, the *Shoah* has assumed a kind of iconic or paradigmatic status, becoming a reference point against which other sufferings and tragedies are measured (and found wanting). The practical consequence of this is a distorting mythologisation of contemporary Jewish realities, as those in *Diaspora* are made to feel guilty for not having done enough to prevent the Holocaust, and the message is conveyed that Israel, ever-threatened with 'a second holocaust', is therefore free of moral considerations that might inhibit its efforts to save itself.[13]

Ellis' views about the Holocaust and the need for Israel to move beyond Zionism, to a pluralistic outlook that offers all citizens, Jewish and Palestinian, 'a formal constitution and bill of rights', are controversial and would be rejected by many. Yet, as with the theological writings of Maybaum, Teitelbaum *et al.*, they are the opinions of a man who has been deeply challenged by the encounter with the *Shoah*. For Ellis, stepping beyond a model of Jewish life that equates Jewish 'innocence' and 'redemption' with a historical movement from 'Holocaust' to 'State of Israel' is also about the revival of Judaism's prophetic heritage, and a reaching out towards a future that is 'Jewish in context and efficacious in reality'.[14]

More widespread in their acceptance than the writings of Ellis are the fears that over-concentration on the *Shoah* in Jewish education and communal expression can lead to a neglect of the full extent of Jewish culture, and that young people in particular may be led to develop distorted understandings of Jewish identity. At worst, future generations may have little sense of active participation in the *continuing* story of Judaism - a religiously oriented lifestyle may be regarded as something belonging to an increasingly remote past. Orthodox rabbi Ephraim Oshry sums up the fears of some religious Jews concerning the potential distortion of Jewish identity and Judaism by Holocaust memorialisation:

> What does it mean when what we've retrieved from the past are sentimental curiosities which are nothing more than anthropological artifacts – fodder for the Jewish nostalgianiks whose relationship to Judaism is measured in terms of glass cases in a museum?[15]

Writing from a quite different perspective, scholar Arnold Eisen suggests that nostalgia is the most widespread reason for Jewish practice in America today.[16] Observance may attest to a desire to connect with an elusive past, a 'lost community'. The challenge for religiously committed Jews is to find ways to build upon the sense of longing for connectedness and community that encounter with the *Shoah* prompts in many young Jews today.

The State of Israel

Since its proclamation in May 1948, the State of Israel has faced acute problems of survival, on economic and military fronts. There have been numerous devaluations of the Israeli shekel, five Arab-Israeli wars and several periods of sporadic Palestinian *intifada* (uprising) in the years following the Declaration of Independence. Life in Israel, then, requires some form of sacrifice on the part of most of its citizens. Whilst emigration from Israel is not unusual, the continued energy and perseverance of most suggests that something other than individual satisfaction and material gain is at stake for residents.

An examination of Judaism's key texts reveals in part why Israel commands such commitment on the part of its Jewish inhabitants, who form around eighty per cent of the population. In the Bible, acquisition and possession of the land is inextricably bound up with the Jews' status as a chosen people, which is something of a paradox, given the universalizing tendencies manifest in scripture (the Noahide laws) and liturgy (the *alenu*). In Genesis 12:1-2, Abraham is told by God to travel to Canaan, where he will become 'a great nation'. Later, when the enslaved Hebrews are led from Egypt by Moses, their destination is once more the Promised Land:

> I am the LORD....I will take you to be My people, and I will be your God. And you shall know that I, the LORD, am your God who freed you from the labors of the Egyptians. I will bring you into the land that I swore to give to Abraham, Isaac, and Jacob, and I will give it to you for a possession (Exodus 6: 6-8)

The special character of the land of Israel is reflected in a host of *mitzvot* which can only be observed there, including the laws of sabbatical and jubilee years (mentioned below in the section on the Environment)

Sample Origins of Israelis, 2002

The countries of origin of the 120 members of the Fifteenth *Knesset* (Israeli parliament), which comprises 13 Israeli Arabs and 107 Jewish members.

Country of Birth	Number of *Knesset* Members
Brazil	1
Denmark	1
Germany	3
India	1
Iraq	3
Israel	74
Morocco	10
Poland	2
Romania	5
Tunisia	1
Former USSR	15

(source: *Knesset Members of the Fifteenth Knesset* - www.knesset.gov.il current in June 2002).

Whilst not representative of Israelis in general, these figures do illustrate vividly the newness (nearly 40% of members were born outside the country) and the diversity of modern Israel (members were born in the Americas, Asia, Africa, and Europe). They also attest to the increased confidence of Sephardi and Oriental Jewry within Israel (described in chapter three.) Forty years earlier, the Fourth *Knesset* had a small percentage of Israeli–born members; over 90% originated in European Ashkenazi communities. Jews born in North Africa (who mostly immigrated in the 1950s and 1960s) constitute nearly a tenth of members today. More recent immigrants represented in the *Knesset* include those from the former Soviet Union, most of whom immigrated in the 1990s. Their presence in government and administration contrasts with the absence of the *Beta Israel* (see Afterword) who immigrated in the 1980s and 1990s.

regulations relating to the harvest (Deuteronomy 26:1-11), and the system of Temple sacrifices. The Hebrew Bible teaches that God makes the land of Israel available to the people so that they may live in peace and justice.

The enforced exile from the land that followed the war with Rome in the first century CE was regarded as a monumental tragedy. Nationalistic opposition to Roman rule continued to fuel armed rebellions for some time later. In 132-135 CE a revolt was led by Simon Bar Kokhba, whom Rabbi Akiva, a prominent early sage, probably regarded as a king-messiah.[17] After Bar Kokhba's death, most early rabbis opposed direct military action, teaching that loss of the land was the result of Jewish sinfulness and that redemption in the form of resettlement would be brought about only by an eschatological messiah figure, who would be able to re-build the Temple and gather all nations into God's plan. The rabbis did, however, continue to stress the special sanctity of the land. The *Mishnah* (*m.Kelim* 1.6) says that 'the land of Israel is holier than any other land'. This, and other ideas drawn from Joel 4:2, fostered the view that Israel was the preferred place of residence for living Jews, and the ideal resting-place for the dead. (Some pious *Diaspora* Jews still try to arrange burial in Israel or have a small bag of soil from the land placed in their grave.)

In addition to its outplaying in rabbinic thought, love of the land of Israel or 'Zion' was expressed beautifully in songs, poetry, and art. The philosopher-poet Judah ha-Levi (author of the *Kuzari*, discussed in chapter five) believed that the redemption of the Jews would be brought about through their return to Israel. He eventually died in Egypt, *en route* to the land. This poem, which is rich in biblical imagery ('Zion'; 'Edom'), expresses ha-Levi's personal desire to make *aliyah*, or 'go up' to Israel. It evokes the traditional conviction that a life in *Diaspora* must inevitably also be one in *galut*, or exile from one's true home:

> My heart is in the East, and I in the depths of the West.
> My food has no taste. How can it be sweet?
> How can I fulfil my pledges and my vows,
> When Zion is in the power of Edom, and I in the fetters of Arabia?
> It will be nothing to me to leave all the goodness of Spain.
> So rich will it be to see the dust of the ruined sanctuary.[18]

Since Biblical times there have always been Jewish communities in the land of Israel, but for many centuries the population of the *yishuv* ('settlement') in Palestine was small. Most settlers were religiously motivated, and had left their *Diaspora* homelands out of a desire to live in a land which facilitated fuller observance of the *mitzvot*. Others had more unusual views. For example, when Rabbi Judah Hasid and his students made the journey from Poland in 1700, they did so expecting to witness the miraculous return to earth of Shabbatai Tzvi – a view not welcomed by existing *yishuv* residents.

The modern state of Israel is not just a fulfilment of ancient longings and dreams. In sharp contrast to the yearnings of ha-Levi, this poem, 'Tourists', by Yehuda Amichai (1924-2000) expresses the tensions felt by modern Israelis who cannot escape Jerusalem's status as a city of holiness and history, and yet also long to pursue a normal, everyday life there:

Tourists
Visits of condolence is all we get from them.
They squat at the Holocaust Memorial,
They put on grave faces at the Wailing Wall
And they laugh behind heavy curtains
In their hotels.
They have their pictures taken
Together with our famous dead
At Rachel's Tomb and Herzl's Tomb
And on the top of Ammunition Hill.
They weep over our sweet boys
And lust over our tough girls
And hang up their underwear
To dry quickly
In cool, blue bathrooms.
Once I sat on the steps by a gate at David's Tower, I placed my two heavy baskets at my side. A group of tourists was standing around their guide and I became their target marker.
"You see that man with the baskets? Just right of his head there's an arch from the Roman period. Just right of his head." "But he's moving, he's moving!"
I said to myself: redemption will come only if their guide tells them, "You see that arch from the Roman period? It's not important: but next to it, left and down a bit, there sits a man who's bought fruit and vegetables for his family."[19]

In the late nineteenth century, nationalism and the persistence of antisemitism gave added impetus to those Jews who wished for a 'return' to the land of Israel. Dismissing the hope of Jewish equality in an egalitarian society as unrealizable, Zionists argued that only a national Jewish homeland would solve the 'Jewish problem', and overcome antisemitism. Their views gained credibility following the Dreyfus affair. When French Jew Alfred Dreyfus was wrongly imprisoned for betraying his country to Germany, it became apparent that, despite emancipation, anti-Jewish prejudice persisted, even in the land that was popularly regarded as the birthplace of the Enlightenment. Journalist Theodor Herzl (1860-1904) the founder of political Zionism, formulated his programme for a state of Jews after reporting on the Dreyfus trial:

> The Jewish Question still exists....This is true in every country, and will remain true even in those most highly civilized – France itself is not an exception – till the Jewish Question finds a solution on a political basis....We are a people – One People. We have honestly striven everywhere to merge ourselves in the social life of surrounding communities, and to preserve only the faith of our fathers. It has not been permitted to us....In countries where we have lived for centuries we are still cried down as strangers; and often by those whose ancestors were not yet domiciled in the land where Jews had already made experience of suffering....
>
> We are one people – our enemies have made us one in our despite....Yes, we are strong enough to form a state, and a model state.[20]

Many early Zionists were religious, but not all religious Jews were (or are) Zionists. *Charedi* groups like *Neturei Karta*, led today by Rabbi Amram Blau, base their opposition to the modern state on the grounds that Zionism seeks to create and maintain a Jewish state through ordinary political, as opposed to messianic, efforts. They refuse to participate in Israeli elections and in some cases decline state money such as social security payments. There is also a tradition of liberal religious critique of Israel, based on the idea that Judaism is a *universal* religion, and (especially in the early years of the movement, in the nineteenth century) a fear that nationalism could incite antisemitism. A significant British proponent of anti-Zionism was Claude Montefiore (1858-1938), one of the founders of Liberal Judaism. He argued that Jews should be seen as a religious community, not an ethnic one, and that 'Zionism and Zionistic activities

... depress Judaism by putting nationality first and religion second.' [21]

To many Jews today, including Liberal and other Progressive Jews, Montefiore's anti-Zionism seems dated. He died in 1938, before the Nazis implemented 'the Final Solution'. However, Montefiore was correct in his recognition that what characterizes both religious and secular Zionists is the recourse to essentially non-religious conceptions of Jewish national identity. Modern Zionism developed in the context of post-Enlightenment Europe. It is not a straightforward extension of the traditional Jewish yearning for the land of Israel. Zionism draws crucially on modern concepts like that of the nation state. The increasingly large numbers of Jews who made *aliyah* from the mid-nineteenth century onwards were predominantly influenced by the rise of a secular Jewish nationalism.

Israel is a Jewish state in the sense that its population is predominantly Jewish. It is also a secular state, a democratic republic in which justice is administered in municipal courts by judges appointed by a President. Under the provisions of the Foundations of Law Act (1980):

> Where a court finds that a question requiring a decision cannot be answered by reference to an enactment or a judicial precedent or by way of analogy, it shall decide the same in the light of the principles of freedom, justice, equity and peace of the heritage of Israel,[22]

which could be interpreted to imply a desire to base new legislation on *halakhah*. However, the significance of this measure is symbolic (it superseded a pre-Independence linkage of Israeli law with the English legal system) and *halakhah* has little *de facto* role in the Israeli legal system. In practical terms, Judaism's official involvement in the Israeli polity, overseen by the Ministry of Religious Affairs, is restricted to four fairly discrete areas. First, Sabbaths and festivals are public holidays. Second, kosher food is served at public events and in state institutions. Third, the state school system operates both a National Secular and a National Religious stream. And finally, personal status law is determined by rabbinical courts, as was the case during earlier British and Ottoman rule.[23] (The implications of this final point are discussed at some length in chapter four and the afterword of this book.) At other times, however, the religious sensibilities of carefully observant Jews have proved hard for particular governments to ignore. Members of the *Knesset* or Parliament are elected by a form of proportional representation that has tended to result in volatile coalition administrationns. Some of these have collapsed, or come close to doing so, when secular members have acted in a manner offensive to their Orthodox partners.

Outside the realm of policy, classical Jewish sources, which are for the most part religious ones, provide the framework for much Israeli life and culture. The modern Hebrew used in Israel grew out of a language kept alive in liturgical and other literary usages by observant Jews over the centuries. The national symbol (the *menorah*) has unequivocally biblical origins, as does the national flag. The design of the latter (two blue stripes on a white background, with a *magen David*, the 'shield' or star of David, in the middle) also evokes the traditional *tallit* or shawl worn by Jewish males at prayer. On a more personal level, some Biblical names have undergone a revival in the new state (although note the discussion of naming in chapter four). Names like Boaz (a Biblical ancestor of David) and Gideon (one of the Biblical Judges) can represent both a rejection of Yiddish culture, perceived by many Zionists as weak and passive, and an interpretation of the new state as a renewal of Jewish history.

Despite widespread secularity, Judaism is likely to remain a significant feature of Israeli life, informing the cultural milieu, and exercising a determining influence in the lives of a significant number of the Jewish population. But although Judaism is important in shaping Israeli life, Jewish religious expression has also been profoundly shaped by the Israeli experience. Arguably, life in the State of Israel has turned out to be as much about re-defining what Jewish life is as it is about the building of a nation.

Israel's existence inevitably raises questions about the nature and locus of Judaism's continuity, beyond those relating to the sheer survival of its Jewish citizens. Once established, the State of Israel has transformed the basic facts of Jewish existence – its politics, demography and religion. This change has occurred within Israel itself and to a lesser but significant extent, in *Diaspora* as well. One clear example of the impact on Judaism in Israel is the emergence of an Israeli civil religion, the re-definition of traditional religious symbols and practices in the light of statehood. In sociological terms, a civil religion is a commonly recognized set of public beliefs and rites that integrate society, legitimate the social order, and mobilize the population on behalf of certain goals. Liebman and Don-Yehiya argue that in Israel a civil religion exists which blends Israeliness, Jewishness and the religious traditions of Judaism. It has its own beliefs

(Israel is the guarantor of Jewish security; the Jewish people's destiny is moral statehood), symbols (the flag and national symbol, mentioned above), sacred sites (Jerusalem and Masada, as well as memorials like *Yad Vashem*), and so on. There are also special festival days, such as *Yom Ha-Atzma'ut*, the anniversary of the proclamation of Israel's independence, on 5th *Iyyar*. (This day was declared a religious holiday by the Israeli Chief Rabbinate, and is marked by special prayers in the synagogue, and general patriotic festivities elsewhere.) What is at stake in the practice of Israeli civil religion is not simply the attachment of new meanings to older forms, however. Civil religion evidences a shift in Israel from substantive to more openly functional forms of religion; a move away from traditional Jewish forms of meaning to newer ones that are more readily suited to meet the needs of a young but incredibly diverse nation.

The concept of civil religion is not universally accepted by sociologists. Classical civil religion theory is grounded in consensus-oriented views of societies and some social scientists prefer to emphasise the forces of competition and difference. It is certainly not at all clear that Israelis share common attitudes and goals. For example, the early emphasis on the Holocaust in Israeli society may in part reflect the political dominance of its Ashkenazi citizens, which persisted into the late twentieth century. Similarly, groups like *Neturei Karta* regard days like *Yom ha-Atzma'ut* as indicative of the wrong-headedness of the Zionist project, and may even protest its observance by displaying black mourning-flags outside their homes. Finally, there are also significant non-Jewish minorities in Israel. Baha'is, Christians, Druze and Muslims are unlikely to relate to historically Jewish symbols in the same manner as do the majority of the Israeli population.

At the same time as Judaism is undergoing a process of re-definition in Israel, demographic changes taking place in *Diaspora* may in turn affect the orientation of some religious groups towards the state. American Jewry has for some time been affected by high rates of intermarriage. By 1990, fifty-seven per cent of Jews married a partner not born Jewish.[24] Most non-Jewish parties in these marriages do not convert to Judaism (perhaps ten per cent do). For the majority of American Jews who are involved in or born into inter-marriage or conversion-marriage, Jewish identity is arguably likely to be seen as increasingly de-ethnicised – more a matter of personal choice than of the heritage one is born into. The implications of this demographic trend are as yet unclear, but it is *possible* that religious

Jews in America will at some point in the future have less of a sense of attachment to the predominantly secular Jews of Israel than is currently the case.

The Environment

The *Shoah* and State of Israel do not pose questions for Jews and Judaism alone. As was mentioned in chapter five, the creation of Israel in 1948 and subsequent Jewish sovereignty over Jerusalem brought Jews into conflict with the world of Islam, which has a strong geo-political dimension. And the actions of many church members during the *Shoah* means that the events of the Holocaust arguably pose as significant a challenge to Christianity as they do to Judaism.

Just as events which are commonly perceived as Jewish concerns are of great import for other communities, so Judaism is not isolated from global concerns. Pressing issues raised by developments in medical science will be discussed later. In the last twenty years or so, ecological challenges have also asserted themselves. Most Jews live in industrialized societies, but increasingly it is becoming clear that even such 'advanced' countries cannot escape the effects of modern patterns of consumption. Deforestation, desertification, lessening of biodiversity (decreasing range of species and habitats), and ozone depletion impact at the global level. Growing concern for the environment generally also prompts specific questions about human exploitation of other species. Is the hunting of animals permissible? Is a vegetarian diet the only one that makes moral and ecological sense? These are some of the questions that Judaism today seeks to address.

The starting point for a Jewish religious response to environmental concerns is the conviction that the physical world was created by God, and that, in considering this work, God 'found it very good' (Genesis 1:31). Like the story of Noah's Ark in Genesis 7 and 8, the accounts of Creation show an attention to the existence of different kinds of organisms, as do the laws of *kashrut* introduced in chapter four. Coupled with this awareness of biodiversity is the conviction that human beings are at the apex of Creation, because they alone are made in the image of God (Genesis 1:27). Genesis chapter 2 outlines the rights and responsibilities entailed in humanity's special status. While Adam's rulership

The Western Wall, Jerusalem: In contrast to the colourful Dome of the Rock, a bare stone wall is Judaism's most holy site. The Western Wall is part of the retaining wall built round the Second Temple. According to rabbinic tradition the *Shekinah* (Divine Presence) never deserted it; during the Ottoman period it became a pilgrimage site.

Today, the nearby plaza functions as an outdoor synagogue, divided into two areas, one for men, and a smaller one for women. There is a steady stream of visitors but it is busiest on Friday evenings when local *yeshiva* boys celebrate the arrival of *Shabbat*. In the foreground there are a number of police vehicles. For Jews, this area is the Temple Mount, but for Muslims it is the site of Ishmael's near-sacrifice, and the rock associated with Muhammad's ascent into the heavens. Disputes over the territory mean that it has become an obstacle to peace between the two peoples.

of Eden is symbolised by his power to name the other animals (including woman) he is placed in Eden 'to till it *and tend it*' (Genesis 2:15) implying that stewardship, not exploitation, of the created world is what is intended by God. These themes are reiterated and developed in later Jewish literature. For example, Deuteronomy 20:19-20 says, 'when in your war against a city you have to besiege it…only trees that you know do not yield food may be destroyed'. Whereas in its initial context this injunction is a piece of pragmatism rather than a rallying cry for environmentalism, the rabbis expanded the phrase *bal tashchit* (do not destroy, or more accurately, not to destroy) to imply a respect for all creation, and the need to avoid wasteful use of resources. For the fourteenth century Rabbi Aaron Ha-Levi of Barcelona, the concept of *bal tashchit:*

> is the way of the devout and those of good deeds – they love peace, rejoice in that which benefits people and brings them to *Torah*, they never destroy even a grain of mustard, and are upset at any destruction they see. If only they can save anything from being spoilt they spare no effort to do so.[25]

In its linking of reverence for the natural world and observance of *Torah*, Aaron ha-Levi's approach was not new. The Babylonian *Talmud* suggests that, even if humanity is at the high point of the hierarchy of creation, people can learn from the behaviour of animals: 'R. Yohanan observed, If the *Torah* had not been given we could have learnt modesty from the cat, honesty from the ant, chastity from the dove and good manners from the cock' (*Eruvin* 100b). Other texts stress links between observance of the *mitzvot*, careful use of the land (of Israel) and divine favour. Just as domesticated animals are to rest on *Shabbat*, so Leviticus introduces the concept of a sabbath or rest day for farmland, neglect of which will result in exile and loss:

> When you enter the land that I assign to you, the land shall observe a sabbath of the LORD. Six years you may sow your field and six years you may prune your vineyard and gather in the yield. But in the seventh year the land shall have a sabbath of complete rest, a sabbath of the LORD….
>
> ….If…you disobey Me…I will lay your cities in ruin and make your sanctuaries desolate….Then shall the land make up for its sabbath years throughout the time that it is desolate and you are in the land of your

enemies; then shall the land rest and make up for its sabbath years. (Leviticus 25:2-26:34)

Some *Charedi* groups today avoid consumption of produce grown in soil by Jewish farmers in Israel during the seventh year. The *Tanakh* also outlines the concept of a Jubilee year, when all leased land reverts to its original owners and slaves are set free (Leviticus 25:23). (The *Tanakh* and classic rabbinic texts tolerate slavery, but contain measures to ensure its limitation, and to require that slaves are, by ancient standards, treated humanely.)

As with a range of other issues, the creation of the State of Israel has led to a quickening of Jewish discussion and action on environmental matters. Israel is located in a region prone to soil erosion, desertification and water shortage. From the beginning of the twentieth century it has been subjected to increasing population pressures and rapid industrial growth, both of which could have a negative impact on the natural environment. Moreover, problems have in some cases been exacerbated by attempts at land development. For example, the draining of the Huleh wetland, which had previously acted as a natural filter for the Kinneret (Sea of Galilee), led to silting and rapid algae growth. It is therefore not surprising that the environment and conservation are significant items on the Israeli political agenda.[26]

There are a host of nature reserves and environmental agencies in Israel. Probably the best known of these is the Jewish National Fund (JNF). Founded at the Fifth Zionist Congress in Switzerland in 1901, the JNF was established to purchase land in Israel. Its blue collection boxes were ubiquitous in many pre-war Jewish homes: at one level, the fund was a practical means of furthering the Zionist dream of statehood, but it also tapped into much older ideas about the connection between the Jewish people and the Land. Today it owns roughly an eighth of the land in Israel and operates a number of projects including water-recycling and reservoir development, and reforestation. Tree-planting is a vital means of preventing further soil erosion, providing shade and countering the growth in carbon dioxide emissions. But for many people, sponsoring a tree in the Promised Land powerfully links the world of nature with important religious concepts. The Jewish National Fund also evokes Biblical law explicitly in its practice of leasing property to individuals and groups, rather than selling it to them in perpetuity.

The emphasis placed on tree-planting and the environment generally in Israel has prompted a revival in the fortunes of one minor religious festival, the New Year for Trees (sometimes known as Arbor Day). In biblical times farmers in Israel were obligated to tithe their crops and set aside a proportion of the annual yield for the poor and the *kohanim* or priests. The date from which tithes were counted was the fifteenth of *Shevat*, in hebrew, *Tu bi-Shevat*. In the twentieth and twenty-first centuries, this day has been re-cast as a celebration of the natural, created world, and a time to demonstrate commitment to responsible stewardship. In Israel, especially encouraged by the JNF, and increasingly also in *Diaspora*, there has been a revival of the practice of planting a fruit tree on the festival day.

Israeli and *Diaspora* Jews share in the wider global concerns about environmental pollution. For secular and Progressive Jews, halakhic precedence for this interest may be desirable but it is certainly not necessary. Perhaps surprisingly, however, Jewish legal sources provide considerable resources which may be extrapolated from ancient Israel to the contemporary situation. The concept of *bal tashchit* has already been mentioned. Similarly, the Biblical book of Numbers envisages town planning to include a 'green belt' around cities (35:2-5). Rabbinic texts including the *Mishnah*, *Talmud*, and *Shulchan Arukh* also discuss the measures necessary to ensure the minimisation of water and atmospheric pollution, and the abatement of noise. Modern Orthodoxy has sought to capitalise on these resources in its efforts to produce policy documents and *responsa* which are 'environmentally friendly'. In Britain, the Board of Deputies Working Group on the Environment promotes this task. However, as Norman Solomon points out, for the carefully observant Jew it is on ethical and ritual grounds, rather than in the interests of conservation *per se*, that decisions on environmental matters ultimately rest. Thus the traditional Jewish opposition to hunting animals for sport has a firmly halakhic basis. Such activity is frowned on insofar as it is destructive and wasteful of natural resources (see above on *bal tashchit*), causes needless distress to the animal, produces a non-kosher carcass, and distracts one from the holy task of *Torah* study. Extrapolating from Leviticus 18:3 (where the Israelites are commanded to refrain from the sexual practices of Egypt and Canaan) it is also argued that hunting for pleasure should be avoided as, since medieval times, it has been the preserve of the wealthy, landed non-Jewish sections of society. To engage in hunting would, in effect, be a form of assimilation to non-Jewish norms.[27]

Developments in Medical Science

Advances in health care and the biological sciences have generated new questions and dilemmas for Jews seeking to pursue the halakhic life. In dealing with these, several thousand *responsa* have been issued, and centres of Jewish education like Yeshiva University in New York and Jerusalem's Hebrew University appoint staff in medical ethics, to explore issues within a Jewish framework. The significance of the challenges posed by modern medicine should not be underestimated. As has been noted throughout this book, the *halakhah* has always needed to be re-applied as situations arise that differ markedly from the ones in which traditional rulings were expounded. But some recent developments, such as genetics, changing ideas about death, and *in vitro* fertilization have even further reaching implications, predicated as they are upon notions about human nature and destiny which differ profoundly from traditional Jewish ones.

Despite the *Mishnah*'s assertion that 'the best among physicians is destined for Gehenna', (*m. kiddushin* 4:14) many famous halakhists, including Maimonides, combined their *Torah* studies with a medical profession. In more recent years, a number of significant developments in, for example, British medical science were the result of the work of Jewish refugees from Nazi Germany.[28] The *Talmud* states that all laws, with the exception of the prohibitions against bloodshed, idolatry, incest and adultery may be over-ridden in order to preserve life (*Sanhedrin* 74a), and even forbids scholars from living in a town which has no doctor to care for its sick. There is, then, a general welcoming in Judaism of improved means of disease prevention, detection, and treatment. Developments in obstetrics and gynaecology, and in transplantation and genetic science, pose the greatest practical and philosophical challenges to traditional Judaism, and it is these areas which will now be considered.

Judaism teaches that nature was created by God for humanity to use to its benefit. But it also holds that any exploitation of the natural world must be responsible; humans are only the stewards of a Creation that is ultimately owned by God. Perhaps unsurprisingly, then, artificial insemination (AI) and *in vitro* fertilization (IVF) are regarded with caution by Orthodox Judaism and a large body of rabbinic literature is devoted to the topics.[29] There is a general consensus that both procedures are permissible where semen and ovum come from married Jewish partners, the insemination is performed outside the woman's period of ritual impurity (the period of menstruation and the seven 'clear' days that follow it), and pregnancy could not otherwise be achieved. A few Orthodox authorities oppose AI and IVF on the grounds that the masturbation necessary to produce the sperm is prohibited (Genesis 38:9-10) but most agree that, since the act is intended to assist conception rather than to prevent it, it is permitted. By extension, sperm banking by men who anticipate infertility following chemotherapy treatment is also regarded as permissible, but is not mandatory.[30] Couples are, however, usually required to undertake a waiting period or to obtain medical proof of the absolute necessity of the treatment before they proceed.

In many cases of assisted conception, either sperm or egg comes from a donor. This is generally because one of the intended social parents is unable to produce sperm or egg, or because adhesions or scars on the ovaries make egg collection difficult or dangerous.[31] Since use of donor material does not involve sexual intercourse, the birth mother is not considered by most rabbis to have committed adultery, and any resulting children will not be *mamzerim* (singular, *mamzer*, 'illegitimate'[32]). But many strictly Orthodox authorities consider the use of donors in AI or IVF to be prohibited, for a variety of reasons grounded in *halakhah*.

The general policy in many countries of preserving the anonymity of sperm and egg donors sits uneasily with *Torah*, which places a large emphasis on biological inheritance when determining an individual's status. For example, many rabbis, especially in Israel, believe that the processes of gestation and parturition, rather than genetic inheritance, are determinative of a child's halakhic status. Being delivered of a Jewish woman makes one legally Jewish. But a child carried by a Jewish woman but conceived with a donor egg from a non-Jew is held by some to require a formal conversion. Similarly, a considerable body of rabbinic opinion judges that children conceived with a Jewish donor's sperm are halakhically his (in respect of inheritance, support, custody and other laws).[33] Moreover, use of unknown egg or sperm means that the AI or IVF child runs the risk (albeit a small one) of committing incest with the donor's other offspring.

Since many of the halakhic disagreements centre around the anonymity of the donor, Conservative Judaism permits donor insemination subject to the couple's knowing either the identity of the donor, or information about the donor's genetic make-up and character. Prospective parents are also required to undertake counselling in order to work through issues that may arise from their differing genetic relationship to the child. Reform and Liberal Judaism leave family planning issues to the couple concerned. However, one recent guide to Reform Judaism in Britain suggests that donor insemination be avoided, because of its potentially harmful emotional consequences for parents and child, and that adoption is a preferable option for couples who cannot have children themselves.[34] Perhaps surprisingly, one of the most radical solutions to infertility was proposed in a *responsum* from Orthodox Rabbi Moshe Feinstein, who argued that use of donor sperm was permissible if the donor was *not* Jewish. Under pressure, this judgement was later withdrawn, but doctors report that, in America, traditional Jews prefer non-Jewish sperm donors.[35] Similarly, in Israel, where the government encourages citizens to have children, single mothers are not stigmatized, and fertility treatment is state funded, special non-Jewish sperm banks are used by the carefully observant. In such arrangements, the Jewish mother ensures the halakhic status of the offspring, and the possibility of their committing incest in the future is drastically lessened. At the same time, potential difficulties in relation to inheritance are averted as the *halakhah* simply does not acknowledge the existence of the non-Jewish biological father.

Here, in the area of human fertility, is a clear example of the ways in which new technologies pose questions that challenge the nature of Jewish continuity in the twenty-first century. The high value traditionally placed on children in Jewish communities, together with the tendency to delay the decision to start a family amongst Jews in North America and Western Europe, means that more and more Jewish couples are likely to want to overcome the halakhic restrictions (by meeting or ignoring them) and use AI or IVF to conceive. But any resulting proliferation, if not of *mamzerim*, then of children of uncertain halakhic status, may create increased boundaries between different Jewish sub-cultures, with some Orthodox and *Charedi* groups being disallowed from marrying the members of other denominations. (See also Afterword.)

When Louise Brown became the first child to be born as a result of IVF in 1978, it had already been twenty-one years since the first heart transplant.[36] Kidney transplants had been undertaken since the 1950s, and corneal grafting to restore sight to a diseased or damaged eye had been pioneered successfully in 1905. Like AI and IVF, organ transplantation has raised many ethical, legal and political problems. Is it responsible to enhance a seriously ill patient's life in this way, particularly when other therapies may be available? Does the removal of organs from living or dead donors require permission? If so, from whom and by what means – voluntarily, or in response to request? How should the considerable costs of the procedures be met? By society? The patient? Such dilemmas reflect the extent to which transplant surgery has brought into question the whole status of the body: is it a commodity, disposable like any other piece of property? Or, does the donation or vending of organs and tissue reify the body in a dangerous and de-humanising way? Jewish religious thought is certainly not untouched by these general concerns. But the halakhic stance on organ transplantation centres around two key issues: the risk posed to the living donor's life; and the definition of death, which raises particularly acute problems when applied to heart transplants.

In the first of these cases, the *halakhah* is fairly straightforward. If there is no risk, or small risk to life, then there is no prohibition on organ donation, provided that the donor's consent is freely given. A potential objection to donation could be made on the grounds that such a procedure transgresses the command to 'take utmost care and watch yourselves scrupulously' (Deuteronomy 4:9; 4:15). However, other elements in Jewish tradition suggest that one may undertake some risk to save the life of another, by (for example) donating a kidney:

> The Jerusalem Talmud concludes that one is obligated to place oneself even into a possibly dangerous situation [to save another's life]. It seems logical that the reason is that the one's [death without intervention, i.e., the kidney recipient] is a certainty, whereas [the donor's] is only a possibility.[37]

A majority of *responsa* allow, but do not require, live donors to subject themselves to a degree of risk in order to save the life of a dying person. Most religious and secular Jews would agree that someone who donates an organ in this way has performed a true *mitzvah*.

Whilst many kidney transplants use organs from living donors, most organs used in transplant surgery are from brainstem-dead, heart-beating cadaveric donors, from whom multiple organs are taken. These donations present Jews who seek to live in accordance with *halakhah* with problems of the most serious order. In chapter four, the prohibitions against desecrating the corpse and delaying burial were discussed. These rules, which would seemingly count against organ removal, may be over-ridden in the attempt to preserve life. Traditionally, this principle has been invested with tremendous plasticity, and many authorities will permit the removal even of the cornea, not usually regarded as a life-sustaining organ, on the grounds that a blind person may fall and be killed. But heart transplants remain highly controversial in carefully observant circles. As discussed in chapter four, Jewish law traditionally defines death as the cessation of respiration and absence of a heartbeat. But, because only a heart that is collected from a donor whilst still beating can be used in transplant surgery, the procedure usually requires that the donor is attached to a respirator prior to the organ's removal, preservation and chilling (cardioplegia). The halakhic question then arises: is it permissible to prolong artificially the 'life' of the donor in order to facilitate heart transplantation, and subsequently to shut off the donor's respirator? Such a query was posed by the late former Chief Rabbi of Britain, Immanuel Jakobovits, shortly after the first heart transplant operation was carried out in South Africa in 1967. The *responsum* issued by Rabbi Yaakov Yitzchock Weiss, condemned the procedure as murder. Other concerns relate to the recipient of the new heart. What is his or her status in the period between the removal of the diseased heart and the implantation of the new one? Because the heart is regarded as the seat of life, one's *chezkat chayyim* or 'hold on life' is arguably lost at this point in the procedure.[38] Is he or she halakhically dead? Has his or her spouse therefore been bereaved? Is remarriage required once the patient is alive again? Similar questions apply to open heart surgery, where the patient's own heart is temporarily disconnected from his or her circulatory system.

A noticeable minority of Orthodox authorities regards these problems as rendering heart transplantation as at best morally repugnant, and at worst, doubly murderous of donor and recipient. However, in 1987 the Israeli Chief Rabbinate ruled that brain-stem death may be a halakhically valid definition, on the grounds that it is the brain-stem which controls respiration.[39] This move has allowed heart transplantation in Israeli hospitals, and more widely amongst the religiously observant Jewish population. The development of totally artificial hearts for transplantation into dying patients may also offer hope to those needing surgery which is acceptable within the framework of Jewish law, since at the very least it would obviate the difficulties linked to organ collection.

Within the last decade, developments in genetics have brought medical science closer to the goal of being able to eliminate or radically ameliorate experience of a number of diseases, including some of those currently tackled by transplantation. The diagnosis of genetic disease (including the preimplantation screening of IVF embryos, testing of embryos and foetuses *in utero*, and diagnosis of an individual's predisposition to genetic disease) and gene therapy (the 'engineering' of genetic change in living subjects) are amongst the procedures that have become possible in the industrialized nations where most Jews live. The number and availability of new genetic techniques is likely to increase in the future, especially in view of the recent completion of the project to map the human genome or chromosomal blueprint. As would be expected, given the diversity of Judaism in the modern era, a range of halakhic and extra-halakhic factors come into play in debates surrounding genetic science.

The concept of heredity is found in a number of Judaism's classical sources. In Genesis 31:10, Jacob is aware of the transmission of characteristics from animal parents to offspring. The *Talmud* rules that a man may not marry a woman whose family members suffer from epilepsy or leprosy, on the grounds that these diseases may pass to any children (*Yevamot* 64b) whilst marriage between individuals with diverse physical characteristics is praised (*Bekorot* 45b) indicating that the early sages had a concept of eugenics through selective mating. The theological idea that Jews particpate in *tikkun olam*, the repairing or completion of the world, can also be held to imply that responsible genetic science is a legitimate pursuit. In Britain, a member of the Chief Rabbi's cabinet welcomed the government's recent decision to permit the regulated cloning of embryos, stating that 'the spirit of Jewish law welcomes any technological advances which have the potential of enhancing human life'.[40] Genetic science also brings practical benefits. Like many national, ethnic and other population groupings, different Jewish communities seem to have a genetic predisposition to certain conditions. Among Ashkenazi Jewry, these include certain forms of breast cancer, and Tay-Sachs disease. Tay-Sachs is a congenital disorder in which an enzymal deficiency leads to progressive mental and motor deterioration, resulting in death at about three years of age. Approximately one in thirty Ashkenazim and one in three hundred non-Jews carries the recessive Tay-Sachs gene. Therefore, an Ashkenazi Jew has a much higher risk of having children with the disease than is generally the case, especially if he or she marries another Jew.[41]

Screening for the Tay-Sachs gene is welcomed by the Jewish community. A *responsum* of Rabbi Moshe Feinstein summarises the general attitude:

> ...it is advisable for one preparing to be married, to have himself [sic] tested. It is also proper to publicize the fact, via newspapers and other media, that such a test is available. It is clear and certain that absolute secrecy must be maintained to prevent anyone from learning the result of such a test performed on another. The physician must not reveal these to anyone...these tests must be performed in private, and consequently, it is not proper to schedule these tests in larger groups as, for example, in Yeshivas, schools, or similar institutions. [42]

In fact, some mass screening programmes do take place, arranged by communal organisations. But care is taken to ensure that participation is voluntary.

Despite the availability of tests, pregnancies of course still occur in which the genetic profile of the foetus is unknown: one or more parent may have failed to go for screening. Moreover, for the observant Orthodox, the probability that some children may be born with Tay-Sachs or any other genetic condition does not permit a couple to ignore the *mitzvah* of procreation. In such instances, amniocentesis and early abortion of an affected foetus is permitted by some, but not all, halakhic authorities. Traditionally, abortion is sanctioned in Jewish law only where the mother's life is at stake, or where continued pregnancy poses a serious threat to her physical or mental health. Other factors, such as the ability to support the child financially, or its likely state of health once born, are not admissible. Most authorities do not therefore allow the abortion of a Tay-Sachs child. But in a creative decision born of compassion, Rabbi Saul Israeli (Jerusalem Rabbinical Court) and medical ethicist Rabbi Eliezar Waldenberg have suggested that the anxiety caused to a woman carrying such a child is sufficient to permit an abortion should one be sought: 'The present knowledge that the child will deteriorate and die in infancy, although the birth itself will be safe for her, gives her genuine mental anguish now'.[43]

Screening and amniocentesis become unnecessary where successful cures are developed. Since Tay-Sachs is linked to the deficiency of a specific enzyme, it seems theoretically possible to develop and administer a synthetic substitute and thereby control its symptoms. This is likely to be especially welcomed by those Orthodox and *Charedi* groups which do not favour contraception or abortion. Gene therapy, the introduction of properly functioning genes to correct the effect of defective ones, is also on the horizon. Much more debate is needed on what the implications of genetic science are for Jewish continuity. But it seems likely that ways will be found for religious Jews of all denominations to gain positive benefit from research and interventions that are carefully and responsibly undertaken.

Notes

[1] J. Sacks, *Will We Have Jewish Grandchildren?: Jewish Continuity and How to Achieve It*, Vallentine Mitchell, 1994.

[2] R. Rubenstein, *After Auschwitz: Radical Theology and Contemporary Judaism*, New York: Bobbs-Merrill, 1966, p. 153.

[3] Y. Eliach, 'The Holocaust: A Response to Catastrophe Within a Traditional Jewish Framework', in Y. Gutman and G. Greif (eds), *The Historiography of the Holocaust Period: Proceedings of the Fifth Yad Vashem International Historical Conference, Jerusalem, March 1983*, Jerusalem: Yad Vashem, 1988, p. 731.

[4] See Neusner and Avery-Peck (eds), *Judaism*, pp. 246-247.

[5] N. Solomon, *Judaism and World Religion*, Macmillan, 1991, p. 181.

[6] E. Berkovits, *Faith After the Holocaust*, New York: Ktav, 1973; I. Maybaum, *The Face of God After Auschwitz*, Amsterdam: Polak and Van Gennep, 1965.

[7] E. L. Fackenheim, *The Jewish Return to History: Reflections in the Age of Auschwitz and a New Jerusalem*, New York: Schocken, 1978, pp. 22-24.

[8] N. Glazer, *American Judaism*, Chicago: University of Chicago Press, 1957, p. 143.

[9] D. Marmur, *Beyond Survival: Reflections on the Future of Judaism*, Darton, Longman and Todd, 1982.

[10] D. Marmur, 'The Future of the Jews', in J. A. Romain (ed.), *Renewing the Vision: Rabbis Speak Out on Modern Jewish Issues*, SCM Press, 1996, p. 175.

[11] R. Gordis, *Judaic Ethics for a Lawless World*, New York: Jewish Theological Seminary, 1986, p. 112.

[12] J. Neusner, *Death and Birth of Judaism: The Impact of Christianity, Secularism and the Holocaust on Jewish Faith*, New York: Basic Books, 1987, p. 280.

[13] M. H. Ellis, *Beyond Innocence and Redemption: Confronting the Holocaust and Israeli Power: Creating a Moral Future for the Jewish People*, San Francisco: Harper and Row, 1990, pp. 36-37.

[14] Ibid. pp. 192-193.

[15] Oshry, *Responsa from the Holocaust*, p. viii.

[16] Eisen, *Rethinking Modern Judaism*, p. 14.

[17] Grabbe, *Judaism*, Vol. 2, pp. 579-581.

[18] D. Goldstein (ed.), *The Jewish Poets of Spain, 900-1250*, Harmondsworth: Penguin, 1965, p.128.

[19] 'Tourists' from *Great Tranquility: Questions and Answers* by Yehuda Amichai, translated by Glenda Abramson and Tudor Parfitt, copyright ©1983 by Yehudi Amichai, is reprinted by permission of HarperCollins Publishers inc.

[20] Mendes-Flohr and Reinharz, *Jews in the Modern World*, pp. 422-423.

[21] 1918 paper, in E. Kessler (ed.), *An English Jew: The Life and Writings of Claude Montefiore*, rev. ed., Vallentine Mitchell, 2002, p. 143.

[22] Hecht *et al.*, *Introduction to Jewish Law*, p. 411.

[23] N. Solomon, *Judaism and World Religion*, p. 119.

[24] S. Sharot, 'Judaism and Jewish Ethnicity: Changing Interrelationships and Differentiations in the Diaspora and Israel', in E. Krauz and G. Tulea (eds), *Jewish Survival: The Identity Problem at the Close of the Twentieth Century*, Transaction Publshers, 1998, p. 96.

[25] Quoted in N. Solomon, 'Attitudes to nature', in S. Kunin, *Themes and Issues in Judaism*, Cassell, 2000, p. 231.

[26] A. Rose, 'The Environment: Israel's Remarkable Story', p. 86 and U. N. Safriel, 'The Regional and Global Significance of Environmental Protection, Nature and Conservation and Ecological Research in Israel,' p. 93, both in A. Rose (ed.), *Judaism and Ecology*, Cassell, 1992.

[27] N. Solomon, 'Attitudes to Nature,' pp. 228-229.

[28] D. Pyke, 'Contributions by German Emigrés to British Medical Science', *Quarterly Journal of Medicine* 93 (2000), 487-495.

[29] See E. N. Dorff and L. E. Newman (eds), *Contemporary Jewish Ethics and Morality: A Reader*, Oxford: Oxford University Press, 1995; and F. Rosner, *Modern Medicine and Jewish Ethics*, second edition, New York: Yeshiva University Press, 1991.

[30] J. D. Bleich, 'Sperm Banking in Anticipation of Infertility', in E. Feldman and J. B. Wolowelsky (eds), *Jewish Law and The New Reproductive Technologies*, Hoboken: Ktav, 1997, pp. 139-154.

[31] R. Winston, *The IVF Revolution: The Definitive Guide to Assisted Reproductive Techniques*, Vermilion, 2000, pp. 4-5.

[32] A child born as a result of incest, or an adulterous relationship between a married woman and a man other than her husband, is a *mamzer*. *Mamzerim* may not marry legitimate Jews, and the status passes down the generations. Progressive Judaism no longer recognises the status.

[33] Rosner, *Modern Medicine and Jewish Ethics*, p. 110.

[34] E. N. Dorff, 'Artificial Insemination, Egg Donation and Adoption', *Conservative Judaism* (Fall 1996); Romain, *Faith and Practice*, p. 209.

[35] Dorff, 'Artificial Insemination', pp. 20-21.

[36] For a survey of transplantation practice see R. C. G. Russell, N. S. Williams and C. J. K. Bulstrode (eds), *Bailey and Love's Short Practice of Surgery*, 23rd edition, Arnold, 2000, pp. 125-146

[37] Joseph Karo on Maimonides' *Mishneh Torah*, quoted in Rosner, *Modern Medicine and Jewish Ethics*, p. 287.

[38] Rosner, *Modern Medicine and Jewish Ethics*, pp. 291-292.

[39] Hecht *et al.*, p. 414.

[40] Rabbi Chaim Rapoport, quoted in S. Baum, 'Rabbinical support for embryo cloning', *Jewish Chronicle*, 4 August 2000, p. 7.

[41] Rosner, *Modern Medicine and Jewish Ethics*, pp. 169-170.

[42] Ibid., p. 175.

[43] D. M. Feldman, 'This Matter of Abortion', in Dorff and Newman (eds), *Contemporary Jewish Ethics and Morality*, p. 389.

Afterword: Who is a Jew?

This short book is now almost at an end; the broader task of *Understanding Judaism* is necessarily ongoing. All religions and cultural movements are subject to change and Judaism, despite its strong emphasis on tradition, has been shown to be no exception. Chapter six reviewed some of the topics which seem likely to influence the future development of Judaism. New media and technologies will also have an as yet barely predictable impact. For example, the contemporary move to digitalise source-texts like the *Talmud* and *responsa* may profoundly affect those Judaisms which have embraced modernity. In the past, variations in *minhag* or custom developed in part because of the inevitable selectivity and incompleteness of a local rabbi's knowledge of *halakhah*. Computer networking may foster a trend towards uniformity of interpretation and practice, at least within particular movements or denominations. There is a risk that the rich expressiveness of local *minhag* surrounding rites of passage, for example, may be lost, as ceremonies are planned according to the advice offered in guides to standardised legal procedure. At the same time, non-contiguous communication via the Internet may make future debates between scholars even further removed from the original nature of the *oral Torah* than were the written *responsa* of, say, Maimonides' day. However, an issue even more fundamental than the likely impact of modern technologies upon the *halakhah* currently occupies the most significant place on the Jewish agenda: "Who is a Jew?"

Who is a Jew? How may the term 'Jew' be defined? From the standpoint of traditional Judaism, the answer is relatively straightforward. According to *halakhah*, a Jew is someone born of a Jewish mother, or someone who undergoes an acceptable form of conversion to Judaism. End of discussion. However, Jewish life today does not fit with the halakhic model in this instance, as in many others. Divisions over the nature of Jewish identity (as opposed to debates over the nature of Jewish religious expression) are currently deep enough for writer David Landau to be able to claim that, 'The Jewish People is likely to split in two within the next three decades over the question, "Who is a Jew?"[1]

A range of factors has conspired to precipitate the 'identity crisis' in contemporary Judaism. (It is interesting to note that the psychoanalyst who coined the phrase 'identity crisis', Erik Erikson, was highly ambivalent towards his own Jewishness.[2]) On the one hand, there are differing insider and outsider definitions of 'Jew'; and the relationship between 'Jew' as metaphor or symbol and Jews as historical agents is by no means straightforward. Judith Lieu has explored the extent to which, in order to shape its own identity, early Christianity had also to construct the identity of the 'Other', i.e. of the Judaism within which it was born. Whilst being informed by actual contacts with Jews and Judaism, writers like Justin Martyr and Melito of Sardis (mentioned in chapter five) created a literary and psychological image of 'the Jew' which was in large part a creation born from their own specific needs, including the requirement to justify the retention by the church of the Hebrew Scriptures without a continuing observance of the *mitzvot*.[3] In later periods (as chapter five also illustrated), 'Jew' has frequently been used by Judaism's Christian and Muslim detractors as a synonym for 'dishonest', 'corrupt', even 'devil', 'anti-Christ' or 'sub-human'. At the same time, the oppressors' construal of Jewishness has been subject to modification, as is illustrated by the case of the *conversos* or New Christians of medieval Spain and Portugal. At first, the authorities granted these converts citizenship, and many achieved good positions within Iberian society. Jewishness was implicitly regarded as a religious matter and, having publicly renounced Judaism, the *conversos* were no longer seen as Jews. However, by 1449 the *conversos* were the object of new suspicions. Some had continued to adhere to Jewish religious practices in secret, which was a source of concern, but the new opposition was construed in explicitly *racial* terms and laws known as *limpieza de sangre* or 'purity of blood' were passed to restrict their advancement.[4] Finally, as was explored in chapter three, for some Enlightenment thinkers, Jews were symbolic of problematic forms of difference that obstructed attempts to dismantle the *ancien regime* and establish the nation state according to rational principles. What threatens to split Jewry today, however, is not the fluctuating definition of Jewishness by other religious and ethnic groups. Marked *internal* Jewish divisions over the "Who is a Jew" question are proving serious in their implications.

Chapters three and six explored some of the pressures on Jewish religious life today. One of the practices frequently (and somewhat crudely) used as an index of Jewish assimilation to non-Jewish norms is inter-

Karaite Kenesa in Vilnius, Lithuania

In North America, the Karaites or Karaim have adopted the label 'Karaite Jews'; they have traditionally been regarded (by themselves and others) as belonging to the Jewish people. However, in Eastern and Central Europe, Karaites avoided persecution as Jews after petitioning first the Tsars, and later the Nazis, to be recognised as a separate ethnic group. This changing self-definition was reflected in the nineteenth century shift from Hebrew to Judeo-Tatar as the language of prayer, and is visible in the architecture of this kenesa. Built in the early twentieth century, closed in 1949 by the Soviet authorities, and reopened in 1993, its style reflects the increasing prominence European Karaites have given to their Crimean origins.

-marriage. Although in the *Purim* story Esther marries a non-Jew and becomes the means for God to save the Jewish people from annihilation, the *Tanakh* frowns upon such relationships (Deuteronomy 7:3-4; Ezra 9 and 10). Judaism's halakhic sources sanction only those marriages in which both partners are Jewish, yet intermarriage between Jew and non-Jew is increasingly common. This is particularly the case in North America, Britain, and Commonwealth nations such as Australia and Canada, but the problem is not unique to the West. For example, under the Soviet regime, the anti-religious policies in the USSR created a situation in which, in the postwar era, many Russian Jews lacked knowledge of Jewish religion and culture. Nevertheless, as Jews they were subject to lingering hostility and occasional violence, and so it was that when Mikhail Gorbachev finally permitted their free emigration in 1989, upwards of half a million left for Israel. Among the ranks of these Russian citizens who had 'Jew' stamped in their passports were many who were either party to or products of mixed marriages. Intermarriage is a reality throughout the Jewish world.

As mentioned in chapter four, Progressive Judaism has sought to respond to intermarriage by adopting a sympathetic approach to spouses who wish to convert, or, more strictly speaking, become proselytes to Judaism. (The traditional rabbinic stance was to discourage would-be converts; proselytisation was an offence punishable by the Christian authorities in the early medieval period.) Where conversion does not happen, other strategies may be deployed to try to ensure that the Jewish partner and any offspring are not lost to the Jewish community. Around forty per cent of Reform rabbis in America will officiate at mixed marriages, and a further thirty per cent who refuse to do so will refer the couple to another rabbi who will.[5] Controversially, certain groups within Progressive Judaism are now willing to regard as Jewish any child of a mixed marriage who self-identifies and acts publicly as a Jew. Patrilineal or matrilineal descent is sufficient for Liberal Judaism in Britain, as it is for the American Reform movement. If the marriage is between a Jewish man and a non-Jewish woman, this situation results in an intriguing paradox: today there are numbers of people with Jewish fathers and non-Jewish mothers, who are not regarded as Jewish in *halakhah* but who essentially lead more observantly and emotionally Jews lives than, say, the non-observant Orthodox Jew who is halakhically kosher but attends synagogue once a year, if at all.

This lack of congruency between the halakhic and Progressive models of Jewish life is not merely an intriguing academic point. Particularly in the State of Israel, Jewish identity and definition is an acute political issue. In 1950, the *Knesset* passed the Law of Return, granting Jews worldwide the right to immigrate to Israel and immediately receive citizenship. Almost at once, the question arose as to whether this provision extended to those who had only a Jewish father. The situation was a sensitive one, particularly in view of the fact that some survivors of the *Shoah*, who had been persecuted by the Nazi regime as Jews, fell into this category. In 1958, the Minister of the Interior ruled that anyone sincerely declaring him- or herself Jewish should be regarded as such. This was a far broader position than any Jewish religious movement could countenance at the time, and it led the National Religious Party (NRP) to resign from the coalition government. There then followed a lengthy period of consultation and uncertainty. In 1959 the directive of the previous year was revoked and the authority of *halakhah* in matters of personal status re-emphasised. However, in 1962 this position was once more challenged. Brother Daniel Rufeisen, a converted Jew who had become a Catholic monk, claimed Israeli citizenship. His case relied on the fact that halakhically speaking, a Jew remains a Jew even if he or she adopts beliefs and practices that differ widely from Jewish norms. The Israeli Supreme Court rejected this appeal to *halakhah* and ruled that, for the purposes of the Law of Return, 'Jew' referred to those traditionally regarded by Jews as such, and did not apply to a convert to Christianity.

The secular approach to Jewish identity adopted in this instance was reinforced in the Shalit case, when a Jewish man married to a non-Jew successfully fought to have his Israel-born children registered as Jews. Like the 1958 directive, this liberalising decision led to fierce controversy. Eventually, in 1970, the Ministry of the Interior was entrusted to the NRP who immediately sought to alter the Law of Return to end the uncertainty and satisfy secular and religious Israelis alike. The amended legislation defined 'Jew' as 'a person born of a Jewish mother or who has become converted to Judaism and is not a member of another religion'. It also extended 'the rights of a Jew' to 'a child or grandchild of a Jew, the spouse of a Jew, the spouse of a child of a Jew, and the spouse of a grandchild of a Jew, except for a person who has been a Jew and voluntarily changed his religion'. Subtly, this wording extended Israeli citizenship to the (halakhically speaking) non-Jewish child or grandchild of a Holocaust survivor, and to the married partner of a Jew, but it did not challenge the right of the *halakhah* to define Jewish identity.

The amended version of the Law of Return prevented any repetition of the Brother Daniel case, but at the same time it did not clearly define either 'member of another religion' or 'conversion', and this failure has given rise to further problems. For example, in the 1980s, two Messianic Jews, both of whom were born to Jewish mothers, petitioned to become Israeli citizens under the Law of Return. Like other Messianic Jews (or Hebrew Christians) they argued that accepting Jesus of Nazareth as their messiah constituted a completion or fulfillment of their Judaism, rather than adoption of another religion. However, the High Court rejected this argument on the grounds that belief in Jesus was not compatible with Judaism as popularly defined and legally established in the Brother Daniel and Shalit cases. This decision met with widespread support. Generally speaking, Jews do not regard Messianic Jews as Jewish, but view them simply as Christians.[6] Far more controversial is the issue of conversion *to* Judaism, and it is this which, together with the Progressive recognition of patrilineal descent, threatens to split Judaism and the Jewish community today.

Orthodox Judaism has consistently declined to recognise non-Orthodox conversions as satisfactory. At certain fundamental levels, Orthodox Judaism rejects Progressive Judaism's claim to authenticity (see chapter three) and so by definition also rejects Progressive conversion. More specifically, this is because not all Progressive movements demand that the candidate fulfil the traditional halakhic requirements for conversion, which are: acceptance of the *mitzvot*, immersion in a *mikveh* and, for males only, circumcision. Moreover, from an Orthodox perspective non-Orthodox rabbis cannot constitute a proper *bet din* or religious court to approve the conversion. However sincerely undertaken then, a Reform or Reconstructionist conversion is an exercise in futility and the candidate is, by Orthodox standards, as non-Jewish as she or he was before.

Conversely, the secular courts in Israel have persistently refused to limit the scope of valid procedures to those performed within the strict boundaries of *halakhah*. In particular, non-Orthodox conversions carried out in the *Diaspora* (not in Israel, where as is the case in all matters of personal status, such as marriage or divorce, the conversion must be Orthodox to carry full legal weight[7]) are regarded as sufficient to establish Jewish identity for the purposes of the Law of Return. This has resulted in a complex situation where individuals who have undergone non-Orthodox conversion outside Israel, or whose mothers did so, may be registered as Jewish when first immigrating, but later find themselves (and their children) unable to marry a Jew in Israel unless they are willing to undergo a further conversion. It is estimated that over one hundred thousand of Israel's citizens currently fall into this category. Unable to marry in their own country, these people often opt to do so abroad. By the mid-1990s such weddings accounted for approximately ten per cent of marriages registered by the Ministry of Interior.[8]

As recently as 1995, it seemed that some kind of resolution might be possible. Hava Goldstein, a Brazilian who immigrated to Israel, and underwent a Reform conversion there, applied for citizenship under the Law of Return, and wished to have her Jewishness recognised on her identity card. The Israeli Supreme Court ruled that the Interior Ministry should do this, implicitly recognising non-Orthodox conversions contracted *inside* Israel. However, without the agreement of the Orthodox rabbinate, the situation remains in flux. In spring 2002, the 'conversion crisis' returned to the headlines. By-passing questions about the validity of different conversions and the Law of Return, the Supreme Court focused on the Ministry of Interior and its role in registering the status of Israelis. It determined that the Ministry's job was an administrative, not a judicial, one, and that the only circumstance under which registration as Jewish could be refused was when it was *clear* that the applicant's claim was false. Where there is doubt or ambiguity regarding the claim (as in the case of a conversion accepted by some but not all Jewish authorities) the Registrar must accept the application and register the applicant as a Jew. However, for the Interior Minister at the time (a member of the Orthodox *Shas* party) such a move was unconscionable. He declared the decision a scandal, and suggested the Ministry would delay the processing of the identity cards of non-Orthodox converts until legislation could be prepared which would assert the exclusive right of Orthodox leaders to determine who is a Jew. In short, whereas the Israeli courts see Israel as the country of the Jewish people, for the Orthodox establishment (not for all Orthodox Jews), Israel is the country of the Jewish religious community. So, at the start of the twenty-first century, there is no settled agreement about what form of conversion or descent is necessary in order for one to be defined as a Jew.

The dynamic equilibrium that exists between *halakhah* and secular law in the State of Israel means that most public discussion of the "Who is a Jew?" controversy has centred around the competing answers offered by the Orthodox and Progressive groupings. However, it is not only between the various 'modern' forms of Judaism that disagreement persists. In recent years the traditional *Beta Israel* ('House of Israel', formerly known as Falashas) have also found themselves the victims of conflicting models of Jewish identity. As the twentieth century progressed, the *Beta Israel* experienced worsening oppression at the hands of the Marxist regime that controlled their Ethiopian homeland. In a daring move, the Israeli Government secretly airlifted several thousand people to Israel in the early 1980s. The project, known as *Operation Moses*, was hailed as a triumph of the Zionist spirit:

> It may be said that this is one of the most daring and wonderful acts of self-redemption that our country…has ever known….we are one people, tied to an ancient and splendid faith, and no physical force and no external difference can divide us.[9]

However, despite these inclusivist statements, once in Israel the *Beta Israel* were caught up in a struggle for recognition. On the one hand, the *Beta Israel* considered themselves Jewish. Community traditions traced their origins to the migration of Jews at the time of the Assyrian and Babylonian exiles, 'after Jeremiah the prophet', and a *responsum* of the sixteenth century halakhist Rabbi David ben Abi Zimra declared that they were 'without doubt from the tribe of Dan'.[10] On the other hand, the Orthodox authorities in Israel queried their Jewishness: were they perhaps instead a *Judaizing* group, whose practices were derived primarily from the Bible, or from the Ethiopian Orthodox church, rather than from Judaism itself? Without doubt, much of the *Beta Israel* religion was non-Talmudic in character. The *Beta Israel* used the Bible in Ge'ez (ancient Ethiopic) but had relatively little knowledge of Hebrew and also recognised a sizeable number of (from the Talmudic perspective) extra-canonical works. Most of their Sabbath laws were based on the Book of Jubilees, a text from the second temple period, which was part of the canon of the Ethiopian Church. So, whilst rabbinic Judaism regarded sexual intercourse between husband and wife as a legitimate 'Sabbath joy', perhaps even a 'duty', for the *Beta Israel* it was a practice forbidden on pain of death.[11] Similarly, in addition to celebrating *Shabbat*, the new moon, and other festivals in common with early Judaism, they observed the festival of St. Mikael (St. Michael) and believed in spirit possession. Indeed, until the twentieth century, when the need to counter Christian missionary activity prompted European and North American efforts to encourage the *Beta Israel* to bring their religious practices closer to those of rabbinic Judaism, they were led by celibate monks.

Ultimately, although the *Beta Israel* regarded themselves as Jewish, Orthodoxy's definition of 'the Jew' was dominant. Whilst recognised as Jews for the purposes of the Law of Return, the *Beta Israel* found themselves marginalised in Israeli society. Their children were sent to separate schools, their religious leaders were not recognised unless they retrained in Orthodox *yeshivot*, and adults were required to undergo a form of conversion ceremony (ritual immersion, the acceptance of the *mitzvot* or commandments, and, until 1984, a symbolic 'recircumcision' of males) as a prerequisite for marriage. During the past twenty or so years the *Beta Israel* have faced pressures to assimilate to white Israeli (particularly Ashkenazi) norms in order to gain social acceptance and respect. At one level, Orthodoxy's treatment of the *Beta Israel* could be regarded as a purely religious move, designed to uphold and strengthen *Torah*-true Judaism. That it was in part due also to racism seems likely. In 1996, it emerged that blood donated by the *Beta Israel* had been thrown away secretly, for fear of HIV infection. However, what is also at stake in the case of the *Beta Israel*, and in the plight of non-Orthodox converts who fall foul of Israeli religious courts, is Orthodoxy's struggle to assert itself as the guardian of Judaism and exercise authority over other groups that also claim the power to define 'Jew'.

Where, then, does the future lie for Judaism? Is it, as the Landau quotation suggests, destined to be practised by groups of people who, for the first time in Jewish history, no longer regard one another as Jews? Does the disagreement about conversion and descent mean that in the future Judaism will no longer be in any sense an ethnic religion? What are the implications of this for the discussion at the start of this book, which tried to understand Judaism in terms of a people bound by a shared sense of history; a *community of meaning*?

The different movements within Judaism are themselves aware of the dangerous possibility of irrevocable fracture over the question, "Who is a Jew?" Being religiously pluralist in outlook, Reform and other Progressive movements hope for a time when Orthodoxy will recognise as Jews all those whom they accept. More pragmatically, efforts continue to gain for Progressive authorities the same legally enshrined right to decide personal status issues that is enjoyed by the Ashkenazi and Sephardi Orthodox in Israel. In particular, there have been calls for the introduction of a Law of Religious Freedom in Israel, to safeguard the freedom of religion and conscience originally envisaged in Israel's Declaration of Independence and called for by the United Nations' Universal Declaration of Human Rights. If this does not happen, then Progressive Judaism continues to run the risk of being sidelined as a *Diaspora* experiment that has failed to negotiate the 'test' of Jewish nationhood. At the other end of the spectrum, while some Orthodox leaders have tended to adopt an increasingly hardened approach in this matter, others are willing to explore potential solutions to avert what Reuven Bulka has termed 'the coming cataclysm'.[12]

Chief Rabbi Jonathan Sacks adopts a historical perspective on Jewish unity. Sacks cites two precedents illustrating the possible course of inner Jewish conflict. The first is the tension between the rabbinic schools grouped around the first century sages, Hillel and Shammai. According to the *Talmud* they disagreed to the extent that 'the *Torah* became as two *Toroth*' (*Sanhedrin* 88b). However, the *Mishnah* notes that, despite their differences, the schools of Hillel and Shammai did not refrain from marrying one another (*m.Eduy* 4:8). An ultimate breach was avoided. The second is the conflict between early Judaism and nascent Christianity. Early Christians were Jewish in origin and continued to be regarded as such by their non-Christian counterparts. However, a final break came when the Christian community ceased to require its Gentile members to meet the halakhic requirements for conversion. At this point, the rabbis viewed Christianity as a different and alien religious community. The problem for contemporary Jews is, Sacks warns, that unlike the disagreements between Hillel and Shammai, the Orthodox-Reform rift is already advancing along the path taken by Jews and early Christianity. Differences over the interpretation of the *halakhah* will not split Jewry, but the Progressive overturning of the halakhic system itself may do so.[13]

In attempting to avert potentially irreparable schism, Sacks advances a position that he calls 'halakhic inclusivism'. He suggests that Orthodoxy take a more positive, proactive approach to both Progressive Jews and the non-Jewish partners of Jews. Unless Orthodox leaders do so, they will be guilty of engaging in the same piecemeal approach to the *mitzvot* that they criticise in Progressive Judaism. As Bulka phrases it:

> An individual who chooses to commit the self to keeping the *Shabbat*, to adhering to the kosher code, but at the same time chooses to be less than strict with regard to such imperatives as "love that which pertains to your neighbour as if it pertains to yourself", actually indulges in the same process as the Reform....that of making value judgements concerning what is important in the *Torah* and what is not.[14]

In other words, for Bulka, Orthodoxy needs to understand that it cannot enforce a return to tradition; if it wishes non-Orthodox Jews to be attracted to the halakhic life, it needs to model more successfully the moral and intellectual integrity that characterise a life structured around *Torah*.

'Halakhic inclusivism', of the type advocated by Sacks and Bulka, might manifest itself in a variety of practical ways. For example, the Orthodox authorities in Israel could make it easier for non-Orthodox converts to undergo a subsequent Orthodox conversion. According to Rashi, Hillel himself accepted as proselytes those whom he felt would eventually accept the whole of Jewish law, even if they did not do so at the time of their application. A similar approach could be used to accept non-halakhically oriented Progressive converts into the Orthodox fold. Other options could include the recognition that, although Progressive conversion is not, in Orthodox eyes, halakhically valid, it does have some positive value, perhaps conferring on the would-be proselytes a kind of 'intermediate Jewish identity', and functioning as an important gesture signalling solidarity with the Jewish people. Finally, other suggestions for creative Orthodox responses to the conversion problem have included proposals for a 'theological clearing-house'. This institution would be responsible for the instruction and rabbinical examination of candidates for conversion to the full variety of different Jewish movements. Referring communities would have opportunities to provide distinctive input into their own candidates' programme, but all groups would agree to a standardised basic approach incorporating the need for circumcision, ritual immersion and a (broadly defined) acceptance of the commandments.[15]

Lest anyone doubt that these proposals constitute a shift from the current Orthodox position, it is worth noting that some authorities have refused to accept proselytes whose decision to convert is motivated by a desire to marry (on the grounds that such a decision is not really free or voluntary). Other groups have gone further and, in the case of the Syrian Sephardim, refuse to accept converts at all, whilst some Orthodox authorities have shunned contacts with Progressives not just officially, but socially, too.[16] Seen in this light, any move to recognise Progressive conversion as having even minimal value, or to involve Orthodox rabbis in the education of non-Orthodox proselytes, is radical. The difficulty with halakhic inclusivity however, is that it collides (as Sacks acknowledges) with the rationalist, pluralist sensibilities of the non-Orthodox.

From a pluralist perspective, halakhic inclusivity denies non-Orthodoxy's understanding of itself. Reform and Reconstructionist converts see themselves as Jewish – not as 'Jew-ish' or 'Jewish style'. They wish to be accepted by Orthodoxy for what they are, not for what they might (potentially) become. Proposals to standardise conversions across Judaism, or to make it easier for non-Orthodox converts to undergo a 'halakhically valid' rite are also problematic. Implicitly, they require the non-Orthodox groups to accept the Orthodox conception of itself as the only reliable guardian of normative Judaism.

For Sacks, this clash of world-views should not cause offence to the non-Orthodox. Reform Judaism has, he says, never derived its legitimacy from Orthodox recognition. Moreover, when considering the various proposals, the emphasis should be placed on their practical consequences, i.e. the creation of a *modus operandi* which can hold Jewish diversity in tension and in unity, rather than on the philosophical or political implications abstracted from them. However, this seems a little naïve. In particular, many non-Orthodox Jews would deny that pluralism and *halakhah* are necessarily distinct. Conservativism, Reform, and Reconstructionism all assert that the halakhic system possesses value – even primary value – for Jews, yet the latter two in particular also maintain that commitment to *halakhah* can co-exist with an acceptance of inner Jewish diversity.

Ultimately, the same factors that have given rise to the "Who is a Jew?" controversy also work against its easy solution. The modern era has offered Jews unprecedented opportunities for freedom and empowerment. The result has been that some Jews have accepted modern philosophies and modes of discourse, while others have not. This impacts not just on their attitudes towards religious life and thought, but also on their very construction of Jewish identity. Moreover, in the face of this diversity, Judaism lacks a centralised body with sufficient authority to impose, or at least advocate, a definitive answer to the question, "Who is a Jew?"

All this might be thought to imply that Jewish unity, and therefore perhaps also Jewish continuity, is at an end. In ten or twenty years' time will a book titled *Understanding Judaism* appear hopelessly dated? Will it be necessary to speak of *Understanding Judaisms*, or of *Understanding Orthodox* or *Reform Judaism*? Such conclusions are perhaps overly pessimistic. For example, some of the current pressures could be eased if Israeli state law distanced itself from the *religious* debate on conversion. The 1970 amendment to the Law of Return conferred 'the rights of a Jew' on those with Jewish fathers only, without offering a judgement on the religious debate about descent. Given the role of religious parties in Israel's coalition governments, change is never easy. Conceivably further modifications could be introduced that whilst accepting non-Orthodox conversions as evidence of the proselyte's sincere wish to identify with the hopes and destiny of Israel's citizens (and therefore as demonstrating fitness for citizenship) do not pretend to make a judgement on the religious implications of the conversion. Such a practical measure would not of course solve the problem of conversion, but it would at least disentangle and distance it from some of the complicated political issues.

Other factors also argue for the continued unity and survival of not just Jews, but of Judaism itself. Whilst their fortunes have fluctuated, at the start of the twenty-first century none of the major forms of Jewish religious expression is on the verge of disappearance. *Charedi* and Orthodox groups are undergoing something of a revival, both intellectually and statistically speaking. Conservativism, Reform, and Reconstructionism face very real dilemmas, but are also growing in maturity and confidence. In Britain, Liberal Judaism celebrated its centenary in 2002. These groups have all found new ways to speak to an increasingly global and mobile Jewish community. And although many Sephardi and Oriental Jews experienced the trauma of having to leave their historic homelands in the late twentieth century, they have been able to enjoy growing social and economic successes in Israel and North America, and to give voice to their own distinctive forms of Judaism. On the secular, political front, the State of Israel has survived for over fifty years. It is now a major influence that both complements and challenges *Diaspora* existence. Although the possibility of fracture is very real then, the resources that can be deployed to work for Jewish unity and renewal are also great.

And Jewish history itself attests to the fact that the Jewish people, even when exiled and dispersed, and subject to the influence of a diversity of non-Jewish cultures, can retain a sense of unity.

Although Orthodox and Progressive forms of Judaism are fundamentally quite different in spirit, in their own way, each hopes to foster a sense of tolerance and unity amidst the diversity that is Jewish life today. If this shared desire can be kept to the fore, then it may yet be possible to resolve the "Who is a Jew?" controversy. In the twenty-first century as in the past, Jewish continuity will inevitably be not about the replication of the traditions of earlier generations – their strengths and their follies – but about the active construal of identity. Jewish continuity and unity will of necessity entail Jewish creativity.

Notes

[1] D. Landau, *Piety and Power: The World of Jewish Fundamentalism*, New York: Hill and Wang, 1993, p. 291.

[2] See briefly P. F. Langman, *Jewish Issues in Multiculturalism: A Handbook for Educators and Clinicians*, Northvale, NJ: Jason Aronson, 1999, pp. 71-91; 277-278.

[3] J. M. Lieu, *Image and Reality. The Jews in the World of the Christians in the Second Century*, Edinburgh: T. and T. Clark, 1996, pp. 1, 11–12.

[4] The combination of outward adherence to Christianity and private commitment to another religion was not unique to the *conversos*. *Moriscos* privately maintained Muslim practice and belief; most were expelled in 1619.

[5] R. Bulka, *The Coming Cataclysm: The Orthodox Reform Rift and the Future of the Jewish People*, second edition, New York: Mosaic Press, 1986, p. 44.

[6] D. Cohn-Sherbok, *Messianic Judaism*, Cassell, 2000, pp. 198-200.

[7] Israeli law follows the practice during the British Mandate, which in turn was influenced by Ottoman law. Each religious community has jurisdiction over the personal status (marriage, divorce, conversion) of its members. For a discussion of the place of *halakhah* during the Mandate and of many of the cases in this Afterword see Hecht, *Jewish Law*, pp. 397–419.

[8] M. Boyden, 'The Challenge for Reform Judaism in a Jewish State', in J. A. Romain (ed.), *Renewing the Vision: Rabbis Speak out on Modern Jewish Issues*, SCM Press, 1996, p. 205.

[9] Shimon Peres, quoted in D. Kessler, *The Falashas. A Short History of the Ethiopian Jews*, third edition, Frank Cass, 1996, pp. xi-xii.

[10] M. Corinaldi, *Jewish Identity: The Case of Ethiopian Jewry*, Jerusalem: The Magnes Press, 1998, pp. 13; 46.

[11] Ibid., p. 62.

[12] Boyden, 'The Challenge', p. 203; Bulka, *The Coming Cataclysm*.

[13] J. Sacks, *One People? Tradition, Modernity, and Jewish Unity*, Littman

Library of Jewish Civilisation, 1994, pp. 186–187.

[14] Bulka, *The Coming Cataclysm*, p. 112.

[15] Ibid., p. 81; Sacks, *One People?*, pp. 188–194.

[16] S. Z. Lieberman, 'A Sephardic Ban on Converts', *Tradition*, 23:2 (1988), 22–5.

Appendices

1. Judaism and Jewish Culture on the Internet

The Internet is a valuable resource for anyone seeking to understand contemporary Judaism. Many hard-to-find source materials relating to Jewish history are also available online. However, web-based material should be treated as critically as that delivered by other means. For example, it is good practice to identify:

– the author of the site;
– his or her purpose in creating and maintaining the site; and,
– the currency of the material presented,

before making a judgement about the accuracy and reliability of its content. The following sites (all current at the time of going to press) are intended to serve as an introduction to some of the resources available on the Internet today.

Gateways and Other General Sites

Judaism and Jewish Resources http://shamash.org/trb/judaism.html gateway site with links to many sites of academic or practical interest; maintained by Andrew Tannenbaum.

Tracey Rich's *Judaism 101*, http://www.jewfaq.org takes a slightly different approach, offering a basic online encyclopedia of basic information on Judaism.

For historical resources, try the *Internet Jewish History Sourcebook*, http://www.fordham.edu/halsall/jewish/jewishsbook.html, a well organised and referenced site maintained by Paul Halsall in the History Department of Fordham University.

Schoolteachers may be interested to visit the Judaism corner of RE-XS, the Religious Education Exchange Service http://re-xs.ucsm.ac.uk, maintained by St Martin's College, Lancaster, and the REsite, http://allre.org.uk . Both of these are gateway sites, containing a smaller number of focused links, their purpose being to support religious education in British schools. The latter includes a useful section on using information technologies in Religious Education.

Judaism in Britain Today

http://www.unitedsynagogue.org.uk the United Synagogue's website
http://www.chabad.org/ Chabad-Lubavitch in Cyberspace (international site)
http://www.refsyn.org.uk/ Reform Synagogues of Great Britain
http://www.ulps.org Union of Liberal and Progressive Synagogues

Individual synagogues may also maintain their own sites: for example, http://www.coolshul.org – run by the innovative Saatchi Synagogue, or http://www.wls.org.uk, which is the website for West London Synagogue, the first reform synagogue in Britain.

International Sites

Distinctively North American groupings are represented at:
http://www.uscj.org United Synagogues of Conservative Judaism
http://rj.org/ Reform Judaism
http://www.jrf.org/ Jewish Reconstructionist Federation website
http://www.utj.org Union for Traditional Judaism

For a more global approach:
http://www.wjc.org.il/ the World Jewish Congress site includes information on Jewish communities of the world, from Afghanistan to Zimbabwe
http://www.haruth.com/JewsoftheWorld.html offers a slightly more eclectic collection of links

The *Shoah* (Holocaust)

General sites:
http://remember.org/ A Cybrary of the Holocaust
http://www.nizkor.org/ The Nizkor Project

Museum and memorial complexes:
http://www.yadvashem.org.il/ Yad Vashem website
http://www.ushmm.org United States Holocaust Memorial Museum
http://www.bethshalom.com Beth Shalom Holocaust Memorial Centre,
England

Israel

http://www.israel.org/mfa/home.asp State of Israel website, from
the Ministry of Foreign Affairs
http://www.knesset.gov.il The Knesset (Parliament of Israel) website,
in English and Hebrew
http://www3.haaretz.co.il/eng/htmls/1_1.htm Ha'aretz Daily
Newspaper – Online English Edition
http://www.jpost.com/ Jerusalem Post Internet Edition
It is also possible to visit http://www.israelradio.org/english.html and
listen to Kol Israel (Voice of Israel), the Israeli radio overseas broadcasting
service

Jewish/Non-Jewish Relations

http://www.jcrelations.net jcrelations.net is a comprehensive site
covering Christian-Jewish relations and maintained by the International
Council of Christians and Jews
http://www.cjcr.cam.ac.uk Centre for Jewish-Christian Relations,
Cambridge
http://www.interfaith.org.uk/ the Interfaith Network for the United
Kingdom links many interfaith groups and organisations

2. Jewish Holidays in 5764 (2003-2004)

In the Jewish religious calendar, years are numbered from 3761 BCE, traditionally believed to be the date of the world's creation.

This chart gives the start dates for festivals discussed in this book; carefully observant Jews will also mark a number of other fasts and celebrations.

HOLIDAY	JEWISH DATE	SECULAR DATE
Rosh Ha-Shanah	Tishri 1	September 27, 2003
Yom Kippur	Tishri 10	October 6, 2003
Sukkot	Tishri 15	October 11, 2003
Shemini Atzeret	Tishri 22	October 18, 2003
Simchat Torah*	Tishri 23	October 19, 2003
Chanukah	Kislev 25	December 20, 2003
Tu Bi-Shevat	Shevat 15	February 7, 2004
Purim	Adar 14	March 7, 2004
Pesach	Nisan 15	April 6, 2004
Yom Ha-Shoah	Nisan 27	April 18, 2004
Yom Ha-Atzma'ut	Iyyar 5	April 26, 2004
Shavuot	Sivan 6	May 26, 2004
Tisha Be-Av	Av 9	July 27, 2004
Erev Rosh Ha-Shanah	Elul 29	September 16, 2005

*Jews in Israel (and progressive Jews in the *Diaspora*) observe this festival on the preceding day.

In 5765 (2004-5), Rosh Ha-Shanah falls on September 16, 2004 and Pesach begins on April 24, 2005.

Glossary

Agunah   (plural, *agunot*)   a woman barred from re-marrying because of insufficient proof of her husband's death or his refusal to give her a divorce

Aliyah   'ascent', being called to read from scripture in the synagogue, or, in contemporary Zionist parlance, making immigration to the Land of Israel

Amidah   'standing', one of the principal prayers of the Jewish liturgy

Amora (plural *amora'im*)   'expounders'; sages whose discussions are recorded in the *Talmud*

Ashkenazi (plural, *Ashkenazim*) Jews whose ancestors came from Germany surrounding countries. The name derives from Ashkenaz (Genesis 10.3) which medieval commentators identified as Germany

Avodah   'service'

Bar mitzvah/Bat mitzvah   'son/daughter of the commandment', having attained religious maturity

Baraitot   external or outside things - especially a tradition attributed to a *tanna* but not found in the *Mishnah*

Berakhah	*benediction or blessing*
Berit or *brit*	covenant, an agreement between two parties
Bet din	'house of law', i.e. court of religious law
Beta Israel	an ethnic group, originating in Ethiopia, which claims Jewish origins
Bimah	platform in the synagogue from which the *Torah* is read
Chollah	plaited loaf of bread, eaten on the Sabbath and other festivals
Chametz	leaven
Chanukah	'dedication', winter festival of lights
Chanukiah/Chanukah	nine-branched candlestick used at
Charedi (plural, *charedim*)	a carefully observant Jew; sometimes called 'ultra-orthodox'
Chavurah (plural, *chavurot*)	'fellowship'; a small group that comes together for religious study and celebration, associated in particular with Reconstructionist Judaism
Charoset	a sweet paste-like food eaten at the *seder*
Chasid (plural, *Chasidim*)	'pious'; a God-fearing person; especially a member of the movement founded in the eighteenth century by the Baal Shem Tov

Chazan	a cantor; a community official who leads the synagogue prayer service.
Cheder	'room'; the name given in Britain to a (supplementary) Hebrew school for children. Previously the name used in Eastern Europe for an elementary school offering traditional Jewish education to boys
Cherem	a ban; the strongest form of excommunication from membership of a Jewish community and its rights and privileges
Chuppah	(wedding) 'canopy'
Dayyan	a judge in a rabbinic court
Dhimmi	non-Muslim communities (e.g. Jews or Christians) living under Muslim rule or protection
Diaspora	Jewish communities outside the Land of Israel
Eretz Israel	the Land of Israel
Galut	'exile'; also a traditional name for the *Diaspora*
Gaon (plural, *geonim*)	'excellency" name given to the heads of the two Babylonian academies in Sura and Pumbedita, which exercised considerable authority over the Jewish world between the seventh and eleventh centuries

Gemara	a 'teaching'. An alternative name for the *Talmud* used in the medieval period by printers wishing to deflect the authorities' attentions from what was seen as an anti-Christian text
Get	a bill of divorce
Goses	a dangerously ill person
Haftarah	the reading from the Prophets in the synagogue service on the Sabbath and festival days
Haggadah	non-legal material in rabbinic literature; also, the text recited before and during the *Seder*
Halakhah	from Hebrew meaning (prob.) to walk. The legal tradition of Judaism. Often used as a collective noun but may also refer to an individual law or ruling
Hallel	'praise'; Psalms recited liturgically, especially during festivals
Haskalah	the Jewish Enlightenment
Kabbalah	'tradition'; the Jewish mystical tradition
Kapparot	a rite of individual atonement, practiced in some Orthodox communities on the eve of *Yom Kippur* and involving the symbolic transfer of sin to a fowl, which is then slaughtered
Karaites	group dating from the 8th century CE, characterised by their rejection of the

	Talmud and other rabbinic literature
Kashrut	religious dietary laws
Ketubbah	a wedding contract
Kiddush	prayer (and accompanying ritual) inaugurating a Sabbath or festival
Kippah	skull-cap
Kittel	white garment worn on *Yom Kippur*
Kol Nidrei	annulment of 'all vows'; prayer (and service) on the eve of *Yom Kippur*
Kosher	'fit'; used particularly to refer to food prepared in accordance with dietary laws
Ma'ariv	evening prayer
Mamzer	an illegitimate child, born as the result of adultery or incest
Maror	bitter herb, eaten at the *seder*
Masorti	'traditional'; name of Conservative Judaism in the United Kingdom and Israel
Matzah (plural, *matzot*)	unleavened bread
Megillah	scroll (especially of Esther, read at *Purim*)
Menorah	seven-branched candlestick
Mezuzah (plural, *mezuzot*)	'door-post'; the parchment scroll fixed

	to door-post of the house
Midrash	traditional rabbinic method of Bible exegesis. Can also be applied to the genre of literature which the method produces
Mikveh	ritual bath used for cleansing after contact with the dead, menstruation, and as part of the ritual of conversion
Minhag	custom
Minyan	quorum of ten adults required for public worship. Orthodoxy counts men only towards the *minyan*; most progressive Judaisms count women, too.
Mishnah	'teaching'; the collection of Oral Law compiled by Judah Ha-Nasi in the late 2nd/early 3rd century CE. Also applied to an individual teaching within that collection
Mitzvah (plural, *mitzvot*)	a commandment (positive or negative). Sometimes used to denote any good deed
Mohel	a circumciser
Neilah	'closing'; final service on *Yom Kippur*
New Religious Movements	generic term referring to the thousands of religious movements emerging worldwide in the period since World War II. Many are syncretistic and their success may be attributed to rapid social change, increased contact between

	cultures, and the challenges arising from the loss or absence of community, amongst other factors
Niddah	a menstruating women, traditionally considered ritually impure
Olam ha-Ba	the world to come; the hereafter
Pesach	Passover; festival commemorating the Exodus from Egypt
Piyyut (plural, *piyyutim*)	liturgical poem (typically added to the set prayers in the medieval period)
Purim	'lots', festival celebrating the story of averted genocide, recounted in Esther
Rabbi	teacher, especially of religious law
Responsa	latin term for the Hebrew, *she'elot u-teshuvot*, 'questions and answers', exchanges of letters in which one party consults another on a halakhic matter
Rosh Chodesh	New Moon
Rosh ha-Shanah	New Year, literally, 'Head of the Year'
Sacrament	an event or object regarded as an occasion for the presence of God
Seder	'order', the home service held on the first night (or first two nights) of *Pesach*
Sefirot	Kabbalistic name for the ten emanations or manifestations of God's attributes in the universe

Sephardi (plural, *Sephardim*)	Jew whose ancestors came from Spain or related oriental countries. The term comes from the place Sepharad (Obadiah 1.20) which early commentators identified with Spain
Sha'atnez	'counterfeit'; fabric containing a mixture of wool and linen, forbidden in the *Torah*.
Shabbat	Saturday, the Jewish Sabbath
Shacharit	morning service
Shadkhan	a marriage broker or matchmaker
Shavuot	festival commemorating the giving of the Torah on Sinai
Shechitah	ritual slaughter of animals, prescribed by Jewish law
Shekhinah	the Divine Presence
Shema	'hear'; Deut. 6:4-9, 11:13-21 and Num. 15:37-41, recited twice daily
Shivah	'seven'; seven day period of mourning after burial of a relative
Shoah	'catastrophe'; used to refer to the murder of six million Jews by the Nazis during World War II
Shofar	ram's horn, blown especially at *Rosh ha-Shanah*

GLOSSARY

Shtetl	*(Jewish) small town*
Simchat Torah	festival commemorating the completion of the annual cycle of reading the Pentateuch
Sukkot	the festival of tabernacles, or booths
Synagogue	congregational meeting place, used for worship and other activities
Tallit	prayer shawl
Talmud	rabbinic works, one Palestinian and one Babylonian. The teachings of the *amora'im* which take the form of a commentary on the *Mishnah*.
Talmud Torah	*Torah* study
Tanakh	the Hebrew Bible. The name is an acrostic derived from the first letters of each of the three divisions of the Bible: Torah, Nevi'im and Ketuvim
Tanna (plural, *tannaim*)	'teacher' or 'rehearser' whose words are recorded in the *Mishnah*
Tefillin	'phylacteries', leather boxes containing scripture passages and worn during morning prayer
Terefah	'torn'; food that is non-kosher because of a defect in the animal
Teshuvah	repentance
Theodicy	the justification of the existence of an

	omnipotent, benevolent God, despite the presence of evil and suffering in the world
Torah	'teaching' or 'instruction' often translated, perhaps inaptly, as 'law'. May be applied to an individual teaching / law or to a body of laws, especially the Pentateuch or first section of the *Tanakh*
Tosefta	literally, 'addition' especially used of tannaitic law which supplements the *Mishnah*
Tu bi-Shevat	New Year festival for trees
Tzaddik	a righteous person or, in *Chasidism*, a charismatic leader
Yamim Noraim	'days of awe'; ten days of repentance from Rosh ha-Shanah to Yom Kippur
Yeshivah	institution for the traditional study of *Torah* (particularly *Talmud*) for its own sake (rather than as preparation for rabbinical ordination), open to males aged eighteen and above
Yom ha-Atzma'ut	(Israeli) Independence Day
Yom ha-Shoah	Holocaust Memorial Day
Yom Kippur	Day of Atonement

Bibliography

Affron, C., 'Honoré de Balzac (1799-1850)', in J. Barzun and G. Stade (eds), *European Writers. The Romantic Century. Volume 5: Johann Wolfgang von Goethe to Alexander Pushkin*, New York: Charles Scribner's Sons, 1985, pp. 635-657.

Agus, A., 'This Month is for You: Observing Rosh Chodesh as a Woman's Holiday', in E. Koltun (ed.), *The Jewish Woman: New Perspectives*, New York: Schocken, 1976, pp. 84-93.

Aitken, J., 'Jews and Christians Take Counsel', *Church Times*, 20 October 2000, pp. 15, 17.

Alpert, R. T., and Staub, J. J., *Exploring Judaism: A Reconstructionist Approach*, Wyncote: The Reconstructionist Press, 1997.

Arberry, A. J. (trans.), *The Koran*, Oxford: Oxford University Press, 1983.

Assaf, S., *Teshuvot haGe'onim*, Jerusalem: Darom, 1928.

Barton, J., 'The Significance of a Fixed Canon of the Hebrew Bible', in M. Saebo (ed.), *Hebrew Bible/Old Testament. The History of Its Interpretation Vol. 1 From the Beginnings to the Middle Ages (Until 1300)*, Göttingen: Vandenhoeck and Ruprecht, 1996, pp. 67-83.

Bat Ye'or, *The Dhimmi: Jews and Christians Under Islam*, Associated University Presses, 1985.

Baum, S., 'Rabbinical support for embryo cloning', *Jewish Chronicle*, 4 August 2000, p. 7.

Belcove-Shalin, J. S. (ed.), *New World Hasidim: Ethnographic Studies of Hasidic Jews in America*, New York: State University of New York Press, 1995.

Ben-Ami, I., *Saint Veneration Among the Jews in Morocco*, Detroit: Wayne State University Press, 1998.

Berend, N., *At the Gates of Christendom: Jews, Muslims, and 'Pagans' in Medieval Hungary, c. 1000 – c. 1300*, Cambridge: Cambridge University Press, 2001.

Berkovits, E., *Faith After the Holocaust*, New York: Ktav, 1973.

Berkovits, E., 'The Centrality of Halakhah', in J. Neusner (ed.), *Understanding Rabbinic Judaism: From Talmudic to Modern Times*, New York: Ktav, 1974, pp. 63-70.

Bleich, J. D., 'Sperm Banking in Anticipation of Infertility', in E. Feldman and J. B. Wolowelsky (eds), *Jewish Law and The New Reproductive Technologies*, Hoboken: Ktav, 1997, pp. 139-154.

Borowitz, E. B., *Liberal Judaism*, New York: Union of American Hebrew Congregations Press, 1984.

Boyden, M., 'The Challenge for Reform Judaism in a Jewish State', in J. A. Romain (ed.), *Renewing the Vision. Rabbis Speak Out on Modern Jewish Issues*, SCM Press, 1996, pp. 203-211.

Brandt, W. I. (ed.), *Luther's Works*, Volume 45, Philadelphia: Fortress Press, 1971.

Braybrooke, M., *Christian-Jewish Dialogue: The Next Steps*, SCM Press, 2000.

Brown, D., 'Refusal to Say a Short Sentence Lands Israeli Husband a Long One', *The Guardian*, 22 February 1993, p. 1.

Bulka, R., 'Orthodoxy Today: An Analysis of the Achievements and the Problems', in his *Dimensions of Orthodox Judaism*, New York: Ktav, 1983, pp. 7-32.

Bulka, R., *The Coming Cataclysm: The Orthodox Reform Rift and the Future of the Jewish People*, second edition, New York, Mosaic Press, 1986.

Bulka, R., *Jewish Marriage: A Halakhic Ethic*, New York: Ktav, 1986.

Carmi, T.; Schulman, G. (trans.), *At The Stone of Losses*, Manchester: Carcanet New Press, 1983.

Central Conference of American Rabbis (ed.), *The Union Haggadah: Home Service for Passover*, New York: Central Conference of American Rabbis, 1923.

Chatterjee, M., *Gandhi and his Jewish Friends*, Macmillan, 1992.

Chatterjee, M., *Studies in Modern Jewish and Hindu Thought*, Macmillan, 1997.

Chaucer, G., *The Canterbury Tales*, Oxford: Oxford University Press, 1998.

Chill, A., *The Minhagim: The Customs and Ceremonies of Judaism, Their Origins and Rationale*, New York: Sepher-Hermon Press, 1979.

Coggins, R. J., *Haggai, Zechariah, Malachi*, Sheffield: JSOT Press, 1987.

Cohen, J., 'Medieval Jews on Christianity: Polemical Strategies and Theological Defense,' in E. J. Fisher (ed.), *Interwoven Destinies: Jews and Christians Through the Ages*, New York: Paulist Press, 1993, pp. 77-89.

Cohen, J. R., 'Women's Roles in Judeo-Spanish Sephardic Song', in S. S. Swartz, and M. Wolfe (eds), *From Memory to Transformation: Jewish Women's Voices*, Toronto: Second Story Press, 1998, pp. 49-61.

Cohick, L. H., 'Melito's *Peri Pascha*. Its Relationship to Judaism and Sardis in Recent Scholarly Discussion', in H. C. Kee and L. H. Cohick (eds), *The Evolution of the Synagogue: Problems and Progress*, Harrisburg, PA: Trinity Press International, 1999, pp. 123-140.

Cohn-Sherbok, D., *Modern Judaism*, Macmillan, 1996.

Cohn-Sherbok, D., *Messianic Judaism*, Cassell, 2000.

Cook, C. (ed.), *Pears Cyclopaedia 2000-2001*, Harmondsworth: Penguin, 2000.

Cook, J. M., 'Persia', in B. M. Metzger and M. D. Coogan (eds), *The Oxford Companion to the Bible*, Oxford: Oxford University Press, 1993, pp. 582–583.

Corinaldi, M., *Jewish Identity: The Case of Ethiopian Jewry*, Jerusalem: The Magnes Press, 1998.

Crone, P., and Cook, M., *Hagarism: The Making of the Islamic World*, Cambridge: Cambridge University Press, 1977.

Danby, H. (trans.), *The Mishnah*, Oxford: Clarendon, 1933.

Davidman, L., and Stocks, J., 'Varieties of Fundamentalist Experience: Lubavitch Hasidic and Fundamentalist Christian Approaches to Contemporary Family Life,' in Belcove-Shalin, J. S. (ed.), *New World Hasidim: Ethnographic Studies of Hasidic Jews in America*, New York: State University of New York Press, 1995, pp. 107-133.

Dawidowicz, L., *The War Against the Jews 1933-1945*, Harmondsworth: Penguin, 1977.

de Lange, N. R. M., 'Jewish Attitudes to the Roman Empire', in P. D. A. Garnsey and C. R. Whittaker (eds), *Imperialism in the Ancient World*, Cambridge: Cambridge University Press, 1978, pp. 255-281.

de Lange, N. R. M., *Judaism*, Oxford: Oxford University Press, 1986.

Deshen, S., and Zenner, W. (eds), *Jewish Societies in the Middle East*, Washington: University Press of America, 1982.

Dickens, C., *Oliver Twist*, Harmondsworth: Penguin, 1985.

Dinur, B., 'The Origins of Hasidism', in G. D. Hundert (ed.), *Essential Papers on Hasidism: Origins to Present*, New York: New York University Press, 1991, pp. 86-204.

Dobrinsky, H. C., *A Treasury of Sefardic Laws and Customs: The Ritual Practices of Syrian, Moroccan, Judeo-Spanish and Spanish and Portuguese Jews of North America*, revised edition, New York: Yeshiva University Press, 1998.

Dorff, E. N., and Newman, L. E. (eds), *Contemporary Jewish Ethics and Morality: A Reader*, Oxford: Oxford University Press, 1995.

Dorff, E. N., 'Artificial Insemination, Egg Donation and Adoption', *Conservative Judaism* 26 no. 1 (Fall 1996), 3-60.

Dubnow, S., 'The Beginnings: The Baal Shem Tov (Besht) and the Center in Podolia', in G. Hundert (ed.), *Essential Papers on Hasidism: Origins to Present*, New York: New York University Press, 1991, pp. 25-57.

Du Maurier, G., *Trilby*, Harmondsworth: Penguin, 1994.

Eisen, A. M., *Rethinking Modern Judaism: Ritual, Commandment, Community*, Chicago: University of Chicago Press, 1998.

Elazar, D. J., and R. M. Geffen (eds), *The Conservative Movement in Judaism: Dilemmas and Opportunities*, New York: SUNY Press, 2000.

Eliach, Y., 'The Holocaust: A Response to Catastrophe Within a Traditional Jewish Framework', in Y. Gutman and G. Greif (eds), *The Historiography of the Holocaust Period: Proceedings of the Fifth Yad Vashem International Historical Conference, Jerusalem, March 1983*, Jerusalem: Yad Vashem, 1988, pp. 719-735.

Ellis, M. H., *Beyond Innocence and Redemption: Confronting the Holocaust and Israeli Power: Creating a Moral Future for the Jewish People*, San Francisco: Harper and Row, 1990.

Fackenheim, E. L., *The Jewish Return to History: Reflections In the Age of Auschwitz and a New Jerusalem*, New York: Schocken, 1978.

Feldman, D., 'Was Modernity Good for the Jews?', in B. Cheyette and L. Marcus (eds), *Modernity, Culture and 'the Jew'*, Cambridge: Polity Press, 1998, pp. 171-187.

Feldman, D. M., 'This Matter of Abortion', in E. N. Dorff and L. E. Newman (eds), *Contemporary Jewish Ethics and Morality: A Reader*, Oxford: Oxford University Press, 1995.

Feldman, E., and J. B. Wolowsky (eds), *Jewish Law and the New Reproductive Technologies*, Hoboken, NJ: Ktav, 1997.

Fishbane, S., 'Jewish Mourning Rites: A Process of Resocialisation', in J. N. Lightstone and F. B. Bird (eds), *Ritual and Ethnic Identity: A Comparative Study of the Social Meaning of Liturgical Ritual In Synagogues*, Waterloo, Ont.: Wilfred Laurier University Press, 1995, pp. 169-184.

Fishbane, S., 'Contemporary Bar Mitzvah Rituals in Modern Orthodoxy', in J. N. Lightstone and F. B. Bird (eds), *Ritual and Ethnic Identity: A Comparative Study of the Social Meaning of Liturgical Ritual In Synagogues*, Waterloo, Ont.: Wilfred Laurier University Press, 1995, pp. 155-167.

Fisher, E. J. (ed.), *Interwoven Destinies: Jews and Christians Through the Ages*, New York, Paulist Press, 1993.

Flusser, D., *Jesus*, Jerusalem: Magnes Press, 1968.

Forward, M., *Muhammad: A Short Biography*, Oxford: Oneworld, 1997.

Fraser, T. G., *The Arab-Israeli Conflict*, London: Macmillan, 1995.

Freehof, S. B., *Reform Responsa*, New York: Ktav, 1960.

Frymer-Kensky, T., Novak, D., Ochs, P., Fox Sandmel, D., and M. A. Signer (eds), *Christianity in Jewish Terms*, Boulder, Col.: Westview Press, 1999.

Gager, J. G., 'The Parting of the Ways: A View from the Perspective of Early Christianity', in E. J. Fisher (ed.), *Interwoven Destinies: Jews and Christians Through the Ages*, New York: Paulist Press, 1993, pp. 62-73.

Gaon, S. (ed.), *Book of Prayer of the Spanish and Portuguese Jews' Congregation, London*, Four Volumes, Oxford: Oxford University Press, 1971.

Garnsey, P., and Saller, R., *The Roman Empire: Economy, Society and Culture*, Duckworth, 1987.

Geertz, C., "'From the Native's Point of View": On the Nature of Anthtropological Understanding', in R. T. McCutcheon (ed.), *The Insider/Outsider Problem in the Study of Religion*, Cassell, 1999, pp. 50-63.

Geffen, R. M. (ed.), *Celebration and Renewal: Rites of Passage in Judaism*, Philadelphia: Jewish Publication Society, 1993.

Glatzer, N. N. (ed.), *Language of Faith: A Selection of the Most Expressive Jewish Prayers*, New York: Schocken, 1975.

Glazer, N., *American Judaism*, Chicago: University of Chicago Press, 1957.

Glick, L. B., *Abraham's Heirs: Jews and Christians in Medieval Europe*, Syracuse: Syracuse University Press, 1999.

Goldstein, D. (ed.), *The Jewish Poets of Spain 900-1250*, Harmondsworth: Penguin, 1965.

Goodman, D. G. and Miyazawa, M., *Jews in the Japanese Mind: The History and Uses of a Cultural Stereotype*, Free Press, 1995.

Goodman, P. (ed.), *The Yom Kippur Anthology*, Philadelphia: Jewish Publication Society, 1971.

Gordis, R., *Judaic Ethics for a Lawless World*, New York: Jewish Theological Seminary, 1986.

Grabbe, L. L., *Judaism from Cyrus to Hadrian*, two vols, Minneapolis, Fortress Press, 1992.

Gray, D. P., 'Jesus Was a Jew', in M. Perry and M. Schweitzer (eds), *Jewish Christian Encounters Over the Centuries: Symbiosis, Prejudice, Holocaust, Dialogue*, New York: Peter Lang, 1994, pp. 1-25.

Gutman, Y. and G. Greif (eds), *The Historiography of the Holocaust Period: Proceedings of the Fifth Yad Vashem International Historical Conference, Jerusalem, March 1983*, Jerusalem: Yad Vashem, 1988.

Habermas, J., 'Modernity and postmodernity', *New German Critique* 22

(1981), 3-14.

Halevi, J., *The Kuzari: An Argument for the Faith of Israel*, New York: Schocken Books, 1964.

Halivni, D. W., *Revelation Restored: Divine Writ and Critical Responses*, Boulder: Westview Press 1997.

Hammer, R. (ed.), *The Jerusalem Anthology: A Literary Guide*, Philadelphia: Jewish Publication Society, 1995.

Hecht, D. *et al.*, *Introduction to The History and Sources of Jewish Law*, Oxford: Clarendon Press, 1996.

Heilman, S. C., *Defenders of the Faith: Inside Ultra-Orthodox Jewry*, New York: Schocken Books, 1992.

Heilman, S. C. *Synagogue Life: A Study in Symbolic Interaction*, New Brunswick: Transaction Publishers, 1998.

Hengel, M.; Bowden, J. (trans.), *Judaism and Hellenism*, SCM Press, 1981.

Hertzberg, A., *The French Enlightenment and the Jews*, New York: Columbia University Press, 1968.

Heschel, A. J., *God in Search of Man. A Philosophy of Judaism*, John Calder, 1956.

Heschel, A. J., *The Prophets*, New York: Harper and Row, 1962.

Heschel, A. J., 'No Religion is an Island', in R. A. Rothschild (ed.), *Jewish Perspectives on Christianity*, New York: Continuum, 1996, pp. 309-324.

Heschel, S., *Abraham Geiger and the Jewish Jesus*, Chicago: University of Chicago Press, 1998.

Hilton, M., *The Christian Effect on Jewish Life*, SCM Press, 1994.

Himmelfarb, M., 'The Parting of the Ways Reconsidered: Diversity in Judaism and Jewish Christian Relations in the Roman Empire "A Jewish Perspective"', in E. J. Fisher (ed.), *Interwoven Destinies: Jews and Chrisitans Through the Ages*, New York: Paulist Press, 1993, pp. 47-61.

Hirsch, S. R.; Elias, J. (trans.), *The Nineteen Letters*, Jerusalem: Feldheim, 1995.

Hitler, A.; Mannheim, R. (trans.), *Mein Kampf*, Boston: Houghton Mifflin, 1962.

Hundert, G. D. (ed.), *Essential Papers on Hasidism: Origins to Present*, New York: New York University Press, 1991.

Jacobs, L., *We Have Reason to Believe*, third edition, Vallentine Mitchell, 1965.

Jacobs, L., 'Electricity', in his *The Jewish Religion: A Companion*, Oxford: Oxford University Press, 1995, p. 143.

Jacobs, L., 'Shulhan Arukh', in his *The Jewish Religion: A Companion*, Oxford: Oxford University Press, 1995, pp. 466-467.

Jacobus, H., 'Getting Together', *Jewish Chronicle*, 11 August 2000, p. 22.

Joyce, J., *Ulysses*, Harmondsworth: Penguin, 1992.

Kaplan, D. E., (ed.), *Contemporary Debates in American Reform Judaism: Conflicting Visions*, London: Routledge, 2001.

Kaplan, M. M., *Judaism as a Civilisation: Toward a Reconstruction of American-Jewish Life*, New York: Thomas Yoseloff, 1934.

Kasimov, H., *No Religion is an Island: Abraham Joshua Heschel and Interreligious Dialogue*, Maryknoll: Orbis, 1991.

Kee, H. C., and L. H. Cohick (eds), *The Evolution of the Synagogue: Problems and Progress*, Harrisburg, PA: Trinity Press International, 1999.

Kessler, D., *The Falashas. A Short History of the Ethiopian Jews*, third edition, Frank Cass, 1996.

Kessler, E. (ed.), *An English Jew: The Life and Works of Claude Montefiore*, revised edition, Vallentine Mitchell, 2002.

Kimelman, R., 'Birkhat ha-minim and the Lack of Evidence for an Anti-Christian Jewish Prayer In Late Antiquity', in E. P. Sanders (ed.), *Jewish and Christian Self-Definition. Vol. 2. Aspects of Judaism in the Graeco-Roman Period*, SCM Press, 1981, pp. 226-244.

Klein, I., *A Guide to Jewish Religious Practice*, New York: JTS, 1979.

Koltach, A. J. (ed.), *The Concise Family Seder*, New York: Jonathan David, 1987.

Krauss, S.; Horbury, W. (rev. and ed.), *The Jewish-Christian Controversy From the Earliest Times Until 1789. Vol. 1. History*, Tübingen: J.C.B. Mohr, 1995.

Krauz, E., and Tulea, G. (eds), *Jewish Survival: The Identity Problem at the Close of the Twentieth Century*, New Brunswick: Transaction Publishers, 1998.

Kugelmass, J., 'Green Bagels: An Essay on Food, Nostalgia and the Carnivalesque', *YIVO Annual* (1990), pp. 57-80.

Kunin, S., (ed.), *God's Place in the World: Sacred Space and Sacred Place in Judaism*, Cassell, 1998.

Kunin, S. (ed.), *Themes and Issues in Judaism*, Cassell, 2000.

Landau, D., *Piety and Power: The World of Jewish Fundamentalism*, New York: Hill and Wang, 1993.

Langman, P. F., *Jewish Issues in Multiculturalism: A Handbook for Educators and Clinicians*, Northvale, NJ: Jason Aronson, 1999.

Latham, R. (ed.), *Pepys' Diary*. Vol. 1, The Folio Society, 1996.

Leibowitz, Y.; Goldman, E. (ed.), *Judaism, Human Values and the Jewish State*, Cambridge Mass.: Harvard University Press, 1992.

Levine, J. L., 'Why People in the Sunbelt Join a Synagogue: Jewish Religious Preference in Palm Beach County', in D. E. Kaplan (ed.), *Contemporary Debates in American Reform Judaism: Conflicting Visions*, London: Routledge, 2001, pp. 56-65.

Lieberman, S. Z., 'A Sephardic Ban on Converts', *Tradition*, 23:2 (1988), 22–5.

Liebman, Charles S., and E. Don-Yehiya, *Civil Religion in Israel*, London: University of California Press, 1983.

Lieu, J. M., *Image and Reality. The Jews in the World of the Christians in the Second Century*, Edinburgh: T. and T. Clark, 1996.

Lightstone, J. N., and Bird, F. B. (eds), *Ritual and Ethnic Identity: A Comparative Study of the Social Meaning of Liturgical Ritual in Synagogues*, Waterloo, Ont.: Wilfred Laurier University Press, 1995.

McCutcheon, R. T. (ed.), *The Insider / Outsider Problem in the Study of Religion: A Reader*, Cassell, 1999.

Magonet, J., *Manna*, Number 60 (Summer 1998) un-numbered insert.

Marcus, I. G., *Rituals of Childhood: Jewish Acculturation in Medieval Europe*, New Haven: Yale University Press, 1996.

Markham, I. (ed.), *A World Religions Reader*, Oxford: Blackwell, 1996.

Marmur, D., *Beyond Survival: Reflections on the Future of Judaism*, London: Darton Longman and Todd, 1982.

Marmur, D., 'The Future of the Jews', in J. A. Romain (ed.), *Renewing the Vision: Rabbis Speak Out on Modern Jewish Issues*, SCM Press, 1996, pp. 173-181.

Maybaum, I., *The Face of God After Auschwitz*, Amsterdam: Polak and Van Gennep, 1965.

Maybaum, I., *Trialogue Between Jew, Christian and Muslim*, Routledge and Kegan Paul, 1972.

Maybaum, I., *Happiness Outside the State: Judaism, Christianity, Islam: Three Ways to God*, Oriel Press, 1980.

Meggitt, J. J., *Paul, Poverty and Survival*, Edinburgh: T. and T. Clark, 1998.

Mendes-Flohr, P., and Reinharz, J. (eds), *The Jew in the Modern World: A Documentary History*, second edition, Oxford: Oxford University Press, 1995.

Metzger, B. M., and M. D. Coogan (eds), *The Oxford Companion to the Bible*,

Oxford: Oxford University Press, 1993.

Meyer, M. A., *Response to Modernity. A History of the Reform Movement in Judaism*, Oxford: Oxford University Press, 1988.

Michael, R., 'Antisemitism and the Church Fathers', in M. Perry and M. Schweitzer (eds), *Jewish Christian Encounters Over the Centuries: Symbiosis, Prejudice, Holocaust, Dialogue*, New York: Peter Lang, 1994, pp. 101-130.

Morris, B., *Anthropological Studies of Religion: An Introductory Text*, Cambridge: Cambridge University Press, 1987.

Neusner, J., *Death and Birth of Judaism: The Impact of Christianity, Secularisation and the Holocaust on Jewish Faith*, New York: Basic Books, 1987.

Neusner, J. (trans.), *The Mishnah: A New Translation*, New Haven: Yale University Press, 1988.

Neusner, J., and Avery-Peck, A. J. (eds), *The Blackwell Reader in Judaism*, Oxford: Blackwell, 2001.

Oshry, E., *Responsa from the Holocaust*, New York: Judaica Press, 1989.

Pawlikowski, J. T., 'Jesus – A Pharisee and the Christ', in M. Shermis and A. E. Zannoni (eds), *Introduction to Jewish-Christian Relations*, New York, Paulist Press, 1991, pp. 174–201.

Pearl, C., *Rashi*, Peter Halban, 1988.

Perry, M., and Schweitzer, M. (eds), *Jewish Christian Encounters Over the Centuries: Symbiosis, Prejudice, Holocaust, Dialogue*, New York, Peter Lang, 1994.

Popkin, R. H., 'Spinoza and Bible scholarship', in D. Garrett (ed.), *The Cambridge Companion to Spinoza*, Cambridge: Cambridge University Press, 1996, pp. 383-407.

Porter, S. E., and B. W. R. Pearson (eds), *Christian-Jewish Relations Through the Centuries*, Sheffield: Sheffield Academic Press, 2000.

Pyke, D., 'Contributions by German Emigrés to British Medical Science', *Quarterly Journal of Medicine* 93 (2000), 487-495.

Rabinowicz, H., *Hasidism and the State of Israel*, Rutherford: Fairleigh Dickenson University Press, 1982.

Rich, D., 'Why I Back Euthanasia', *Manna*, Number 62 (Autumn 2000), pp. 9-11.

Romain, J. A., *Faith and Practice: A Guide to Reform Judaism Today*, RSGB, 1991.

Romain, J. A. (ed.), *Renewing the Vision: Rabbis Speak Out on Modern Jewish Issues*, SCM Press, 1994.

Romain, J. A., *Till Faith Do Us Part: Couples Who Fall in Love Across the*

Religious Divide, Fount, 1996.

Rose, A. (ed.), *Judaism and Ecology*, Cassell, 1992.

Rose, A. (ed.), 'The Environment: Israel's Remarkable Story', in A. Rose (ed.), *Judaism and Ecology*, Cassell, 1992, pp. 81-88.

Rosenbaum, I. J., *The Holocaust and Halakhah*, New York: Ktav, 1976.

Rosenzweig, F., 'Teaching and Law', in N. N. Glatzer (ed.), *Franz Rosenzweig - His Life and Thought*, New York: Schocken, 1961, pp. 234-242.

Rosner, F., *Modern Medicine and Jewish Ethics*, second edition, New York: Yeshiva University Press, 1991.

Rubenstein, R., *After Auschwitz: Radical Theology and Contemporary Judaism*, New York: Bobbs Merrill, 1966.

Ruether, R. R., *Faith and Fratricide*, New York, Seabury Press, 1974.

Russell, R. C. G., Williams, N. S., and Bulstrode, C. J. K. (eds), *Bailey and Love's Short Practice of Surgery*, twenty-third edition, Arnold Publishers, 2000.

Sacks, J., *The Persistence of Faith: Religion, Morality and Society in a Secular Age*, Weidenfeld and Nicolson, 1991.

Sacks, J., *One People?:Tradition, Modernity and Jewish Unity*, Littman Library of Jewish Civilisation, 1994.

Sacks, J., *Will We Have Jewish Grandchildren?: Jewish Continuity and How To Achieve It*, Vallentine Mitchell, 1994.

Safriel, U. N. 'The Regional and Global Significance of Environmental Protection, Nature and Conservation and Ecological Research in Israel,' A. Rose (ed.), *Judaism and Ecology*, Cassell, 1992, pp. 90-101.

Saperstein, M., *Moments of Crisis in Jewish-Christian Relations*, SCM Press, 1989.

Schäfer, P., *Judeophobia: Attitudes Towards Jews in the Ancient World*, Cambridge, Mass.: Harvard University Press, 1998.

Schindler, P., *Hasidic Responses to the Holocaust in the Light of Hasidic Thought*, Hoboken: Ktav, 1990.

Schmool, M., and Cohen, F., *British Synagogue Membership in 1996*, Board of Deputies of British Jews, 1997.

Scholem, G., 'Sabbatai Sevi: The Mystical Messiah', in M. Saperstein (ed.), *Essential Papers on Messianic Movements and Personalities in Jewish History*, New York: New York University Press, 1992, pp. 289-334.

Schur, N., *History of the Karaites*, Frankfurt-am-Main: Peter Lang, 1992.

Sered, S. S., *Women as Ritual Experts: The Religious Life of Elderly Jewish Women in Jerusalem*, New York: Oxford University Press, 1992.

Service of the Heart: Weekday Sabbath and Festival Services and Prayer for Home and Synagogue, Union of Liberal and Progressive Synagogues, 1967.

Shai, D., 'Family Conflict and Cooperation in Folksongs of Kurdish Jews', in S. Deshen and W. Zenner (eds), *Jewish Societies in the Middle East*, Washington: University Press of America, 1982, pp. 273-284.

Sharot, S., 'Judaism and Jewish Ethnicity: Changing Inter-relationships and Differentiations in the Diaspora and Israel', in E. Krauz and G. Tulea (eds), *Jewish Survival: The Identity Problem at the Close of the Twentieth Century*, New York: Transaction Publishers, 1998, pp. 87-105.

Shermis, M., and A. E. Zannoni (eds), *An Introduction to Jewish-Christian Relations*, New York: Paulist Press, 1991.

Sherwin, F. (ed.), *Luther's Works*. Vol. 47. Philadelphia: Fortress Press, 1971.

Singer, S. (trans.), *The Authorised Daily Prayer Book of the United Hebrew Congregations of the British Commonwealth of Nations*, Eyre & Spottiswoode Ltd., 1962.

Sklare, M., *Conservative Judaism: An American Religious Movement*, New York: Schocken Press, 1955.

Solomon, N., *Judaism and World Religion*, Macmillan, 1991.

Solomon, N., 'Attitudes to Nature', in S. Kunin (ed.), *Themes and Issues in Judaism*, Cassell, 2000, pp. 219-248.

Solomon, N., 'Jewish Fundamentalism', *The Newsletter of the International Interfaith Centre at Oxford*, No. 12 (December 2000), p. 6.

Soloveitchik, J. B.; Kaplan, L. (trans.), *Halakhic Man*, Philadelphia: Jewish Publication Society, 1983.

Sorkin, D., 'Jewish Emancipation in Central and Western Europe in the Eighteenth and Nineteenth Centuries', in D. Englander (ed.), *The Jewish Enigma*, Open University, 1992, pp. 81-109.

Stendahl, K., *Paul Among Jews and Gentiles*, Philadelphia, Fortress Press, 1976.

Stillman, N. A., *Sephardi Religious Responses to Modernity*, Harwood Academic Publishers, 1995.

Strack, H. L., and Stemberger, G.; Bockmuehl, M. (trans.), *Introduction to the Talmud and Midrash*, Edinburgh: T. & T. Clark, 1991.

Tanakh, a New Translation of the Holy Scriptures According to the Traditional Hebrew Text, Philadelphia: Jewish Publication Society, 1988.

Twersky, I., *A Maimonides Reader*, New York: Behrman House, 1972.

Twersky, I., *Introduction to the Code of Maimonides (Mishneh Torah)*, New Haven:

Yale University Press, 1980.

Ucko, H. (ed.), *People of God, Peoples of God: A Jewish-Christian Conversation in Asia*, Geneva: WCC, 1996.

van Gennep, A.; Vizedom, M. B. and Caffee, G. L. (eds), *The Rites of Passage*, Chicago: University of Chicago Press, 1969.

Vermes, G., *Jesus the Jew: A Historian's Reading of the Gospels*, London: S. C. M. Press, 1973.

Voltaire, *Dialogues et Anecdotes Philosophiques*, Paris: R. Naves, 1939.

Voltaire; Besterman, T. (trans.), *Philosophical Dictionary*, Harmondsworth: Penguin, 1971.

Walters, J. C., *Ethnic Issues in Paul's Letter to the Romans: Changing Self-Definitions in Earliest Roman Christianity*, Valley Forge: Trinity Press International, 1993.

Wengst, K., *Pax Romana and the Peace of Jesus Christ*, SCM Press, 1987.

Weyl, R., 'Convivencia – Enhancing Identity Through Encounter Between Jews, Christians and Muslims: The ICCJ 2000 Annual Conference in Seville, Spain (2-6 July)', *ICCJ News* 25 (Autumn 2000), pp. 1-3.

Whaling, F., *Christian Theology and World Religions*, Marshall Pickering, 1986.

Wiener, M. (ed.); Schlochauer, E. J. (trans.), *Abraham Geiger and Liberal Judaism: The Challenge of the Nineteenth Century*, Cincinnati: Hebrew Union College Press, 1981.

Williams, G. H., *The Radical Reformation*, third edition, Kirksville: Sixteenth Century Journal Publishers, 1992.

Winston, R., *The IVF Revolution: The Definitive Guide to Assisted Reproductive Technologies*, Vermilion, 2000.

Wright, M. J., 'The Nature and Significance of Relations between the Historic Peace Churches and Jews During and After the *Shoah*', in S. E. Porter and B. W. R. Pearson (eds), *Christian Jewish Relations Through the Centuries*, Sheffield: Sheffield Academic Press, 2000, pp. 400-425.

Zimmels, H. J., *Ashkenazim and Sephardim: Their Relations, Differences, and Problems as Reflected in the Rabbinical Responsa*, Hoboken, NJ: Ktav, 1996.

Index

INDEX

INDEX

Printed in the United Kingdom
by Lightning Source UK Ltd.
101996UKS00001B/290